DATE DUE

DEMCO 38-297

Renaissance
Man
from
Louisiana

Arna Bontemps, novelist-playwright. (Moorland-Spingarn Research Center, Howard University; collection Mary O'H. Williamson.)

Renaissance Man from Louisiana

A BIOGRAPHY OF
Arna Wendell Bontemps

KIRKLAND C. JONES

CONTRIBUTIONS IN AFRO-AMERICAN AND AFRICAN STUDIES,
NUMBER 151
Henry Louis Gates, Jr., *Series Adviser*

Greenwood Press
Westport, Connecticut • London

Library of Congress Cataloging-in-Publication Data

Jones, Kirkland C.
   Renaissance man from Louisiana : a biography of Arna Wendell Bontemps /
Kirkland C. Jones.
         p.   cm.—(Contributions in Afro-American and African
   studies, ISSN 0069-9624 ; no. 151)
   Includes bibliographical references and index.
   ISBN 0-313-28013-4 (alk. paper)
   1. Bontemps, Arna Wendell, 1902-1973—Biography.   2. Authors,
American—20th century—Biography.   3. College librarians—United
States—Biography.   4. College teachers—United States—Biography.
5. Afro-Americans—Intellectual life.   I. Title.   II. Series.
PS3503.0474Z73   1992
818'.5209—dc20
[B]   91-47062

British Library Cataloguing in Publication Data is available.

Library of Congress Catalog Card Number: 91-47062
ISBN: 0-313-28013-4
ISSN: 0069-9624

First published in 1992

Greenwood Press, 88 Post Road West, Westport, CT 06881
An imprint of Greenwood Publishing Group, Inc.

Printed in the United States of America

The paper used in this book complies with the
Permanent Paper Standard issued by the National
Information Standards Organization (Z39.48-1984).

10 9 8 7 6 5 4 3 2 1

TO MY MOTHER AND TO THE MEMORY OF MY FATHER

and

To J. Marie McCleary

Contents

Acknowledgments   xi

Chronology   xv

1. Family Background and Birth   1

2. Early Years in Alexandria, Louisiana   21

3. Childhood in Los Angeles   29

4. Coming of Age in California   43

5. Unique Role in the Renaissance   53

6. The Depression Period   69

7. The Chicago Period   85

8. Career at Fisk University   101

9. The Mature Years   153

Notes   173

Bibliographic Essay   193

Index   199

Photo essay follows chapter 5.

Acknowledgments

I am grateful to a number of friends, colleagues, and institutions for their substantial contributions to this study. I am especially grateful to my employer, Lamar University, which made the researching of the study possible during the 1985–86 school term through an internal research grant, and which, during the 1986–87 term gave me a sabbatical that has made possible the preparation of this manuscript. Both the grant and the developmental leave were given through the support of administrators Charles Timothy Summerlin, John P. Idoux, and Charles Turco. I am also grateful to colleagues in the Department of English and Foreign Languages who are always encouraging and supportive, and to "Stu" Hayes, now deceased, for his gracious help with photography.

Several other institutions have aided me immeasurably in this effort: Fisk University, Yale University, Syracuse University, the Amistad Research Center, and the Library of Lamar University, especially its Inter-Library Loans Department. At Fisk I owe special thanks to the Special Collections Department of the University Library; at Yale, to the Beinecke Library and the Manuscripts and Archives Department of the Sterling Memorial Library; at Syracuse to Carolyn A. Davis of the George Arendts Research Library and her staff; and at the Amistad Research Center of New Orleans, to senior archivist Florence Borders and her associates, including Dr. Clifton Johnson.

I am also indebted to a number of other individuals for their gracious help: Audrey N. Jackson, without whose willingness to share her Bontemps materials this study could not have been as encompassing as it is; writer-scholar Arthenia Bates Millican, for sharing what she knows about Bontemps as a teacher of creative writing; Irving Ward-Steinman for sharing his Bontemps correspondence; and Rose Metoyer of the Alexandria Public Library for putting me in touch with him. I am also grateful to my friend and colleague Howard Perkins for reading portions of the manuscript and offering sound rhetorical advice and for assisting with photography in central Louisiana. To Johnny Cal Joseph, who helped arrange the research data, I owe thanks. And to Sue Eakin, formerly of Louisiana State University at Alexandria, for offering encouragement at a crucial juncture, and to her colleague, Mozelle Darbonne, for inviting me to speak in Alexandria at the very first meeting of the Arna Bontemps Society in March 1990.

I am also indebted to Jack Conroy, literary collaborator of Arna Bontemps, for sharing his knowledge of the Bontemps career, and to Donald Gallup, former Curator of the Collection of American Literature at Yale University, for supplying information about Bontemps's tenure there. I am also grateful to John Blasingame and Shirley Mero of Yale's Afro-American Studies Department for their excellent help, and to the ministerial and secretarial staffs of St. Frances Xavier Cathedral of Alexandria and St. Paul the Apostle Church of Mansura, Louisiana, for invaluable assistance with genealogy. To my colleague Betty Taylor Ashe Thompson of Texas Southern University for making the original manuscript of her dissertation on Bontemps's fiction available to me, and for sharing her experiences as a student of Bontemps while he was at the peak of his career at Fisk.

I would also like to thank the following persons at Fisk for special help and encouragement: President Henry Ponder and his former assistant, Robert Crigler; Veonie McKinney of Housing; Ann Allen Shockley, noted author and Director of Special Collections, for her research assistance and for permission to quote from her unpublished work on the life of Bontemps; Beth Howse, also of Special Collections, for her cooperation; and Marian Roberts, Sue Chandler, and Greg Engleberg, all of the library staff. To Pearl Cresswell of the Carl Van Vechten Art Gallery and Museum for listening and for sharing her knowledge of the Bontemps career and for aiding me in obtaining an audience with the writer's oldest child, I am deeply grateful. I am also grateful to Vander Harris of the Physical Plant and to members of the campus security force, who took me to Greenwood Cemetery where the poet is buried, and to the Bontemps home on Geneva Circle. I am grateful to Earl Hooks of the Departments of Art and Photography for sharing Bontemps artifacts and offering suggestions about photographs, and to Leslie M. Collins, longtime teacher in the Department of English and cousin of Arna Bontemps, for granting me an interview.

I honor the memory of Ida Cullen for taking time to talk with me about Arna Bontemps's role in the Harlem Renaissance and about the history of *St. Louis Woman* and for allowing me to quote from the Countée Cullen Papers, and for the large envelope full of letters and artifacts that her attorney gave to me after her death. And I am no less appreciative of help given me by members of the Bontemps family: to Alberta Johnson Bontemps for inviting me into her home and for granting me a recorded interview, and to her daughter, Joan Bontemps Williams, for extending similar courtesies. I am also indebted to Hattie Roy Bontemps of New Orleans, who granted me an interview and permitted me to examine important artifacts, and to Ruby Bontemps Troy, who shared family obituaries and who granted me several telephone interviews. Thanks are also due to my friend Arthur L. Tolson, son of poet Melvin B. Tolson, for permission to quote from his father's letters and for his constant encouragement in this and other research projects. I am grateful, too, to my friends Clarence Guthrie and Roger Clayton of Newark for taking me to Troutbeck, the place where the NAACP was born, which became a favorite haunt of Arna Bontemps during the Harlem years.

I also owe a debt of thanks to my friend Ralph Wooster, Dean of Faculties at Lamar University, for encouraging me during the submission process, and for aiding in more tangible ways with the final preparation of this manuscript. And to Minnie Lomax, without whose typing and editing this book would not exist. And I am grateful to Bobbie Scott Williams, who grew up in Bontemps's hometown and to her mother, Ethel Scott, who still lives less than a block from the original site of the Bontemps birthplace, for sharing news items and other artifacts from Alexandria. I extend sincere thanks to my friend and colleague Onita Estes-Hicks, Chair, Department of English at the State University of New York at Old Westbury, for assistance with finding a publisher and for refusing to allow me to panic during the permissions phase.

Of course, any defects that may appear in this manuscript, both in form and content, are my own.

Chronology*

October 13, 1902   Born at Alexandria, Louisiana; given name, Arnaud.

1906   Moved to Los Angeles, California, with his family.

1917   Attended San Fernando Academy, a prep school, until 1920.

1923   Received A.B. degree from Pacific Union College, Angwin, California.

1924   Taught at Harlem Academy in New York City until 1931. Published first poem, titled "Hope."

1926   Married Alberta Johnson. Awarded Alexander Pushkin Prize for his poem "Golgotha is a Mountain," published by *Opportunity* (Journal of Negro Life).

1927   Awarded Alexander Pushkin Prize for his poem "The Return." Awarded *Crisis* Poetry Prize—the first presented by the magazine—for poem, "Nocturne at Bethesda."

1931   Taught at Oakwood Junior College until 1934. First published novel, *God Sends Sunday*.

1932   Awarded *Opportunity* short story prize for "A Summer Tragedy."

1935   Moved to Chicago where he taught at Shiloh Academy until 1938.

1936   Published *Black Thunder*, his first historical novel.

1938   Granted Rosenwald Fellowship for creative writing and traveled in Caribbean until 1939.

1939   Published *Drums at Dusk*, a second historical novel.

1941   Published *Golden Slippers: An Anthology of Negro Poetry for Young Readers* (his first anthology).

*Does not reflect all published works.

1942   Granted Julius Rosenwald Fellowship to pursue the "Negro in Illinois" project in Chicago.

1943   Received M.L.S. degree from the University of Chicago. Appointed Full Professor and Head Librarian, Fisk (served until 1964).

1945   With Jack Conroy, published *They Seek a City*.

1946   Premiere of musical drama *St. Louis Woman*, written with Countée Cullen; adapted from *God Sends Sunday*.

1948   Published *The Story of the Negro*.

1949   Granted Guggenheim Fellowship for creative writing.

1954   Granted Guggenheim Fellowship for creative writing.

1956   Awarded Jane Addams Children's Book Award for *Story of the Negro*; Runner-up for Newbery Award.

1964   Named Acting Librarian of Fisk University—while new librarian was being sought—and Director of University Relations until 1965.

1966   Returned to Chicago where he taught literature and history at the University of Illinois' Chicago Circle campus until 1969.

1967   Jointly with Jack Conroy, received the James L. Dow Award for *Anyplace but Here*.

1969   Received honorary L.H.D. degree from Morgan State University in Baltimore, Maryland.

1969   Appointed Writer-in-Residence at Fisk University, where he began research for his autobiography.

1972   Named Honorary Consultant to the Library of Congress in American Cultural History. Published *The Harlem Renaissance Remembered*.

1972   Returned to his birthplace, Alexandria, Louisiana, where he visited his birth house and finished research in Rapides and Avoyelles parishes for projected autobiography, *A Man's Name*.

1973   Received honorary L.H.D. degree on May 17 from Berea College, Berea, Kentucky.

1973   Died June 4, in Nashville, Tennessee, at age seventy.

Chapter 1

Family Background and Birth

The artistic and scholarly endeavors of Arna Wendell Bontemps, his role in the Harlem Renaissance, his contributions as a teacher-administrator, and his impact on the community of African-American writers have received almost no attention from scholars, with the exception of two or three doctoral dissertations and a few memoirs. Sharing their birth years, Bontemps and Langston Hughes were soul mates, and Hughes wrote in 1949 the most accurate available nutshell assessment of Bontemps's literary sensibility, describing him as

one of America's simplest yet most eloquent writers dealing in historical materials, as his historical novels and his "The Story of the Negro" prove. His prose is . . . readable, . . . yet rich in poetic overtones and the magic of word music. . . . I have known Arna Bontemps for more than twenty years and have collaborated with him on children's books, plays, and the editorship of a recent anthology, *The Poetry of the Negro*. I know him to be a very thorough and conscientious worker, methodical, giving a certain number of hours every day to his writing, and a fine literary craftsman. His factual prose is not dry, but full of warmth and poetry. And he has both tolerance and humor.[1]

Arna Bontemps was born in Alexandria, Louisiana, in what is sometimes referred to on both sides of his family as "Cajun Country." He was of Creole stock. Some of his European ancestors were descendants and cultural relatives of certain original French settlers of the southern United States, especially Louisiana. Others of his ancestors eventually sailed to the United States from the West Indies, landing at New Orleans and working their way inland to Avoyelles and Rapides parishes. Some of this group remained in New Orleans. The name Bontemps, of course, is French, meaning "good times." And these forebears of Arna Bontemps spoke the brand of French patois spoken by most Louisiana Creoles of the region and of their time. Jack Conroy, the American author who was Bontemps's close contemporary, at age eighty-eight reported to the present writer that Arna sometimes "said something about his roots."[2] Conroy knew Bontemps well, for they collaborated for a number of years, and agrees that not all of Bontemps's relatives in Louisiana were black and that those who were had been at one time owned by a comedian on the French stage who called himself Bontemps, or "Mr. Good Times."[3] Whether that was his real name we do not know. It is a fact, though, that Bontemps is a common name in France and other French-speaking communities.

The French family that at first owned the Bontemps slaves had evidently emigrated to Haiti from France. Once there, they acquired slaves and began to intermarry with them. Exactly what caused the mulatto Bontempses, the offspring of this mixture, to move to Louisiana will probably remain a mystery. Whether they separated themselves in some way from the owning family and fled to Louisiana without their blessings, or whether they were brought to the United States by the owning family is not entirely clear. But we do know that for several decades prior to the Civil War they resided in Louisiana and were classified as "free blacks" or "free persons of color." Conroy conjectured that these former slaves came to Louisiana on their own.[4]

There is, however, some evidence to suggest that they were brought to the States by their owners and that they shed their slave status shortly before arriving in Louisiana or shortly thereafter, for Louisiana court, land, and church records from as early as 1821 designate particular members of the Bontemps and Pembrooke families "free persons of color," using the French labels "un homme de color libre" or "une femme de color libre." Others are described on early census records with a "W" for white, while some bear the labels "Mu" for mulatto or "B" for black. A significant number of these persons of mixed blood were griffes, mixtures of one mulatto and one black parent. Many times no race is indicated on passenger manifests and census records, which implies that the person was probably white or thought to be. After these Bontemps men, both the former French slaves and their white relatives, arrived in North America, their blood became even more mixed than before, as these men began to intermarry with Native American women.[5]

Prior to and during the Civil War, Louisiana was the province that had the greatest number of free persons of color. For many reasons, most of which lie outside the purview of this book, the greatest numbers of the free persons of color in Louisiana at this time, with the exception of those in Orleans Parish, an urban area, were to be found in such rural regions as Avoyelles and Rapides parishes, where Arna Bontemps's direct progenitors settled. It is significant that throughout the antebellum period those free people of color who lived in the Louisiana Territory remained a basically rural people, with the greatest numbers of them living in eight inland and Mississippi River parishes where the largest slave populations could also be found.[6]

In 1860 Alexandria, Arna Bontemps's birthplace, had a total population of 1,461. Of this number 131 were "free Negroes," 350 were slaves, and the remaining 980 were white.[7] This free black population was mainly composed of mulattoes. According to the Eighth Census of the United States, conducted in 1860, 15,158 of the 18,647 free persons of color were mulattoes.[8] Most of the Louisiana Bontempses and Pembrookes fit into this category. A smaller group were quadroons, octoroons, and griffes. During most of the nineteenth century, the Bontemps and Pembrooke men in Louisiana owned their own farms, for census records refer to them most often as "planters" instead of "sharecroppers" or "itinerant" farmers. A comparison of census and land records in several courthouses in Avoyelles and Rapides parishes shows that the smallest number of acres listed beside one of these farmers' names is sixty. These freedmen were not only planter-aristocrats, but some of them cast their lots in the professions; others were skilled artisans. The Bontemps men, for example, have been brick and stone masons for as long as they have been in this country.

In short, as far as was possible, given legal and social restrictions placed upon free blacks in Louisiana, they were found in every walk of life. Like others of their class, they originated during the French and Spanish colonial periods. This proud group was much better off than were their slave cousins, but they were denied full rights of citizenship because of the stigma of the "Negro" label. They could own property, testify in court, make wills and, in rare cases, vote when their voting could aid some cunning politician.[9] The Bontempses and Pembrookes became devout members of the Catholic Church, an allegiance they maintained until around the turn of the century, when some members of these families were attracted to particular Protestant denominations. Some became Methodists; others became Seventh-day Adventists.

Many of these freedmen were enterprising and had much of the instinct of the entrepreneur. In May 1862 one Hyppolite Bontemps, "f.m.c." or free man of color, attended a land auction conducted by a public auctioneer and purchased for five dollars a parcel of land that was adjacent to his own farm.[10] About a month earlier, Hyppolite purchased a designated tract of land "for the sum of $51.00, he being the last bidder."[11]

Hyppolite Bontemps became the Father of Paul Bismark Bontemps and paternal grandfather of Arna Wendell Bontemps. These land purchases were made approximately one year after Hyppolite's marriage in Avoyelles Parish to Euphemie Laurent. Their marriage certificate, written entirely in French, shows in the left-hand margin that he was a free man of color and that she was a free woman of color.[12] Neither the bride nor the groom could read or write, but both made their marks above their names, or "marque," as the French text reads. The marriage took place in late March or early April 1861.[13]

From all indications, Euphemie Laurent, the first wife of Hyppolite Bontemps, died early, for she was not the mother of all of Hyppolite's children. Her name drops out of all records a short time after their marriage. From the list of offspring that census records of 1880 and 1900 assign to Hyppolite, it is unlikely that she died much prior to the 1880 census, for the 1890 census, destroyed by fire, is not available.

Hyppolite Bontemps was born in Avoyelles Parish in 1835 to Noel and Rosalie Bontemps.[14] Hyppolite had an older sister, Eugenie, born to his parents on November 16, 1823, although she was not baptized until 1824. He also had several brothers. While still in his twenties, Hyppolite married his first wife, Euphemie Laurent (sometimes spelled Euphenise in parish records) and, true to Catholic tradition they started their family immediately. On November 11, 1861, approximately nine months after their marriage, their first child, Louis Fenelon, named after two of Hyppolite's father's brothers, was born and baptized a little less than a month later. Their second child, a son Arthur, was born two years later on November 14, 1863. Paul Bismark Bontemps, father of the writer Arna Bontemps, was the last child born to Hyppolite.

Noel Bontemps, Hyppolite's father, was still alive in 1880, but his wife Rosalie was deceased. He is listed at age seventy-six by the 1880 census and as married again to a forty-eight-year-old woman named Marguerite whom he married in the year of the census. Also enumerated in his household is a young grandson, Nathan Bontemps, age sixteen. Nathan is either one of Paul Bontemps's older brothers or a cousin. It is not likely that Hyppolite and Euphemie Laurent Bontemps were ever divorced, considering that they were married by the Church, and considering the strictness at this time of the Church's teaching against divorce, as well as the stigma attached.

The Louisiana census of 1880 shows Hyppolite still residing in Avoyelles Parish but married to a different woman.[15] His age is listed as forty-two, which does not accord with his birth year (1835) as recorded elsewhere. If this is his correct age, then he was probably born around 1838 or 1839, though parish records give his birth year as 1835.[16] The 1838 date would have made him close to twenty-two when he married the first time (1861) and accords with the age of forty-two listed by the 1880 census taker, who lists his wife's name as Edvise and gives her age as forty-three. Hyppolite's occupation is listed as farmer; his wife is described as "keeping house."

It is interesting to note that not all of his offspring were living in the house with him, a practice that census records for the state throughout the nineteenth century and into the twentieth reveal as common. He kept at home the older children who could give him a good day as farm laborers. Listed in his household in 1880 were a nineteen-year-old daughter, Juliet, and a seventeen-year-old son, Jolite. Both are described as field hands. This census shows that Hyppolite and at least a portion of his family were living in an area of Avoyelles Parish called "Bayou Rouge Pharrie." The census record lists his color as mulatto and his wife Advise's color as black. This is the background into which Arna Bontemps's father was born.

Paul Bismark Bontemps, who was to become the father of the writer Arna Wendell and his sister Ruby Sarah, was in 1880 living with an uncle in Avoyelles Parish and is described "mulatto male," aged nine.[17] The uncle's name is Laurent DuClaire. And in the same year his brother Victor Bontemps, described by the census as ten years of age, was living with a different household, relationship not reported. This could be the result of the European tradition of apprenticeship that these Creoles followed. At age seven, the sons would have been apprenticed out to a reliable relative or family friend to learn a trade. In the case of Arna's father Paul, it was brick and stone masonry, a craft the Bontemps males had followed for generations. The ancestry of Arna Bontemps is especially interesting to trace, for as census records reveal, many of the Bontempses and Pembrookes, male and female, had the same first names. Among the males on both sides of the family the following names appear in successive generations: Nathan, Arthur, Eugene, Victor, and Joseph, and of course, Paul. Among the females of both families one finds in a similar pattern the names Euphemie, Caroline, Eugenia, Sarah, and Elizabeth, most occurring in several variant spellings. Among all branches of the Bontemps family, African-American, Caucasian, and Native American, the name Paul for male children is a decided favorite; with Nathan, Alexander, and Victor tied for second place. Paul and Alexander were kept by Arna Wendell Bontemps when he named his two sons.

Lists transcribed from original passenger manifests in the archives of the U.S. Customs Service in New Orleans show a Frenchman named Alexandre Bontemps arriving at New Orleans in 1837 aboard the ship *Fortunata*, which he boarded at Le Havre, the seaport closest to Paris. The most significant fact about the passenger manifests is that they show several sea captains with the last name Bontemps who were operating schooners and sailing vessels between New Orleans and ports in Europe and South America.[18] These manifests show T. Bontemps, J. Bontemps, and S. Bontemps, all operating a schooner named *Sarah Ann* between the years 1834 and 1839, making runs between Tampico and New Orleans. These are the three Bontemps brothers who came to New Orleans from France by way of Haiti, and it is not unlikely that they were related to the Alexandre Bontemps mentioned previously.

One of the three sea captains eventually settled in Mississippi, while the other two remained in Louisiana. Since these men were experienced sailors who owned at least one vessel, it was probably on board one of their vessels that the African-American branch of the Bontemps family came to Louisiana. Arna Bontemps's widow, Alberta Bontemps, knows the story of these three brothers, for in a recent interview she commented, ''there were three brothers, all from France. One settled in Mississippi; the other two settled at New Orleans. This was in the first part [half] of the nineteenth century.''[19]

The variant spellings of the Bontemps surname as it appears on various written records can prove a matter of much confusion to the researcher. In Louisiana census reports for 1860, 1880, and 1900, and on passenger manifests from several decades earlier than 1860, it appears as Bontemps, Bontin, Bantin, Bontempo, Bonton, Bunton, Buntin, Bentin, Banton, Benton, Bonte, and Bontins. These variant spellings were used by many of the large number of cousins in the state. But on close examination, one finds that the immediate relatives of Arna Bontemps, as far back as 1821, and probably before this time, spelled their last name Bontemps.[20] Variant spellings of the Pembrooke name also abound but are not as numerous as variants of Bontemps. Census records between 1860 and 1900 show these variants: Pemmbrook, Penbrook, Pembroke, Pembrose, Pembrook, Pembrick, and Pembrooke. Ruby Bontemps Troy, the writer's sister, has provided in a letter written from Huntsville, Alabama's Oakwood College— where she was director of admissions for many years and where she still works part-time—the spelling Pembrooke, the one her family has preferred for several generations.[21]

The Bontempses and the Pembrookes, those who did not remain in New Orleans, tended to congregate in central Louisiana, within a thirty- or forty-mile radius of Alexandria. I was surprised to find that not a single Bontemps or Pembrooke is listed in Father Hebert's famous thirty-three-volume record of settlers of southwest Louisiana.[22] A search of each volume of this scholarly work, which covers the years 1756–1904, reveals that there were in the southwestern region of Louisiana Bonins, Bonnets, Bonsalls, and Bonvillains, but not a single Bontemps. And among the persons with last names beginning with "P" are Pennisons, Penns, Peppers, and Pempletons, but no Pembrookes, not even in a variant spelling. A number of prevailing conditions kept these freedmen in the Alexandria-Pineville-Marksville area of central Louisiana. Prime reasons were the abundance of available farm lands and a climate conducive to producing a variety of staple crops—rice, beans, corn, sweet potatoes, and sugar cane. Furthermore, they sought an area where they could be themselves, keeping their dignity as human beings.

Sterkx has described this group of "free Negroes" as a whole and gives an account of particular conditions with which they were forced to cope during the antebellum and postbellum periods. He reports that there was never a time when they were not intimidated by ever-increasing anti–free Negro forces, especially during and after the 1850s, when the race question became a more contentious issue than it had ever been.[23] There was always a small but vocal minority among the white population whose sole desire, it seems, was to rid the state of this class of "free blacks," whom they regarded as troublemakers: bad examples for the slaves and too proud not to take offense at ill treatment.

To better comprehend the extent to which specific freedoms were denied both "free blacks" and slaves in Louisiana, one needs to consult the state's "Black Code," a set of laws adopted as early as 1724 by the state's Superior Council.[24] Even the Roman Catholic Church made a difference in its treatment of these parishioners and their white counterparts, for early church records show that this group was commonly referred to as "gens de couleur libre," with individual members of the class referred to as "negre libre" or "negresse libre." It was a liability to be "colored," and an even worse stigma to "act colored." This explains, perhaps, why Arna Bontemps's father Paul was so intent on erasing reminders of discrimination in his home state, and why he objected so strenuously to his son Arna's "acting colored," a point to be treated more fully in a subsequent chapter of this biography.

The Bontempses were a particularly proud group, supersensitive about their privacy. They had found that many times they were even more defenseless in this environment than their relatives who were still slaves. Census records show that they were not only proud but high-strung, capable even of belligerence, for they rarely cooperated with census takers, often refusing to answer offensive questions or deliberately giving ludicrous or wrong answers as a means of venting their hostilities toward a dominant power structure.

The mulattoes among the group were more numerous than both the blacks and the whites, and they probably resented inquiries about race and color; such questions as census takers were required to ask. They sometimes refused to supply their ages, and more often than not, the category on the census form titled "relationship to above" bears such responses as "not reported," "not available," or "no relationship given." Moreover, the space under "occupation" is for the adult Bontempses often left blank. A good example would be Hyppolite Bontemps of Rapides Parish, listed in the 1880 census. He is obviously a relative of the younger Hyppolite Bontemps who is enumerated the same year in Avoyelles Parish and whose age is given as forty-two.[25] This elder Bontemps's age is given as fifty-seven, indicating that he would have been an uncle or cousin to the younger Hyppolite, the father of Paul Bismark Bontemps, and grandfather of Arna.[26]

On the other hand, it seems that the Pembrookes were not as abrasive as the Bontempses, though they were clearly just as intelligent. There is no evidence in the census records of any of the Pembrookes failing to cooperate with census takers. It would seem, too, that the Pembrookes possessed less of a particular kind of physical stamina than did the Bontempses. Arna Bontemps's own mother, Maria Carolina Pembrooke, died young from a lingering illness, and her oldest sister died in childbirth. And Joseph Pembrooke, her father, did not survive the rigors of relocating. He was in California only a short time before he became sick and died.[27]

It seems, conversely, that the Wards, the relatives of Arna Bontemps's maternal grandmother, were exceptionally strong and that they lived long, active lives. This is certainly true if Sarah Ward Pembrooke, Arna Bontemps's maternal grandmother, is typical of the others, for not only was she a woman of exceptional intelligence and economic acumen, but her longevity is also remarkable. In 1972, approximately one year before he died, Arna Bontemps remarked that this grandmother had died only a few years previously, and that she had been still alive while one of his own daughters was in graduate school in California.[28]

Nathan Pembrooke, maternal great-grandfather of Arna Bontemps, was in 1900 living in Ward I of what later became the township of Alexandria.[29] At the time of the census, Nathan Pembrooke was seventy-eight years old. His wife Elizabeth was seventy-two. By this time, all of their children were grown. Nathan and Elizabeth had several daughters who, because of their married names, are difficult to trace through written records. They did, however, have at least one son, Joseph Pembrooke, from whom Arna Bontemps is descended on his mother's side. Arna himself corroborated this fact only a short time before he died, for he said in a lecture that his grandfather was Joseph Pembrooke and that he was the son of Nathan Pembrooke. Arna admitted to having great difficulty keeping up with the descendants of Nathan Pembrooke.[30]

Joseph Pembrooke, husband to Sarah Ward Pembrooke and grandfather to Arna Wendell Bontemps and Ruby Sarah, his sister, was born on December 27, 1847. In 1900 he was fifty-two years old, meaning that he was approximately fifty-eight when the family moved to California six years later.[31] His Alexandria address is listed on the census as simply "Ward I, Tenth Street," which would place his and his wife's residence at this time near the house built around the turn of the century at Ninth and Winn Streets where Arna Bontemps was born: a two-family dwelling where Joseph and Sarah Pembrooke had moved by 1902, and where their daughter Maria Carolina and son-in-law Paul Bontemps lived. The census records show Joseph Pembrooke's occupation as "farmer," but it is known that he supplemented his income by working as an undertaker's assistant to his brother-in-law Joe Ekomip, his sister Charlotte's husband, who owned a funeral establishment.[32]

Enumerated in the household with Joseph Pembrooke and his wife Sarah, who was forty-five in 1900, were their seven children.[33] Their eldest was a daughter, Mary Ellen (often referred to by her middle name), born May 9, 1872, who was twenty-eight years old and living at home. A second daughter, Charlotte (referred to most often as Clotilde, her middle name), was born May 4, 1875 and was twenty-five years old and living at home. Their third child, who was to become the mother of Arna Bontemps, was Maria Carolina, listed simply as Maria C. on census records. This daughter, who became in 1901 the wife of Paul Bismark Bontemps, was born on March 4, 1879, and was twenty-one at the time of the 1900 census.

Then came the fourth Pembrooke child, another daughter named Lourania. This is the "Aunt Ludie" to whom Arna and his sister Ruby have affectionately referred from time to time. She was born on July 28, 1881 and was nineteen years old in 1900. The fifth child and youngest daughter was named Anna J., the writer's "Aunt Anna," who was three years younger than her sister "Ludie," for she was born on July 6, 1884 and was sixteen at the time of the 1900 census. Next on the list came the first son, Nathan Ward, who is Arna's "Uncle Ward," whom he mentioned so frequently.[34] Born September 7, 1887, this uncle's age was given as twelve on the 1900 census. His younger brother, the "baby" of the family, was John Douglas, also known by his middle name. Appearing last on the list, he was born on April 7, 1891 and was nine when the 1900 census was taken.

Many of the facts listed above are corroborated by the unpublished "Autobiography of Anna J. Stokes," Arna Bontemps's mother's sister, and by the obituary of Sarah Ward Pembrooke, written by Ruby Bontemps Troy, the first two sentences of which read: "Grandma was born in White Sulphur Springs, Louisiana. She was the daughter of Charlotte and Joseph Ward."[35] This accounts for her naming the second daughter Charlotte, for it was her own mother's name, and it corroborates the "Charlotte" listed on the 1900 census.[36] Arna Bontemps, too, said of this grandmother, about six months before he died, that her marriage certificate proved that she was born approximately eleven years before the end of the Civil War; that she had some familiarity with a school near Pineville, of which General William Tecumseh Sherman, President of Louisiana State University from 1859–1861, was once principal; and that the school was also near White Sulphur Springs, a town which no longer appears on the map of Louisiana.[37]

Sarah Ward, who became Arna Bontemps's maternal grandmother, had been one of a large number of children born to her parents. There were three sons and two daughters who survived to adulthood, though some confusion surrounds their names and sexes. One written source lists their names in this order: Philo, Sarah, Jane, Charles, and Joseph, R.[38] During the Civil War Sarah Ward's father died, while still a young man and while his family was still residing at White Sulphur Springs, a summer resort.[39]

As soon as the war ended, the young mother, Charlotte Ward, moved with her small children into the area that is now known as the City of Alexandria.[40] Sarah, her second child and oldest daughter, grew up there with her brothers and sister Jane. In 1871, when Sarah was approximately seventeen, she married Joseph Pembrooke, who was more than five years her senior. This young Pembrooke was already "an undertaker's assistant and gentleman farmer."[41] In May 1872 their first child was born, and they settled down to rearing a family in an environment attended by difficulties. Sarah Pembrooke and her husband Joe were never able to escape the untoward social climate of Alexandria while their five daughters were growing up, but if conditions were perilous for the young black female growing up in the Deep South, they knew that they were even more threatening to the life and well-being of the young black male. Consequently, the Pembrookes never abandoned their dream of moving North or West where they and their children could enjoy freedom. By 1891, when Douglas, the last child and second son was born, the racial climate in Alexandria had become more threatening than it had ever been.[42]

Sarah Pembrooke was even more ambitious, more industrious, than her husband Joseph. She was a shrewd manager of whatever monies her husband brought home, the kind of bright, hard-working young mother who saw to it that she passed on to her five daughters her domestic skills and that they got all the formal schooling and artistic training available to them. And she must have been pleased that her talented children learned rapidly. At least one of these daughters became a teacher in the public schools of Alexandria. This was Arna Bontemps's mother, Maria (pronounced Ma-rye-a) Carolina. And her youngest sister Anna became a "real modiste," as her niece has described her.[43] Those among the Pembrooke girls who wanted it, received training in art and music. While their daughters were growing up and while their two sons were young boys, Joe and

Sarah Pembrooke watched as their closest friends and relatives left Alexandria, Pineville, Bunkie, Marksville, and Mansura for a better life in California, Illinois, or New York.

By the turn of the century, their desire to flee to freedom had reached almost fever pitch. They had seen so many inequities in the state of their birth that they had by this time despaired of ever attaining the full rights of citizenship in Louisiana, or in any other Southern state. Even Mother Church, at least as the Pembrookes perceived conditions, had failed them, for in this area, where to be a Catholic meant acceptability and prestige, they had learned that where the Church's treatment of its parishioners was concerned there was a noticeable discrepancy between black and white. It is unlikely that in these days the Church had any priests and nuns who were African American, and this fact the Pembrookes may have interpreted as a sign of God's absence in the Catholic community.

These slights were felt even more acutely by some members of the Bontemps clan. The Church had not been strong enough in its objection to injustice to prevent the more sensitive among its parishioners from feeling rejected and alienated. The foreparents of these Bontempses and Pembrookes, like so many of their "free black" counterparts during the antebellum period, had settled in Louisiana because there the laws prohibiting socioeconomic mobility were not as stringent as those of some other Southern states, and "the ones they did have," writes one historian, "were not uniformly enforced."[44] But more than three decades after the Civil War had ended, their dreams of freedom for their grandchildren had not been achieved.

On a whole, the Bontempses and Pembrookes were industrious, law-abiding citizens. But these qualities were not enough in Louisiana to earn for them the respect they felt they deserved. Jim Crow sentiment among whites in the area was increasing with every new day. By 1890, post-Reconstruction disorders had reached their peak in the state. Inferior schools and the terrorist tactics of the Ku Klux Klan—or "White Caps," as they were called—with those of other white supremacist groups had caused Sarah Ward Pembrooke to start making plans prior to 1900 for the entire family to make their exodus to a better land. Her health, too, had not been good in Louisiana, though she worked hard and did not complain. Her husband Joe felt that perhaps another climate would do her good. As for herself, she was determined to see that she and her family enjoyed freedom, if only for a little while. There was livestock and other property to be liquidated. Sarah Pembrooke knew that she would need to save every penny she could, for with sufficient cash on hand she would be able to purchase enough land in another state to assure the family's continuity in the rural lifestyle to which they had grown accustomed. Her dream was to have enough land in their new home to support a truck farm that would sustain livestock and fruit trees to provide food for the family the year round.

Not all of the times in Louisiana, though, had been foul; both the Pembrookes and the Bontempses enjoyed strong family ties and were not without some of the comforts that enhanced the quality of life. Joe and Sarah Pembrooke's youngest daughter wrote as late as 1953 with great joy about their memories of childhood, describing members of her immediate family with tenderness.[45] She described her childhood home as large, with several "extra rooms" and an eight-foot-wide hall and windowsills deep enough for a person to sit on. The house was on one corner of an enclosed acre and had a small lake behind it where the family often went fishing or crawfishing.[46]

Speaking of each of her four sisters and her relationship with them, and of her two younger brothers, Anna revealed that they each had a nickname. She suggested that these nicknames were needed because they had, especially the girls, what she considered "long French names." Her own nickname "Ann" was the sanest of the lot because it derived from her given name. Mary Ellen's nickname was "Nell"; Charlotte Clotilde was called "Laet"; Maria Carolina's nickname was "Ram"; and Lourania had two nicknames, "Ludie" and "Dub." The two boys were nicknamed "Draw" and "Delos," respectively. To keep things from getting dull, they also had a baby to play with, at least for a while. "Laet," the second sister, was separated from her husband and living at home again. Her daughter, "Tam," was raised as Anna's little sister.[47]

A source of particular delight to the Pembrooke children was their maternal grandmother, the former Charlotte Ward, who moved to Alexandria while they were growing up. Anna Stokes wrote that grandmother Charlotte "came from the mixed breeds of South America."[48] She spoke French instead of Spanish, which was the language of nearly everyone in South America, and her father came from the "blue bloods" of England. He had been disinherited by the family and sent away from England because he married a circus rider. Charlotte Ward, the maternal great-grandmother of Arna Bontemps, became this Englishman's second wife.[49] Thus Arna Bontemps had European relatives on both his father's and his mother's sides of the family, the French and the English respectively.

After Charlotte Ward's parents came to the United States, they settled in a Southern resort town where they made huge sums of money. This is the town of White Sulphur Springs. They stored the money in huge wooden kegs and buried it during the Civil War.[50] Sarah Ward Pembrooke remembered her mother's father and was with him, she recalled, when he buried the money, but she was too young when he died to give clear directions about its location. Anna Stokes wrote of how "they plowed the place up without success of finding it," and how her grandmother (Charlotte Ward) became so frightened that she took her children and fled.[51]

The mother of Joseph Pembrooke (father of Arna Bontemps's mother Maria and husband of Sarah Ward) was a full-blooded Cherokee, and his father, a Southern planter, was English. When Joseph Pembrooke pioneered to California in 1906, his father was still alive.[52] Whether this English father was ever married to his mother or whether she was still alive by the time her son left Louisiana is not clear from available records. But the foregoing genealogical information is enough to eliminate most of the confusion surrounding the name Joseph or "Joe" that appears so often on both sides of Arna Bontemps's family.

There is the father of Sarah Ward Pembrooke, Joseph Ward, Sr., and his son by his wife Charlotte, Joseph Ward, Jr. Then there is the writer's mother's father, Joseph Pembrooke. Still another is Joe Ekomip, husband to Sarah Ward Pembrooke's sister Harriet. And on the Bontemps side of the family there were several Josephs in each generation from 1860 until 1900. These Josephs all resided either in Avoyelles Parish or in the adjacent Rapides Parish.

While Joe Pembrooke continued to farm in Rapides Parish and to work part-time for his brother-in-law at the funeral home, his wife Sarah supplemented his income by taking in sewing. As a result, there was enough money available to provide painting and piano lessons for the girls. With five daughters, Sarah had more than enough help with the household chores and was able to spend the larger part of each day in her dressmaker's shop, which was attached to the house in Alexandria, and which her oldest daughter "Nell" helped her operate.

Their volume of business was such that they hired several other women to work in the shop. Sarah was an accomplished seamstress and tried to teach all of her daughters to sew. They all learned the art well; all except "Dub," or "Ludie." This next-to-the-youngest daughter was her mother's pet, as Anna Stokes described her, and was "lazy and pretty" during her childhood and did not take readily to sewing.[53] Joseph Pembrooke was more than a little proud of his wife's sewing skills, for without her help he could not have provided all the finery his five daughters required.

At least one of the daughters, Anna, the youngest, was born in her mother's dressmaking shop.[54] Anna took naturally to sewing and began by making clothes for all of her nine dolls. Since she was not tall enough to sit at a machine to tread the pedal, she stood to sew, running to a machine every time she found one vacant in the shop. By age ten, she was selling her collection of doll clothes to her mother's customers for their children.[55] In the late 1890s, when Anna was around twelve, the family discovered that "Nell," her oldest sister, had been secretly married to a man she had been seeing for years.

Her father, Joe Pembrooke, had repeatedly refused to give his consent to their marriage. "Nell" discovered that she was pregnant but kept her condition a secret, failing to seek the care of a physician. She died in childbirth. The shock nearly killed Joe and Sarah Pembrooke, for they could not absolve themselves of guilt. Sarah was inconsolable and could not concentrate on sewing. The shop was full of unfinished work that she and the deceased daughter had started, and this is how Anna's career as a modiste began, for she stepped in and finished all the work to the delight of the satisfied customers. Her success as a seamstress pleased her parents immensely, for by age fourteen she was earning more per week than most men with families earned.[56]

If Sarah Pembrooke was dissatisfied with life in Alexandria before the death of her oldest child, she was even less contented afterward. Then, to add to her loneliness, by the end of 1901 her second and third daughters, one of whom became the mother of Arna Wendell Bontemps, had both married and left home. So most of the work in the shop fell on Anna's shoulders, and she turned over most of the money she made to her mother. Sarah Pembrooke began to scrimp and save as never before, for she had "heard of a city called heaven" and had decided to make this California "heaven" her home. Heaven for her and her family had never existed in Louisiana.

In November 1901, five years before the move to California, Paul Bismark Bontemps married the woman of his dreams, Maria Carolina Pembrooke, third daughter of Joseph and Sarah Ward Pembrooke.[57] He was an experienced young man of thirty and strikingly handsome with his dark skin, coal-black silken hair and sturdy build. She was a fair-skinned, slender, twenty-two-year-old with an exceptionally pretty face.[58] The marriage license was purchased on November 6, 1901 and was recorded and filed in the Rapides Parish courthouse on the same day of the wedding.[59] The license was signed by the bride, the groom, and the officiating priest, Father L. Minard, Rector of Saint Francis Xavier Church, the same priest who pastored the parish for many years and whose signature appears on the baptismal records of both Arna Bontemps and his sister Ruby.[60]

The signatures of three witnesses appear on this marriage certificate: W. A. Flowers, James Davis, and L. D. Laurent, probably a descendant of one of the Laurents who had witnessed Paul Bontemps's father's marriage to Euphemie Laurent in 1861, some forty years before. The hand is very tremulous, suggesting the writing of an elderly person; hence this Laurent is probably the same Louis Laurent who witnessed Hyppolite's 1861 marriage.

Some of the same signatures representing witnesses at the wedding of Paul and Maria Bontemps also appear, along with others, on the baptismal records of their two children. Interesting to the student of Louisiana culture of that period is the fact that Paul Bontemps was required by law to purchase a bond before he could be issued a license to marry. This nuptial bond was required of all prospective grooms. Paul Bontemps purchased his bond on the day of his wedding and his best man acted as required security for the bond. A portion of the bond reads "know all men by these presents, that P. B. Bontemps, principal, and W. A. Flowers as security, are held and firmly bound to the Governor of the State of Louisiana for the sum of two hundred dollars, for the payment of which we bind ourselves . . . by these presents."[61]

By the time of his marriage, Paul Bontemps had perfected his skills as a brick and stone mason, and his wife had been teaching school in Rapides Parish for at least three years. Maria Bontemps had always been the most literary of the five Pembrooke sisters, all of whom were above average in intelligence. Though born and reared in Alexandria, she spoke with not a trace of a drawl or of the patois that her husband Paul never lost. Her son, in more than one place, corroborated these facts, and mentioned his mother's "literary interest" and that she practiced drawing and had tried to teach her children to draw a bit.[62] And on at least one occasion, Arna Bontemps described his mother as "a real scholar."[63]

Paul Bontemps traveled a great deal, both as a bricklayer, who had to go where the big construction jobs were, and as a member of Claiborne Williams's jazz band. In 1971, while in Alexandria searching for the name of the band Paul Bontemps played with, Arna said that his father played in Williams's band and that the band, even in his later years, meant a great deal to his father, even though his occupation was brick masonry. Williams was one of the great band influences in New Orleans, but he also trained and directed bands in the smaller Louisiana towns.

Bontemps describes a young musician in *Young Booker*, who would go to small towns and teach people as did Claiborne Williams, for whom Arna's father played the valve trombone. Arna also explained why his father had a particular kind of mouthpiece—it was one that would fit both the valve trombone and the baritone horn. Paul Bontemps played them both and never discarded the mouthpiece that Arna blew on when he was a child, "just to see if I could blow it."[64]

During the 1890s the Bontemps family was driven out of Avoyelles Parish by the "White Caps," and some of the immediate descendants of Hyppolite Bontemps moved to nearby Rapides Parish, the area that is now the city of Alexandria. There were three sons, Victor, Charlie, and Paul, Arna's father, who was the youngest. Paul settled in Alexandria; Victor and Charlie chose New Orleans.[65] These three Bontemps brothers, who also had one sister, were all sons of Hyppolite Bontemps by a woman whose first name was Pauline.

Pauline's name does not appear in any of the census records of Avoyelles and Rapides parishes, but it does appear in church records. Arna Bontemps had Pauline identified by his father as the poet's paternal grandmother less than a year before he died, during the period when he was gathering information to use in his autobiography. He confided to a former student who had become his Fisk colleague:

My father's father's name was Hyppolite; he had brothers named Louie and Finilong, and one named Victor. . . . Marksville is where my father was born and Marksville is only about thirty miles from Alexandria, but it's like another world, like a European thing. It was a French-speaking world and my father's father was Hyppolite and his mother was Pauline. . . . I have to use my father's memory for part of it. My father told me that Pauline had lived with an old Frenchman and that they were all free. Well, I was able to verify that because I corresponded with a priest. . . . I tried to find the answer at Marksville [at the courthouse there] and they referred me to Mansura where records were kept prior to the Civil War and . . . the priest there got interested in the questions I gave him and went in and took time to research them and discovered that the only Bontemps prior to the Civil War was Noel, that they had a record of Noel Bontemps. He was a proprietor, as the French word is . . . a land owner. And both Hyppolite and Pauline were listed as free in the book of the free men of color. Now this Hyppolite was born in 1825, so that was quite a long time before Emancipation, so my assumption is that it was just prior to that [to emancipation] that this Noel emancipated Pauline. [Free people could and did own slaves.] And I perused a little further back and found that Noel did have a white wife previously who had died, and a daughter by this previous marriage.[66]

It is obvious, then, that Arna Bontemps's paternal grandmother, Pauline, was a mere girl when the Civil War ended and that she was considerably younger than both Hyppolite Bontemps and his first wife Euphemie Laurent. I have documented already that Euphemie, more than likely, died early. It could be, then, that the Edvise mentioned already, the forty-three-year-old woman living in the house with Hyppolite in 1880 was his third wife, for the census record does not show that they were married during the census year.

One confusing point, though, about this record is that it lists the marriage as the first for both parties, a statement that certainly is not true and which could be another instance of the Bontemps men giving deliberately erroneous information to census takers. The foregoing facts, then, would make Pauline the second wife of Hyppolite Bontemps, possibly his common-law wife, for common-law marriages have been recognized by the State of Louisiana since before Emancipation. At any rate, no written record that documents a formal marriage for the pair has been thus far located.

Arna Bontemps, in the aforementioned interview, also described the conditions in Avoyelles Parish that caused his father's immediate family to settle in Alexandria. "You know in Louisiana," Arna said, "there was great interest in Reconstruction. And we had a lieutenant governor, Pinchback, whom my grandmother [Sarah Ward Pembrooke] knew. But there was a reaction in the nineties, and my grandmother told me how they had the White Caps . . . who had been active in Avoyelles Parish and had driven out the Negroes."[67]

Arna's father Paul Bismark Bontemps had been fortunate indeed where this wave of hostility was concerned, for he was not in Avoyelles Parish with the rest of the family when the worst of the oppression occurred and when his siblings fled to Rapides Parish (Alexandria). In 1890 Paul Bontemps turned nineteen, and by this time he had already left Marksville-Mansura to attend Straight University in New Orleans. Straight was a preparatory school that offered a curriculum from grades three through twelve. It was one of the American Missionary Association schools formed just after the Emancipation Proclamation.[68]

By the time young Paul Bontemps finished his preparatory education, Straight had put some industrial training courses into the curriculum, just the kind of saleable training that would appeal to the pragmatic mind of this young entrepreneur. Like most black schools of the day, Straight had added, under the influence of Booker T. Washington, brick masonry to the curriculum. Paul Bontemps excelled in these courses and had already learned the art as a young boy, for in his own family there were several master brick masons. At Straight he was exposed to the latest technological advancements, and in New Orleans he found many opportunities to earn money as a part-time construction worker. This work experience allowed him to perfect his skills while finishing his schooling. Arna Bontemps described how his father's two older brothers had already settled near New Orleans by the time Paul entered Straight. He also noted that these uncles were probably attracted to the kind of regular instruction offered by Straight University.[69] So Victor and Charlie Bontemps remained in Orleans Parish, where they both married and settled down to rearing their families.

Together with his brothers and the older men of the family, Paul Bontemps had grown accustomed to traveling throughout the state to various construction sites, wherever work was to be found in brick masonry and the other trades. Years later he told his children about having worked throughout the state, wherever the most profitable jobs were, building sugar mills, sugar refineries, railroad depots, or even smaller buildings, when the larger jobs were not available.

It was probably while he was a student in New Orleans that Arna's father met Claiborne Williams and became part of his band. In New Orleans there were many opportunities to earn extra money as a jazz musician. It is not clear from available information, though, just which circumstances caused Paul Bontemps to meet his children's mother, Maria Carolina Pembrooke, though we do know that they met at Alexandria.[70]

It could be that he met her when she was still a girl, while he was helping to rebuild the Saint Francis Xavier Catholic Church in the parish that became an important part of his life after his permanent move to Alexandria. This was in 1894 or 1895, when he was twenty-three and Maria was only sixteen. Or he could have met her several years later after he left New Orleans and had taken up residence in Alexandria. Or it could have been on one of the many road trips with the band, for the *Alexandria Town Talk*—a newspaper which had existed since Reconstruction—carried during the 1890s accounts of the performances of the Claiborne Williams Band in Rapides Parish, a fact that Arna Bontemps alluded to in the fall of 1972 when he visited Alexandria for the last time.[71]

The writer concluded an account of his father's youthful itinerary by saying "he wound up somehow in Alexandria, where he met my mother."[72] We can place Paul Bismark Bontemps in Alexandria after 1894, not only because of his work on the Saint Francis Xavier Church, but also because in 1895 he witnessed the marriage of his sister, Cecelia Bontemps, to William Swann on January 15, 1895. The marriage was performed by Father L. Minard, the same priest who was to perform the marriage ceremony of Maria Bontemps seven years later.[73]

Both Paul Bontemps and his bride were descendants of a class that existed in Louisiana and elsewhere in the South prior to, during, and after the Civil War, and well into the twentieth century. These Louisiana freedmen were no different from that famous group of middle-class African Americans who lived in the neighboring state of Mississippi, especially around Natchez.[74] This was a group of handsome, well-dressed, individuals who, because of their "free" status and their economic acumen, were able to rise above the thousands of other African Americans in the area who remained destitute and uneducated. These descendants of freedmen seized opportunities to start businesses during the last decades of the nineteenth century—such enterprises as the thriving dressmaking establishment of Sarah Ward Pembrooke and the undertaking business of her brother-in-law Joe Ekomip in Rapides Parish. Their free parents, even before the war, though not taught to read and write, learned many saleable skills as carpenters, brick masons, blacksmiths, managers, dressmakers, and cooks. In postwar days many African Americans became teachers, preachers, politicians, artisans, musicians, merchants, farmers, and small businessmen.[75]

So the wedding of Paul and Maria Bontemps brought together two fine minds. Both were skilled in reading and writing, she as a teacher-artist and he as an artisan-musician. Both were from families who for generations had been considered "good livers" in this area of Central Louisiana. But by the time he married Maria, Paul Bontemps already had decided not to remain in the South. His parents and other older relatives could remember the time when terrorists during Reconstruction had driven some of the most vocal African-American politicians away from Rapides Parish and how one of the friends of the Pembrookes, himself a leading politician, had to seek refuge in Arkansas on being driven out of Alexandria.[76]

This public figure knew, as did the older Bontempses and Pembrookes, that as far as darker-skinned citizens were concerned, Reconstruction in Louisiana had been a dismal failure, even in parishes like Rapides that had in 1870 a population approximately 60 percent African American.[77] Joseph and Sarah Pembrooke could remember well how during the summer of 1874 state police and military men had set up an armed camp to keep the peace in Alexandria. There had been unrest ever since the state elections of 1872, because conservatives had screamed election fraud and had tried to ignore the newly elected officers. This move toward the establishment of militant white unity resulted in the founding in 1874 of *Caucasian*, a newspaper that espoused racial hatred.[78] And *The Alexandria Daily Town Talk* was itself far from pro-black, for a perusal of its pages from the 1890s until long after the Bontempses and Pembrookes moved to California in 1906, uncovers an ever-mounting anti-Negro sentiment.

About four months after her marriage to Paul, Maria Bontemps discovered that she was expecting their first child. This was happy news for all of the Bontempses and Pembrookes. Nevertheless, Paul Bontemps was not unaware, even in the midst of his nuptial happiness, that 1902 was a stormy time in Louisiana, for he read every edition of the *Town Talk*, and so did the Pembrookes of his generation; the *Town Talk* was a paper that at that time was published each evening except Sunday.

But the spring, summer, and fall of 1902 was not a peaceful time anywhere, not in the world, not in the nation, not in Alexandria. As Maria Bontemps's delivery drew near, the political climate grew worse instead of better, if newspaper reports of the period are credible. For months prior to October 1902 there had been a nationwide coal strike, with a bitter battle raging between coal miners and their opponents, the coal operators. Violence had broken out in some Eastern and Midwestern cities when coal bosses refused to pay their men union wages.[79]

This was the time when the large railway corporations were enjoying their heyday, and when their activities filled the news. One week before Arna Bontemps was born, the report came out that during the preceding month the cost of living had risen more than 4 percent, wiping out modest gains of the previous August. But foremost in the news were religious conflicts of various kinds and reports of violence throughout the world. More than one fierce theological quarrel had arisen. There were reports of anti-British attitudes among the Boer clergymen, and serious religious conflict threatened all of Great Britain over the Anti-Ritualist Movement. Moreover, civil war had broken out in Colombia.[80]

On Sunday, October 12, the day before Arna Bontemps was born, heading the national news were two stories: the Crown Prince of Siam's visit to the nation's capital city and the coal strike. Heating fuel had become scarce, and federal troops were preparing to go to Wilkes-Barre, Pennsylvania, to stem violence among coal workers there. And in Australia there were also labor problems: workers were not striking; they were being laid off by the thousands. But there were very few African Americans in the national news, and when they did appear it was in connection with either the sensational or the ludicrous.[81]

During the weeks leading toward and including Arna Bontemps's birth, September and October 1902, the *Town Talk* covered state and local concerns. In the first part of September, officials of Rapides Parish were trying to get the citizenry to vote to bring a second cotton factory to the area. They argued that such an addition would provide enough jobs for area residents and a general boost to the economy as well. In late September there had been news about the Rapides cotton crop. The U.S. Bureau of Agriculture had taken steps to gather cotton statistics throughout the parish. This marked the second year that statistical data had been gathered from the ginners, who were asked to disclose the number of bales processed at each gin.[82]

A streetcar strike was brewing in New Orleans and was reported in the *Town Talk* on October 1 under the caption "Streetcar Strike." No cars were moving in New Orleans and there was no news about settling the issues that had caused the walkout. On Monday, October 6, one week prior to Maria Bontemps's confinement, the *Town Talk*'s major story appeared under headlines "New Train Service—over the Southern Pacific into Alexandria." On the day before, "elegant passenger trains" and "splendid freight trains" had come to Alexandria for the first time as part of new regular routes to the area. It was on one of these new trains that the Bontempses and Pembrookes, four years later, would ride to their new home in California. This issue also congratulated the *Town Talk* itself for its successful appeals to the people of the state and to the Southern Pacific Railway, for before this time the only train offering passenger service was a mixed freight and passenger local. Hence this expansion of railway service was a definite sign of progress for the area and it also meant jobs for many citizens of Rapides Parish.

Maria Bontemps's uncle, Joseph Ward, Jr., younger brother of her mother Sarah Pembrooke and grand-uncle to her son Arna, was one of the first African Americans hired as a dining-car waiter after this expansion.[83] This was good news for the family and even better news for young Joe Ward, one who had always been restless. With his new job on the train he would get to see some of the places he had read about in the *Town Talk*. A few years later, around the time that the family was to move to California, Maria Bontemps's own younger brother, Ward Pembrook, was to land a similar job on the same passenger train. Ward had turned fifteen one month before this new train service commenced, and by the time he and his family began to move, piecemeal, to the West, he was approaching nineteen.

Monday, October 13, was remarkable for Alexandria's Bontemps family and for persons throughout the state of Louisiana. Late on the Sunday night before, too late for citizens to get the news, the streetcar strike in New Orleans had ended. The Monday evening edition of the *Town Talk* was full of the news, and on this same day, the *Times Picayune* and the *New York Times* gave fuller treatment of this breakthrough. There was dancing in the streets of New Orleans and widespread rejoicing throughout the state, for this two-week-old strike had effectively tied up transportation and, as a result, all segments of New Orleans's population had suffered.

It was amid this atmosphere of celebration in the state that Paul and Maria Bontemps were given an even greater reason to rejoice. Their first child and only son was born on this day in the two-family dwelling at the corner of Ninth and Winn Streets. Sarah Pembroke was also relieved and her anxiety was brought to an end with the birth of this grandson, for having already lost one daughter to childbirth, she could not rest until her daughter's labor had ceased and mother and baby were well. And as far as Maria herself was concerned, the sight and sound of her firstborn was enough to erase the memory of her travail. Paul Bontemps, equally proud and happy, gave his son a French first name, "Arnaud," to match his French last name, with "Wendell" as a middle name added for good cadence. But this first name, probably because few people could spell and pronounce it correctly, was destined to be clipped "Arna." The *Town Talk* carried no notice of this child's birth.

But if Alexandria was elated by improved train service, and by the end of the New Orleans strike, it was still lamenting the scarcity of paved streets in the city. On the day Arna Wendell Bontemps was born, an editorial reminded city officials that they should try to get more streets paved "as soon as possible."[84] Others in the city were concerned about the racial climate, for race relations in Alexandria in 1902 were not amicable and they were to worsen by the time Arna's sister Ruby was born two years later, reaching the point of intolerance by 1906. African Americans were jeered at and made the objects of jokes, even in sports and the news media. On the very day of Arna's birth, the *Town Talk* reported the news of the day before. On that Sunday (October 12) horseracing fans had enjoyed fine sport at Welch Park, where a large crowd had been present and where the betting had been lively.

But of the day's events the paper's story told an ugly tale: "Snowball and Nigger had a 250 yards run and Snowball won."[85] And the few stories about

African Americans in the news were negative: the death of an elderly manservant who had been "loyal" for years to a prominent family was used as an example to other African Americans of how they should behave; a "Negro" suspected of murdering a white man tracked down by a mob; every robbery blamed on African Americans, even when evidence and suspects were absent.[86]

Arna Wendell Bontemps had been born at a difficult time in an environment that had oppressed his parents and grandparents before him, and that would surely stifle this manchild if it got the chance. But Paul and Maria Bontemps were making plans for their son's future. He was an exceptionally fine baby, and like the parents of Moses, Paul and Maria began to consider ways of hiding their son from the evil that sought to destroy him and against which he would struggle during his entire life.

On the day of young Arna's birth, news had come of a major technological breakthrough at Montreal. Wireless telegraphy had been used by railway stations to communicate with trains traveling as fast as sixty miles per hour.[87] The new Bontemps parents realized that there would be other breakthroughs, other opportunities, and they wanted their son to have a better life than they had growing up in Louisiana. They were also concerned with the more mundane matters of creature comforts. They would need larger living quarters, for the two-family dwelling, now that they had begun to have children, would not do for long. And there were other, more immediate concerns to be considered. The child Arna would have to be baptized and his godparents would have to be chosen. Meanwhile, the baby grew and Joseph and Sarah Pembrooke became doting grandparents. Paul Bontemps continued to take bricklaying jobs out of town, earning extra money with Claiborne Williams's band whenever the could. But young Arna did not suffer, for it was hard to tell who loved him most, his mother Maria or his grandmother Sarah, both of whom showered him with love and the very best of care. Perhaps it was this maternal tenderness that produced in Arna Wendell Bontemps an affable sensitivity that would become his most outstanding trait and which was revealed in his dealings with others throughout his seventy years.

Chapter 2

Early Years in Alexandria, Louisiana

The day had arrived for the baptism of Arna Wendell Bontemps. When their son was four months old, Paul and Maria Bontemps made arrangements with Father Minard to have the baby baptized. There had been the necessary conferences between the priest and the child's parents and godparents, sufficient indication that at least one of the parents, and possibly both, were in good standing with the Church. The date had been set by the parish: the baptism was to occur on February 22, 1903. Of course, godparents had to be selected. The Church required that the infant candidate have an adult sponsor other than his parents who was in good standing with the parish and who was willing, along with the parents, to assume responsibility for the child's religious education. In this rule lay the basis of a conflict that probably signaled the beginning of the end of the Bontempses' and Pembrookes' relationship with the Catholic Church, a break that precipitated four years later.

Leslie Collins, a distant cousin to Arna Bontemps and longtime Professor of English at Fisk University and close friend of the writer, related a story that has been handed down by older relatives from Alexandria, the circumstances of which certainly would have embittered Paul Bontemps toward Catholicism. Collins said that his own mother's sister was Arna's godmother, a Methodist and Arna's mother's first cousin and closest friend. Her name was Ida E. Hines. Collins corroborated the story that there was some kind of conflict involving Arna's mother and the religious godmother at Arna's baptism. Since Arna's father may have been not in good standing (he was baptized Catholic in infancy), and since the godmother chosen by the family was a Methodist, both he (Paul Bontemps) and the godmother (Ida Hines) had to stand behind a partition during the baptism.[1]

Such an incident as this certainly would have been enough to erase any amount

of enchantment with Holy Mother Church that Paul Bontemps might have maintained previously. Despite whatever mix-ups that might have occurred, though,
the baptism did proceed as scheduled. The records of the parish list the birthdate
correctly as October 13, 1902, and the parents' names appear as Paul B. (Bismark) Bontemps and Maria Carolina Bontemps. But the name of the infant Arna
appears in a rendering that is almost ludicrous—"Arnold Wender." In addition
to the parents' names, other names as "sponsors" are John A. Hines, husband
of Ida Hines, and Mrs. J. C. Flowers, wife of the best man at Paul's and Maria's
wedding.[2]

Collins and Bontemps must have discussed this story about events at the
writer's baptism more than once during their thirty years of friendship, for the
subject of Louisiana and his parents' old friends remained a favorite topic of
Bontemps until his death in 1973. It is certain, too, that he found the story
amusing, born diplomat and humorist that he was. But in February 1903, less
than six months after his birth, the young candidate for baptism could not have
cared less about the whole procedure. After the usual family feast and bringing
of gifts to the child were over—customs which were obligatory in this Louisiana
setting—normalcy was restored in the Bontemps household. Young Arna rapidly
and early showed signs of a bright, inquiring mind. His schoolteacher mother
was at home constantly to attend to his physical, emotional, and intellectual
needs, for after the birth of her first child she did not return to the classroom,
mainly because while her son was still a toddler, his sister Ruby Sarah was
born.[3]

This new baby was born on January 20, 1905, when her brother Arna was
approximately four months past his second birthday. Ruby Sarah was baptized
at Saint Francis Xavier Church on March 12, 1905, and Father Minard, the same
priest who had baptized her brother nearly two years before, administered the
sacrament. Her sponsors were Seraphine Laurent, godmother, and Preston Bowman, godfather.[4] Young Arna loved his sister from the beginning, and as they
grew their love for one another also increased. He enjoyed helping to care for
her, and she loved and respected her big brother always. They shared a close
relationship throughout Arna's lifetime, a friendship that began during their
childhood days in Alexandria.[5] Besides his sister, the most important persons
in Arna's life at this time were his parents, his grandmother Sarah, and his "Aunt
Idoo," as he affectionately called his godmother, Ida Hines.

On the whole, Arna's childhood was full of nurture and support, for he was
guided at home by watchful parents, and also had a large yard to play in and
grandparents to spoil him. What more could a small boy want? Writing in 1965,
Bontemps said that his was anything but a squalid childhood. It had not been
varmint-infested, nor had it been marred by the kind of deprivation that had
plagued Richard Wright and that has been conspicuous in so many of the biographies and autobiographies written by Americans.[6] The Arna Bontemps story
was never a "rags to riches" affair, not during childhood, nor even during the
Depression. Although he never seemed to make quite enough money when his

children were growing up, there was usually enough to afford an occasional luxury, and there was always more than enough love in the family from the day of Arna's birth until his sudden death at Nashville. The two-family house in Alexandria in which he was born had been built only a short time before his birth in 1902. It was comfortable and was set on ample land. There were no signs of deterioration in the house itself or in the family structure. The house was situated in downtown Alexandria on one of the city's most select streets, although it was unpaved and poorly drained. But unpaved streets were the rule, not the exception, in Alexandria during the first years of the twentieth century.

Arna's memory of his childhood, even of the earliest days, was remarkable, a memory that stayed with him all of his life. This unusual capacity for recall served him well during his nursery school and kindergarten years and throughout his years as a student. His ability to remember became a hallmark of his career as a writer and as a teacher, creating a tone of nostalgic reminiscence in both his poetry and his prose. During all of his life his ability to remember made his public lectures sparkle. Recalling the earliest days of his childhood, while the family was still in Alexandria, he wrote: "My parents and grandparents had been well-fed, well-clothed, and well-housed, although in my earliest recollections of the corner at Ninth and Winn in Alexandria both streets were rutted and sloppy. On Winn there was an abominable ditch where water settled for weeks at a time."[7] But as most small boys would, Arna chose this mosquito-infested ditch as one of his favorite play spots. The ditch was teeming with crayfish and crawdads and other such life forms to fascinate him.

Arna was especially fascinated by the waterfowl that took their daily baths in the ditch. The ducks and their ducklings, the geese and their goslings were among his favorite friends. As a small boy, he did not seem to mind the muddy banks; in fact, he seemed to prefer this swampy area. His imagination was powerful, even at this tender age. Hence he was seldom bored and would amuse himself for as many hours as the elder Bontempses and Pembrookes would allow. For the child Arna these were simple days, the simplest and most picturesque he was ever to experience, days for which he never stopped longing throughout his life. He has vividly described one of his childhood experiences at the Winn Street ditch during those idyllic days: "I can remember Crazy George, the town idiot, following a flock of geese with the bough of a tree in his hand, standing in slush while the geese padded about or probed into the muck."[8]

The young Arna was enthralled by the whole performance, imagining that these were his very own geese and that Crazy George was his very own clown. He found himself imagining, too, that he was as free as George to play in the mud and water. He had forgotten about time, and home, and who and where he was, when suddenly he felt a firm hand seize him. It was Sarah Pembrooke, his grandmother, ushering him into the house for a bath and a mild scolding. This incident Arna Bontemps always remembered with fondness, for it was on this day that he got his nickname, a priceless possession for any child growing up in Louisiana during the first decade of this century. In her haste to retrieve her grandson from what she considered the baleful influences of the ditch and the town idiot, Sarah Pembrooke shortened Arnaud to Arna, a name she used for the rest of her days and that the writer himself preferred.[9] Arna and his grandmother had been the very best of friends. They laughed together a great deal, and he cherished the nickname she had given him.

From the early years he began to comprehend his place in the family, an important place indeed. Arna also learned early to relate to persons outside his family. There were friends who visited his childhood home whom they all regarded as members of the family. Many of them also had nicknames—"Matt," "Mousie," "Pig," and "Teel." And there were "Pinkie," "Ya-Ya," and several others. Now Arnaud had become Arna, and he was glad. He would not have to pretend any longer that his name was "George." He was now free to let his imagination roam into other areas, to the famous Melrose Plantation near Alexandria and to its famous mansion; to the sugar cane fields that sprawled throughout Avoyelles and Rapides parishes; and to the banks of the Red River at flood time, or to the canebrake beside the Cane River. Whenever he was in a more active mood, he played "bricklayer," pretending he was on a big job with his father, or practiced blowing his imaginary baritone horn or valve trombone, just like the ones his own "Papa" blew with the Claiborne Williams band.[10]

Paul Bontemps, it seemed to the young Arna, was away from home more than he was there during those days. He was often out of town working at brick and stone construction sites, and he continued his "gigs" with Claiborne Williams whenever the job he was working on did not carry him too far from home.[11] How Maria Bontemps responded to her husband's absences is not known, but she had an infant daughter and a growing son to occupy her mind and her time, along with running a household. Paul Bontemps was not the kind of man to squander his money or fail to send money home. But his son did at least intimate that his father's vigor and swaggering good looks tended to make him, during his young adulthood, something of a ladies' man.[12]

Young Arna, however, was not the least bit unhappy about his father's frequent jaunts, for he recalled that by the time he was three his hand was in his grandmother's most of the time: "If we were not standing outside the picket gate waiting for my young uncles to come home from school, we were under the tree in the front yard picking up pecans after one of the boys had climbed up and shaken the branches. If we were not decorating a backyard bush with eggshells, we were driving in our buggy across the bridge to Pineville on the other side of the Red River."[13] Whenever he was not with his grandmother, young Arna was either listening to the stories of ghosts and other folk sensations which his uncles and grandparents frequently told him—the kinds of stories they never seemed to run out of—or playing with his pal Mike McGraw, or with one or more of the many children his own age this Catholic community afforded.

The house on Ninth and Winn was one block from historic Lee Street, and some of Arna Bontemps's fondest memories of his childhood were associated with this street. In those days Lee Street in Alexandria was not the ghetto neighborhood it is today. Lee Street is a long street and the bars and beer joints, when Arna was a child, were much farther from his home than they would be today. Today the blocks closest to Ninth and Winn are dotted with juke joints and neighborhood stores. Just two blocks from the house are two black-owned mortuaries, one facing the other, in the kind of mock defiance that today characterizes the area. When Arna was a small boy, the section of Lee Street nearest his home was lined with impressive, well-kept homes. Farther down Lee Street were the shops, and within walking distance of the Bontemps home, one could catch the streetcar, a delight that Arna remembered all his life.[14] His father would sometimes carry him on his shoulders down Lee Street to the streetcar line.[15]

So while Arna was too young by the time his third birthday arrived in October 1905 to know much about the town of Alexandria as a whole, his bright mind was full of his own neighborhood, and of his family and their friends and relatives.[16] Alexandria was a small boy's paradise. Recalling his childhood there, Bontemps described in July 1972 the family house and its proximity to Lee Street and about its business section. Most three-year-olds would not have remembered such details. But it must be that the details were kept alive in his mind in the same way that most of his knowledge of Alexandria was preserved, through the memories of his older relatives and friends. He related an incident from his childhood:

I remember walking to Lee Street with my older cousin and my young aunts, who'd take me there, you know, and . . . one of my most distinct memories was a small child's tragedy. . . . I was given ten cents to spend when I was on Lee Street. . . . From our house to Lee Street it was a wooden sidewalk which was called down there a banquette. . . . I remember dropping this ten-cent piece . . . through one of the cracks into a hole. That was a tragedy that pained me for a number of years.[17]

Paul Bontemps loved Marksville, his own birthplace, and Alexandria, his youthful stomping ground. But he could no longer wink at the injustices and inequities that he saw daily around him, that he could read about each day in the *Town Talk*. He knew that conditions were worsening throughout the South where opportunities for blacks were concerned, and his greatest fear was that his son and daughter would become the victims of his own procrastination. Hence he resolved to leave Alexandria before it was too late for his children to benefit from the move. By 1905 the precocious Arna was ready for kindergarten,but there were no good kindergartens for him in this segregated town. And his schoolteacher mother could also assess the intellectual needs of her son and daughter and the lack of educational resources in her hometown. Her mother Sarah Pembrooke's attraction to a place of freedom, any place of freedom, had eventually materialized into something more specific for the family. She had by this time made plans to move to California, mainly because some of her closest friends and relatives had relocated there, and because they had begged her to join them. Paul Bontemps was also drawn to California, for he had friends and close relatives there, some in San Francisco, Oakland, and Richmond; others had settled in the Los Angeles area. He had kept in touch with the husband of one of his female cousins who had moved to California and had sent back glowing reports about the weather, the wages, and the schools. This influential friend had not failed to stress in his letters the extent to which greater opportunities existed out West.[18] Another female relative, Paul Bontemps's niece, a daughter of his older brother Victor, had already married a well-known jazz musician in New Orleans and moved to California. Paul was tempted, too, by the frequent offers of a chance to play music with this cousin by marriage if only he would move to California.[19]

But Paul Bontemps had been able to make a good living in Louisiana. Though construction work was not always steady, when he did work his average salary was six dollars a day. This was good money anywhere in the United States in the first decade of this century, but Paul had found the racial climate in Alexandria oppressive. He did not have the ability to wear the mask, to scrape and bow just to get along with white folks, many of whom considered him a "biggety nigger." Arna knew his father well, and he described, years after his father had died and was buried, the conditions that must have made the proud, perceptive Paul Bontemps uncomfortable in the region of his birth; the region that he and his forebears had helped to build. "My father was one of those dark Negroes with 'good' hair, meaning almost straight," he wrote. "In Alexandria," he continued, "his looks, good clothes, and hauteur were something of a disadvantage in the first decade of this century."[20]

Paul Bontemps began to find it increasingly difficult to control his temper when subjected to deliberate personal insults. His concern for his family's welfare had enabled him on more than one occasion to walk away from trouble when it crossed his path. But those who knew Paul Bismark Bontemps also knew that he was capable of fury.[21] Like many other citizens of central and southwest Louisiana, Paul Bontemps decided to relocate in California rather than Chicago because the Southern Pacific Railroad offered direct service to Los Angeles from Beaumont, Texas, a thriving oil town situated just forty miles from the southwestern border of Louisiana. Furthermore, these multicolored African Americans could, in California, escape some of the traditionally prescribed racial roles that had plagued them in the South, while Chicago had proved itself to be, in some ways, just another Jim Crow town.

Thus there was first one attraction and then another for California, first on Arna Bontemps's mother's side of the family, then on his father's side. It would be only a matter of time before they made the actual move. But the sociopolitical climate in Alexandria made this move come sooner than these natives of the Bayou State had expected. By the fall of 1905, what had been primarily threats of racial violence against blacks had begun to materialize in frequent loss of life and property, to say nothing of loss of prestige.[22] Christmas 1905 came and

went for the Bontempses and Pembrookes, and as things turned out, it would
be the last holiday the family would spend as a unit in Alexandria. During the
first six months of 1906, according to the *Alexandria Town Talk*, the situation
worsened for blacks in Rapides Parish. It seems that the editorial and news staffs
of the paper were scouring the country for stories that would denigrate the African
Americans in their midst. These stories they printed in abundance. There was a
report from Livingston, Texas, of a mob "taking" a "Negro" named Ben
Harrison who had been accused of killing a white person. From Muskogee,
Oklahoma, there was a detailed description of the proceedings of the kangaroo
court that had issued the death penalty to a "Negro" named Joe Vickers on a
charge of "assaulting" a Mrs. Bessie Dunbar near Wagoner. In a lighter vein
came stories of all-white minstrel companies that staged in Alexandria such
sketches as "Phrenologist Coon." These shows were invariably described as
"great" successes. And from Chicago came the story of an African American
who allegedly assaulted a ten-year-old white girl. The story described how he
was captured in a swamp and taken to the girl's father's house "where it was
planned to have him identified by the child and then lynched."[23]

On February 1, 1906, the fourth birthday of Langston Hughes, the *Town Talk*
published a story under the caption "Cut Her Throat." The writer went on to
describe a story that had come from Atlanta alleging that a "Georgia Young
Lady" had been assaulted by a "Negro" who had left her in a "dying condition."
A posse of more than a hundred "citizens" were tracking the accused. The
"Young Lady" was too weak to say more than "a tall black Negro was the
perpetrator of the crime."[24]

Not long after this report, an incident occurred on Alexandria's Lee Street
that precipitated the move to the West Paul Bontemps had been contemplating
for several years. Late one evening, he was walking down Lee Street toward
the streetcar line. He had been shopping for the family and his arms were loaded
with packages. Suddenly two white men staggered out of a saloon and blocked
his path, threatening at the same time to "run over the big nigger."[25] Paul
Bontemps never quite understood after the incident what kept him from com-
mitting that night the act of violence that had welled up in his mind. It was
fortunate for his family, though, that he was able to restrain himself once more.
He stepped aside without uttering a sound and allowed his taunters to pass.
Whether he would be able to respond this calmly again to such harassment he
was not sure. Consequently, within the next few days, he and his father-in-law,
Joseph Pembrooke, were on a train bound for California with instructions from
Sarah Ward Pembrooke about the kind of home they were to select for the family.
The others would follow when the time was right.

These facts were summed up admirably by Ruby Bontemps Troy at the death
of Sarah Ward Pembrooke many years later. She wrote:

Because of the unfavorable conditions which prevailed in the South, and because of the
illness of her husband, and because of her desire to give her children a better opportunity

for a full life, Grandma decided to move her family to the far West. Her sons were too young to send on an exploration of the then "wild country" so Grandma sent Papa, the husband of Maria her third daughter, to California to find a place for the family. As soon as Papa found a place, Grandma sent Ward, Mama, Arna and me to be with him.[26]

Just prior to making the move to California, Paul Bismark Bontemps, planning to secure the comfort of his expanding family while they were still in Louisiana, had purchased a spacious lot and had begun raising a new house on it when his precipitous move to California came about. Construction was halted when he decided that he definitely would not rear his family in Louisiana.[27] Paul Bontemps's cup was "full, running over."[28] This was a move that would create in Arna Bontemps a lifelong yearning for a return to the South and to the Louisiana of his birth and early childhood. Hence the nostalgia theme in much of his writing.

Chapter 3

Childhood in Los Angeles

In January it should be winter, thought Paul Bontemps, but he had found ideal weather in Los Angeles. The sunny days and mild temperatures were an agreeable surprise. He had left Alexandria armed with a railroad ticket that would allow him to go as far West as the railroad would carry him, even beyond San Francisco, should he desire to go that far. But it was unthinkable that he should go through Los Angeles without at least stopping long enough to say hello to his relatives and close friends who had migrated there from Louisiana. The train ride had been long and tiresome. In 1906 the trip from Alexandria to Los Angeles by train took almost a week. Hence the layover in the City of the Angels provided a much-needed chance to rest and bathe and eat home cooking. Paul Bontemps also welcomed the chance to explore this part of Southern California and to investigate the availability of suitable housing.

After Paul Bontemps had rested and filled in his friends and relatives "from home" on how everybody and everything in Alexandria were faring, he began to look for a suitable place to live. The decision he made on that winter night in Alexandria as he walked home after the encounter with the two drunks was already beginning to change permanently his own life and the lives of his wife and children. He soon decided that Los Angeles, not San Francisco, would be the place where he would rear Arna and Ruby. Wages for bricklayers were considerably higher in California than they had been in Louisiana.[1] Los Angeles afforded an ample number of good nursery schools and kindergartens to choose from, and the public and private schools were nonsegregated. In addition, the city provided excellent playground and library facilities at various locations, insuring easy access.

So Paul decided to select a house in the Watts section of the city, an area where friends and relatives from Central Louisiana were already residing. Watts was a pleasant, integrated residential community with neat houses and lawns. (That neighborhood, like so many other American neighborhoods of its character, was destined to become a ghetto, but in 1906 the signs of what the area was to become were only barely perceptible.) Nevertheless, when Paul Bontemps compared the muddy streets and Jim Crow customs of Alexandria with this bright new California neighborhood, Watts must have seemed like a heaven on earth. He found just the house for the family, one he was sure Maria would like.

His father-in-law, Joseph Pembrooke, had decided that he was too old to lose his country ways, and had asked his son-in-law to look for a place for him and his wife Sarah that was farther out than Watts, one large enough to allow them to grow enough fruit and vegetables to support a small truck farm. After a few weeks of looking, with the help of friends and relatives, Paul located a farm on the Alameda Highway, just a short drive from where he and his wife Maria with their two children, Arna and Ruby, would be staying. In this rural area the Pembrookes would not be hampered by citified zoning laws.

Paul wrote to his wife in Louisiana frequently during these weeks that grew into months. His letters kept both his wife and mother-in-law apprised of developments in California. Meanwhile, back in Alexandria, Maria Bontemps and her young son Arna watched for the postman to put the letters into their mailbox at Ninth and Winn Streets. Conditions there had worsened in the short time since Paul and Joseph had left for California. Throughout the months of February and March 1906, newspaper accounts of alleged ''assaults'' by ''Negro'' males on white females, and of posses tracking down suspects proliferated. The most sensational news continued to center around the color question. There was an account of a ''Negro'' named Mose Hall who was fined an exorbitant five hundred dollars for allegedly ''insulting a little white girl.''[2] And from Topeka, Kansas, came a detailed story built around the sensational caption ''Negro Robber . . . Fatally Wounds a Woman and Boy.''[3] This was reported during Carnival or Mardi Gras season, the last holiday Maria Bontemps and Sarah Pembrooke would witness in Louisiana.

It was not feasible for the remainder of the family to leave Alexandria all at one time. It was the matriarch herself, Sarah Pembrooke, who engineered their exodus. It would be a gradual departure. ''Oh, Mary don't you weep, don't you moan, oh Mary, don't you weep''; Sarah half-sang and half-hummed this old slave song as she and Maria quietly went about executing the next phase of a plan the elder woman had worked out years before. Her granddaughter described the second phase of the family's departure from Louisiana in these words: ''As soon as Papa found a place, Grandma sent Ward, Mama and me to be with him.''[4] This granddaughter, Arna Bontemps's sister Ruby, was approximately thirteen months old when the family left Alexandria in the spring of 1906.[5] Easter of that year came on April 15. Maria Bontemps, with her two children and younger brother, arrived in Los Angeles just in time to spend Easter with her husband.

This was one of the happiest times of her entire life. At last she was free of the fear she had carried in her heart since becoming a wife and mother in Louisiana, a dread that one day her husband or one of her younger brothers would be killed or maimed—the reason for sending Ward as early as possible to California—for the young black male's existence in the South had grown precarious indeed. Her son Arna later recalled the positive effect this new home seemed to have on his mother: "We moved into a house in a neighborhood where we were the only colored family . . . the people next door and up and down the block were friendly and talkative, the weather was perfect, there wasn't a mud puddle anywhere, and my mother seemed to float about on the clean air."[6]

But from young Arna Bontemps, who was only three and a half when he arrived in Los Angeles, this new home evoked a different response. He liked California well enough, but he liked Alexandria much more. The California speech inflictions were foreign to his ears, and he missed the house where he had been born and had spent so many happy hours. He especially missed his spacious yard at Ninth and Winn Streets. He missed his "Grandma," too, until her arrival a few months later, and he missed his playmates. In short, Arna Bontemps was baffled by the move and about why the family would not be going back home. Writing of his childhood in Alexandria he described how this idyll had come to a "sudden, senseless end at a time when everything about it seemed flawless. One afternoon my mother and her several sisters had come out of their sewing room with thimbles still on their fingers, needles and thread stuck to their tiny aprons, to fill their pockets with pecans. Next . . . we were at the railroad station catching a train to California, my mother, my sister and I, with a young woman named Susy."[7]

It turned out to be a long, expensive, and tiresome trip. Bontemps recalled specific details of this exodus all of his days. The train trip took nearly a week with frequent waits for connecting trains. The lunch that Maria had packed soon ran out, and most of the cold food and beverages they purchased on the train were exorbitantly priced, with non-whites barred from the dining car. Arna never forgot the long layovers that were the most uncomfortable part of the journey, for most of the railway stations between Alexandria and Los Angeles still had segregated waiting rooms that lacked conveniences, and had areas in the rear to which non-whites were confined.[8]

If the train trip from Alexandria to Los Angeles seemed interminable to young Arna, it must have been equally as insufferable for the thirteen-month-old Ruby Sarah. It must also have tested the ingenuity of their mother to keep her two children amused and reasonably comfortable during this five-day journey. Of course, Arna was old enough to be excited about the prospect of seeing his father again as soon as the train pulled into the Los Angeles depot where the big, dark Paul Bontemps would be waiting.

Arna's earliest memory of his father's temperament dated back to his arrival at the Southern Pacific Station in Los Angeles. It was here that he discovered a trait in his father's personality he eventually learned to accept but never quite understood. He wrote of his father: ''He was shy about showing emotion, and he greeted us quickly on our arrival and let us know this was the place he had chosen for us to end our journey. We had tickets to San Francisco and were prepared to continue beyond if necessary.''[9]

This lack of outward elation on the part of his father was something of a letdown to the sensitive, affectionate young Arna. No doubt Maria Bontemps, too, would have appreciated a less perfunctory greeting from her husband, but she had been married to Paul Bontemps long enough to know not to expect a demonstrative greeting from him, and certainly not in public. She knew, though, that he loved her and their two children very much, a devotion which he proved over and over during his lifetime, albeit in his own, unyielding way.

One of young Arna's fondest memories from his brief life in Alexandria was riding on the streetcars. He recalled that his father had taken him for more than one ride on the car as far as it would go down Lee Street and back.[10] And an interesting thing happened concerning the streetcar line in Alexandria near the time that Sarah Pembrooke and the rest of her family were leaving Alexandria for California. On April 12, 1906, while young Arna and the others were en route to California, the streetcars ran on the Lee Street tracks for twelve consecutive hours. On that day in Alexandria Lee Street became a veritable center of excitement on account of its being the first regular day for the running of a newly established streetcar line that extended the service throughout the length of Lee Street, connecting it with several other existing and newly opened lines. Nearly all of this new line had been finished before Maria Bontemps left with her children for California, and Arna recalled during the remainder of his life that just before they left for California one of his older relatives had carried him for a ride on the finished portion of the new tracks. This ride connected to a newly installed track on South Second Street and with the Lee to Cannon Street route.[11]

But a day or two after this last section of the new streetcar tracks in Alexandria was opened, young Arna and his family arrived in Los Angeles. He stated more than once during his lifetime that his grandmother and the rest of the family joined the first group of the clan who had moved to Los Angeles earlier, and that he and his mother and sister had arrived around the time that the great San Francisco earthquake occurred.[12] While some of her loved ones were in Los Angeles feeling the tremors of this huge quake, Sarah Pembrooke was selling the family home in Alexandria, after which she purchased tickets for the rest of her relatives ''sewed the remainder of the money inside her voluminous skirts, and boarded the train for Los Angeles.''[13]

Three or four days after Arna's arrival in Los Angeles with others of his family, he was told by his parents that the earthquake had shaken San Francisco.[14] It had actually happened on the morning of Wednesday, April 18, the third day after Easter 1906. The city had been devastated by the worst quake in its history. In fact, it was one of the strongest ever recorded.[15]

Rebuilding was begun immediately, and it was this effort that came as a direct aid to Paul Bontemps and his family. Builders in San Francisco began hiring every competent brick and stone mason they could find. The hours were long but the pay was good. Paul Bontemps went at once to San Francisco and began laying bricks. He was able to send most of his pay home to Los Angeles, and Maria managed the money well. This eventuality allowed the family to start their new life in Los Angeles on a solid financial footing. Paul continued to work in San Francisco until that Christmas. With the money he earned and Maria saved they would be able to afford tuition at a good private school for Arna. And when Ruby was old enough, they would be able to engage a good piano teacher for her, for the musical impulse had manifested itself in both Bontemps children while they were still very young. Arna, meanwhile, amused himself by "practicing" on the mouthpiece of his father's valve trombone.[16]

Maria Bontemps did not consider returning to the teaching profession after the family moved to California, for her daughter was still quite young. Before her marriage Maria had taught in the public schools of three different Louisiana towns, Lake Providence, Cheneyville, and Alexandria, beginning in a more rural setting and working her way to her hometown, the largest in Rapides Parish. She was a polished young woman. Soft-spoken and somewhat retiring, Maria Bontemps divided her time between her family and her etchings. She was also an accomplished dressmaker, and this activity she could do at home. After the family was settled in California, she began to take in sewing. Before long, she had more customers than she could accommodate.[17] Maria Bontemps, who spoke with not a trace of a Southern drawl or Creole accent, fit well into her new California environment.[18] She kept up correspondence with friends in Alexandria, and with her youngest sister Anna in Chicago.

Before they were in California a full year, the entire transplanted Bontemps–Pembrooke family converted to the Seventh-day Adventist faith. What caused this switch from Catholicism to Adventism is not clear, but it was probably the result of a combination of circumstances. There had obviously been some loss of interest in the Catholic Church prior to their leaving Alexandria. Furthermore, there was no Catholic congregation of the type to which they were accustomed, and the closest one of any kind was not near their new home. It could have been that some of their friends and relatives who had preceded them in the migration had become Seventh-day adherents and influenced the Bontempses and Pembrookes to join their church. The Adventist doctrine, for some reason, appealed strongly to Paul Bismark Bontemps, for soon after his conversion, he became a minister in the Seventh-day Adventist Church.

Meanwhile, both he and his wife Maria worked hard to put the South as far behind them as they could. It is somewhat ironic, though, that they insisted their children get rid of every trace of the South in their speech, especially since Paul Bontemps himself never lost the flavoring of the French patois, his first language.[19] Actually, his exotic looks and strange dialect caused most people he met in California, especially those who had traveled in the Far East, to surmise that he was Ceylonese or of some equally exotic nationality.[20] This undoubtedly caused him much amusement, for in Louisiana no one had ever mistaken him for anything other than what he was; for in Avoyelles and Rapides parishes African Americans who had straight hair and broken French accents were the rule rather than the exception. Paul Bontemps was not especially proud of his African cultural heritage, nor of the French culture that was his, a fact that set him apart from his son and that would be a lasting source of disagreement between them.[21]

It could have been, in fact, Paul Bontemps's desire to obscure his Louisiana roots that contributed to his decision to abandon Catholicism in favor of Adventism. It would seem true, too, that the idea of his being considered an apostate by Holy Mother Church provided him much secret delight. Actually, his feelings about life in Louisiana remained ambivalent, for while he considered the vestiges of his background to be a disadvantage in his new home, he always remembered Louisiana with nostalgia, asserting, from time to time, that if it had not been for the "conditions" he would never have left Alexandria. He even harbored a secret desire to go back and give Alexandria another try. But the thought of his children's future was a sobering one; it always made him glad he had left the South when he did.[22]

But Paul Bontemps kept busy; far too busy, in fact, to brood about what had driven him from his native state. He continued for a number of years, long after the death of his children's mother, to work as a brickmason in Los Angeles. Eventually, though, there came a gradual breaking away from his trade. His growing responsibility as an Adventist minister placed large demands on his time. And his son Arna felt that some of this slowed activity in the building trades coincided with the takeover by the labor unions. "I never heard him talk about it very much," Arna wrote, "but it was attributed by me to the difficulties that arose with . . . the trade unions."[23]

It is a widely known fact that during the 1920s the unions were very hostile to persons of color, especially in the high-paying trades like plumbing and bricklaying. But Paul Bontemps was a highly skilled mason who did a great deal of ornate work.[24] For this reason he was able to continue in the field for as long as he chose to, even though sometimes the unions kept him away from the larger construction sites.[25] His son recalled that one of the big jobs his father worked on was the Los Angeles post office, a project that lasted for about two years. When the large jobs became harder to get, he began working for small building contractors. He would build bungalows and ornamental work on fireplaces, and so on. This, too, continued for a number of years. During this period, 1915–1925, he even built several small buildings by himself, for he was also a master carpenter.[26]

But in the eight-year period from 1907–1915 many changes had come about in the Bontemps–Pembrooke family. Early in 1908 Maria's sister Anna, Joseph's and Sarah's fifth child, joined the rest of the family in California after her parents had sought and won an annulment of her marriage. During her brief marriage, Anna had no trouble at all finding work in tailoring establishments in Chicago.

She had worked in some of the finest dressmaking shops in that city, and that experience was to stand her in good stead for the rest of her working days as a modiste. Her sister Maria had encouraged her in the frequent letters she wrote to learn all she could about making woolen garments for women.

When Arna's "Aunt Anna" arrived in Los Angeles, she found him attending the Ascot Avenue School in Los Angeles—a member of the kindergarten class.[27] Already he was an apt pupil and had new knowledge and skills which he proudly displayed for his aunt. She, in turn, told him stories about Louisiana.

It did not take five-year-old Arna long to realize he was the only African American in his class, a situation that continued through most of his years in school, even during college. This situation made him miss the Louisiana environment and long for the rich folk culture he had appreciated in Alexandria. Consequently Arna developed a tendency to daydream, an indulgence he enjoyed through most of his formative years. In his young mind he began to recall the speech patterns that had fascinated him from his earliest years in Alexandria.

His parents' negative attitude toward Negro dialect did not seem to faze this kindergartener at all. He kept in mind the kinds of verbal exchanges he had heard down South and that, many years later, he was to incorporate into his *Sad-Faced Boy*, an odyssey in miniature in which he deals with Slumber and his two pals, Rags and Willie, three boys who had run away from their Alabama hometown to see the sights of New York City.[28] This book of juvenile fiction, published some thirty-five years after its author entered the Ascot Avenue Kindergarten in September 1907, became the first book by an American author to treat the everyday events in the lives of African-American children in the North.

Moreover, this book was the first in which African-American colloquialisms were expressed in simple, natural terms that allowed their freshness to live. In this book Bontemps successfully abolished the need to mutilate spelling and to create dialect forms that hinder instead of aiding readability. And this linguistic ability had its origins in his childhood days in Alexandria and was nurtured in him during his kindergarten and elementary school years in Los Angeles. Even at this young age he could hear in his mind such passages from *Sad-Faced Boy* as the following:

"Un-hunh," Slumber said aloud. "I got that old gate down pat. You puts your nickel in that there place yonder. Then you pushes that turn-around thing what looks like a wagon wheel with four spokes in it. When the wheel spin around, in you go. It's a mighty fine contraption, too, but I believe I can work it slick as a whistle."[29]

As a child, Arna had begun developing a sensitivity to individual speech patterns that would much later make him a successful writer for children, and his technique would be copied extensively by other writers during his adult years.

Arna's gregariousness manifested itself in his early childhood. On those occasions when Maria Bontemps visited her son's homeroom at school, she found him getting along well in his lessons and with the other children. Maria was amused and pleased to find her son integrated into the group, "holding hands with the others, skipping around the circle when his time came, and generally indicating that he 'belonged.' "[30] As an adult, Arna recalled that during these first months at school he lost in the sand pile a little gold ring—the only one he ever owned.[31]

As Arna adjusted to school and its regimen, his father Paul was adjusting to the rigorous course of study to which he had subjected himself as a prerequisite for the ministry. Probably because of his line of work, Paul Bontemps had, it seemed, deliberately suppressed his cultural and intellectual leanings. He began to express an interest in wide reading and in scholarship, an interest his son suspected his father had all along. No doubt Paul Bontemps realized that if his calling to the ministry were to yield fruit, he would need a humanistic education.[32] His daughter gave the following account of his religious involvement after the move to California: "By 1907 he had united in Los Angeles with the Furlough Track Church of the Seventh-day Adventists. He became a minister not long afterwards, the first Seventh-day Adventist minister of his race in the West, pioneering the Denomination's work in the Watts area of Los Angeles."[33]

But before the end of 1907, tragedy struck the Pembrooke family again when Joseph Pembrooke, Senior, died. This came as a shock indeed, for he had been relatively healthy during most of his sixty years in his native state of Louisiana. But the move to California had taken its toll. He had exhausted himself trying to get his farm on the Alameda Highway in shape. He had farm buildings to erect, planting to do, and grounds to landscape and maintain around the big house and the summer house, to say nothing of the backbreaking labor required to protect his initial investment. He had been in California a little more than a year when he became sick and died.

Arna's sister has described what happened to their grandfather: "The very next year [1907] Grandpa died, so Grandma took Aunt Teal, Ward and Mathilda [a granddaughter] and went back to Louisiana to bury him in the family plot. They remained there until March of 1908 when Grandma sold the rest of her property in Alexandria and returned to California. From that time Grandma remained in or near Los Angeles."[34]

Sarah Pembrooke, it appears, had become a woman of sorrows, acquainted indeed with grief. A short time after her husband's death, Maria Bontemps, her third daughter, became seriously sick. Maria had not been feeling well enough to make the trip to Louisiana with the others to bury her father. And when her mother returned from Louisiana, she found Maria not improved. It was around this time that the entire Bontemps household found it imperative that they move to the country [Furlough Track] for a while. Paul Bontemps, Maria, Arna, and Ruby all went to live on Sarah Pembrooke's farm. The fresh air, they hoped, would be good for Maria, and Paul Bontemps needed someone to care for his wife and two children while he earned a living for them all.[35]

The years between 1908 and 1915, the period the family spent in the rural section of the Furlough Track, were the happiest of Arna Bontemps's entire life.

At first he was too young to comprehend the gravity of his mother's illness. Surely, he believed, Papa will not allow anything to happen to Mama. With Grandma Sarah's fervent prayers, which she prayed aloud as though far off in some lonesome valley, her ailing daughter would soon be all right. Besides, the wholesome meals that Grandma cooked, and the endless string of home remedies from the South would surely make Maria strong again. At his grandmothers's farm the young Arna was not too far removed from his home in Watts, and his school and playmates there, for Watts was an extension of the rural part of the Furlough Track where Sarah Pembrooke had her farm. It is this same area and its "migrant Negroes and Mexican Americans" that the adult Arna Bontemps was to describe in his prologue to *They Seek a City*.[36]

Written in collaboration with Jack Conroy, the book examines the causes of the greatest periods of black migration from the South to Northern cities in the period just after the Civil War, the World War I era, and during and immediately after World War II. Conroy recalls that Arna Bontemps wrote this prologue with no help from him and that it is probably the most autobiographical piece Bontemps ever wrote. Conroy explained recently that "the prologue to Arna's and my *Anyplace but Here* [title of revised version of *City* ... tells of the early settlement of Mudtown and its inhabitants. I recall that Arna told me it was written from his early experiences and he knew all the characters involved."[37]

Sarah Pembrooke's house was not like the makeshift huts that surrounded it. Most of her migrant neighbors were displaced persons indeed. They built tiny adobe homes, for they were not sure how long they would stay there. Others slept in lean-tos and "absurd little shacks" made of tar paper tacked over whatever scrap lumber they could muster. One elderly couple in the area lived in an abandoned treehouse built by neighborhood children. They reached this roost each night on a rickety, homemade ladder.[38] But Sarah and Joe Pembrooke had not planned to move again, hence the house they built was a large, permanent structure patterned after the colonial-style farm homes they had known so well in Louisiana. And they had a spacious. lantern-hung summerhouse on another part of the property, surrounded by pepper trees as was the big house. In the summer house the family staged picnics and invited their friends and neighbors. Young Arna could hardly wait for each Fourth of July to come, for the summerhouse was always decorated with ribbons and bands played under the pepper trees well into the night. But the big house was Arna's favorite of the two, for he enjoyed the spacious rooms and its many fruit trees and the walnut grove nearby.[39]

During these storybook days, Arna had more than a few friends and playmates. There was college-aged James, son of a retired college professor who played the violin and who allowed Arna to listen to him recite Shakespeare. And there were other families who were Sarah Pembrooke's nearest neighbors, those who lived in the dozen or more "substantial cottages" built on the tracts closest to her farm. Among his favorite playmates were the well-dressed, brown-skinned offspring of the cultured YMCA secretary, along with scores of other boys and girls who grew up with him and his sister Ruby. Arna and the other boys his age liked to watch the railroad crews as they placed the original tracks near a grove of eucalyptus trees adjacent to the west side of his grandmother's farm. They liked the sound of the steel rails being driven into the earth. They watched the Mexican section workers settle in, and Arna and the others made friends among their children. He learned to converse with his new friends in their native Spanish, a background experience that would aid him when as a young adult he was asked to teach high-school Spanish at Harlem Academy. These newcomers to the area lived in whitewashed huts the railroad company had built for them.[40] They all laughed and romped and played together and attended one or both of the two little neighborhood churches.

The Furlough Track also had several versions of the "town character" who amused Arna and his friends and whom they mocked while outside their parents' earshot. There was Red Eagle, the broad-shouldered "Negro" who lived a near-hermit's existence. He hardly talked at all to other people and dressed like an Indian, for he had grown up among the Indian tribes of Oklahoma. Red Eagle had become a professional cowboy, and his shack was full of the trappings of his trade—spurs, branding irons, ropes, and knots of every description. Young Arna and a few of his buddies, relying on the former's budding people skills to penetrate Red Eagle's shyness, managed once to secure an invitation to see inside the shack, an experience Arna never forgot. The boys saw all sorts of marvelous objects and examined them, for Red Eagle knew how to fashion utensils of silver. But young Arna was disappointed that Red Eagle knew little about "the ways of black folk," and nothing at all about their songs and laughter."[41]

Arna and his friends also encountered two tall brothers who lived in a small house in a thicket, and whom they nicknamed "The Giants." In his adulthood Arna recalled that for some unexplained reason "these brothers would have no neighborhood children in their yard or climbing their trees. Frequently, in the afternoon when they returned from their work, they would arm themselves with leafy switches, beat through the bushes and branches scare up a half dozen or more brats and drive them off of their lot with shouts and threats and waving arms."[42] The boys were only mildly afraid of these "Giants" who yelled and stomped.

They were terrified, though, of "Tump," the overalled, brogan-wearing woman who walked always in the middle of the road instead of in the footpath, and who was the nemesis of the neighborhood men. Tump worked as a car cleaner in the railroad yard on the other side of the tracks, and she carried a knife. She brooked no questioning from anyone and would sooner fight a man than another woman. Arna and the other boys his age were especially fascinated by the ripeness of Tump's speech and her skill at crapshooting, a game she played with a rough crowd of men, turning the games into brawls whenever she had a mind to.[43]

Arna's fondest memories from his childhood days on his grandmother's farm are associated with other relatives and friends of his family who, after 1910, began gradually to join them in California. One such migrant was Joseph Ward,

Sarah Pembrooke's younger brother and her grandchildren's great-uncle "Buddy." This is the same relative whom an adult Arna Bontemps described as "the little old man who arrived at night" and who got his fill of "Mudtown" in only a few days. He had been thoroughly disappointed with the aspect of the neighborhood after the long, exhausting journey from Louisiana.[44]

Arna had not remembered seeing this uncle in Louisiana but recalled it was about the time of Buddy's arrival in California that he began to pick up comments about Louisiana from the conversations of adult relatives and their friends. Arna learned facts that he had been too young to comprehend before the family left Alexandria. He found out that "Uncle Buddy" had been more than once at the Keeley Institute in New Orleans taking the cure for alcoholism. Arna had seen the framed portrait of this uncle in his grandmother's living room. But when this young mulatto arrived in California a few years after the others had arrived, none of his youth remained, nor were his grace and flare still present. Arna's beloved "Uncle Buddy" was, by this time, a broken, old man. His grandnephew described Buddy's arrival at his sister Sarah's house in this passage—"he entered wearing a detachable collar without a tie. His clothes did not fit. They had been slept in for nearly a week on the train. His shoes had come unlaced. His face was pockmarked. Nothing resembled the picture in the living room."[45]

Despite Buddy's problem, Arna loved and respected him from their first meeting. Full of curiosity, Arna watched as Buddy opened his makeshift luggage and brought out jars of syrup, bags of candy, and Southern goodies his sister had said that she missed in letters she dictated to Arna. Buddy had also brought bags of giant-sized pecans and filé for making gumbo.[46] With such delightful treats in his luggage, what young boy could hold a great-uncle's shabby appearance against him? As the family ate the sweets he brought, Buddy began to recount in his colorful but unaffected manner how he had left things "at home." He described the "conditions," the racial climate, and told who had married and who had died, how the family's teacher friend was getting along, how he had not had a drink or been locked up since his last trip to Keeley Institute. He described graphically the last flood Rapides Parish had experienced when the Red River overflowed the banks of the levee.[47]

Much to the dismay of Paul Bontemps, Arna became the constant companion of his "Uncle Buddy." The elder Bontemps objected to Buddy's frequent use of "nigger," and to his not refraining from using the term in the presence of the family's white friends. All things considered, he felt that the derelict was a bad example for his son, and his status as an Adventist minister was not always enough to remind him not to lose his temper with Buddy. Paul Bontemps refused to accept the types Buddy chose as friends, lumping them into a category he called "don't care folks." Nevertheless, the elder Bontemps was impressed with Buddy's intellect, his ability to quote the whole of Thomas Hood's "The Vision of Eugene Aram," and his spelling and reading skills.[48] The thing that impressed young Arna about this eccentric old uncle was that he was largely self-educated. He had little in the way of formal education, but Arna both recognized and appreciated his superior intellect. "Uncle Buddy" had a similar influence on Arna's developing literary tastes to that exerted on the young Jean Toomer by his own uncle Bismark (Uncle Biz). Toomer, refusing to learn to read at school became, out of defiance, the "class cut-up and the teacher's problem." "Uncle Biz" took the responsibility of educating Jean at home, passing on to him an appreciation of the contemplative's life. And not unlike Arna's father Paul's opinion of Buddy, Jean's grandfather Pinchback considered Bismark's influence to be entirely negative.[49]

Throughout Arna's life he cherished Buddy's memory and the friendship they enjoyed while the writer was still a young boy. Six months before Arna died, he said about this uncle:

He had this unique thing: he had never been to school formally, so far as I know. But he was extremely literate. He was a real nut about reading. He read everything, and he learned [memorized] poetry. He knew much music. He was a fountain of impressions and of information. Things he told me have touched off various speculations in my own mind.[50]

Arna's childhood years in California were enriched by the presence of this uncle, for as an older relative, he proved an extremely important link for the writer to his roots in Louisiana, serving as a kind of long-distance transmitter between Louisiana and California.

But Buddy was not the only relative from Louisiana who had a positive influence on Arna during his boyhood. Some of the other relatives from Alexandria who had a profound influence on him during his childhood were his mother's younger brother, Ward Pembrooke, and his family. The pleasures and inspirations that Arna gained from these relatives remained throughout his life some of his most cherished boyhood memories. Only a few months before his death, the writer said to a group of public-school librarians in his native Alexandria that he felt "constrained" to talk about Alexandria, about Louisiana, and what they had meant to him. Telling them that though he left Alexandria before his fourth birthday, this Louisiana setting was never far from him.

He told of an uncle from Alexandria who had been a dining-car waiter, and how he returned to Louisiana almost every week, bringing back news to California so that the family was never without the place of their birth. He amused the audience by interjecting how Ward brought with him on one of his trips a young woman whom he introduced as his wife, and with them was their young son. Sarah Pembrooke had been so distressed by this well-kept secret that she "almost fell out [fainted]."[51] Ward's son became a beloved playmate of Arna and his other young cousins in California. And although his uncle Ward had died a few years before Arna Bontemps's Alexandrian return, Arna admitted that Ward Pembrooke's communication between Alexandria and Los Angeles had always been a natural part of his growing up in California.[52]

This was the physical and social environment in which Arna Wendell Bontemps grew up. These were the days when he began to discover himself and to learn how to relate well with other people, an activity that became his favorite pastime for the rest of his life. He spent long hours with "Uncle Buddy" among the corn rows, or while tending livestock. This environment fostered the child's developing imagination and encouraged resourcefulness in him. It was an age before the advent of television and sophisticated children's toys. In fact, by present-day standards, Arna Bontemps and his boyhood friends had few playthings except those they or their parents made. This was a world of experiences, both real and vicarious, and Arna, by this time, had discovered the world of books and the aural-oral world of storytelling.

Chapter 4

Coming of Age in California

Arna Wendell Bontemps first knew heartbreak at the tender age of eleven, when his mother, Maria Carolina Bontemps, died of pulmonary tuberculosis on September 30, 1914, two weeks before his twelfth birthday. Maria had not been strong since the birth of her second child, and died at age thirty-six, despite the valiant efforts of her family to make her well again.[1] Her funeral was held on October 2, with the burial following in the Evergreen Cemetery of Los Angeles. Maria's death could not have come at a worse time for Arna. With a birthday approaching, he would sorely miss the love and support his mother had always given him. He would miss the occasional soft word of encouragement he had counted on her to supply, for Maria had become the quiet but unrelenting mediator between father and son, coming to Arna's defense whenever she saw the need. She had slipped quietly away, but from Arna's heart she would never be absent. In adulthood he wrote of her often, and until his own death he rarely sat for an interview or gave a public lecture in which her name did not appear. He always mentioned her with affection and respect, often with tears in his voice.

From 1910 to 1914 Maria Bontemps watched as her son and daughter grew rapidly, and she knew that her health was failing with equal speed. It was during these days of his mother's chronic illness that Arna was able to discover a side of his father's personality that he had not observed previously. Arna knew that Paul Bontemps loved his family, but he was able to observe the extent of his father's devotion and strength when these were put to the test during Maria Bontemps's last years. The adult Arna Bontemps mentioned in more than one place how his father would lay bricks all day and nurse his mother all night, and then see that he and Ruby got to school on time, properly clothed and fed. All of this Paul Bontemps did at a time when the demands of his ministry were heaviest. Of course, without the assistance of his mother-in-law Sarah Pembrooke, he could not have carried on.[2]

After Maria was buried, feeling alone and without a strong ally, Arna became the kind of "lonesome boy" he had depicted in his juvenile piece by that name, and who appears again and again in his fiction. Betty Taylor Ashe in her 1978 doctoral dissertation also perceived some of the underlying causes of this Bontempsian theme, for she wrote: "The lonesome boy theme is autobiographical . . . and many of the author's protagonists are motivated by their feeling of estrangement from their social environment."[3] This theme and its accompanying nostalgic mood stayed with Bontemps throughout his career as a writer and is reflected in both his poetry and his prose. He longed to recapture the joys of home experienced while his mother was alive, and he cherished in his heart the lessons she had taught him.

At age twelve Arna became a voracious reader. Whenever he could escape his playmates for a long enough time, he retired to his room to read; that is, when his father did not interrupt. Now he was spending longer hours at the Watts branch of the Los Angeles Public Library and at the main branch where the selection of books was larger. He devoured *Treasure Island*, *Kidnapped*, *Ivanhoe*, and *Robinson Crusoe*. Other favorites besides Shakespeare and the Old Testament were Twain's *Tom Sawyer* and *Life on the Mississippi*. He also checked out travel books and how-to books in chemistry and popular mechanics.[4] But Arna was by no means a mere bookworm. He was also an avid sports fan and had early begun to master the technical aspects of football, basketball, and baseball, games which remained his favorites long after he stopped playing them. As a boy he injured one of his knees while playing in a friendly game of football, an injury which he aggravated in high-school athletics and which caused him discomfort during his adult years.[5] Young Arna began to discover the vast potential of his own expanding mind, as he read, played, and attended church and school.

He began to develop an interest in history and was especially curious about the history of African Americans. He could read for days, months, even years, and find precious little about his people in the books made available to him. Moreover, he never forgot how in 1912 he encountered that damaging and discrediting article about "the Negro" in the 1911 edition of *Encyclopedia Britannica*. It taunted him during his years as a schoolboy in California, for he was not too young to realize that this article would affect the thinking of all who read it for decades.[6] He longed for authentic writings about African Americans, but at school he would have settled for almost any kind of reading materials on his own background, for he was to lament, many years later, the virtual blackout of reliable information about "Negro Americans" in his school books. Concerning this developing interest in antiquity, he told the following anecdote:

In the year of my twelfth birthday—I sometimes heard it spoken of as the age of accountability—I read in Los Angeles about the celebration of the Centennial of the Battle of New Orleans. This was of pointed interest to me for two reasons. Our transplanted family still had many relatives in Louisiana, and the descriptions of the planned festivities sounded like news from home.

. . . What followed, however, was a strange denouncement that inflicted a lasting hurt. I read later in the Negro press that the ceremonies, brilliant as they were, had been carried out exclusively by white soldiers, white orators, and white school children. . . .

This struck me as a disheartening omission in 1914, and it was clearly in my consciousness when I began to haunt the branch . . . library on Central Avenue just south of Vernon, within the area recently convulsed by rioting [the 1965 Watts riots]. I was seeking a recognizable reflection of myself and my world in the collections of books available to a boy reader going on twelve. What I found was of cold comfort, to say the least. Nothing more inspiring than *Our Little Ethiopian Cousin* was not what I needed or expected. He was not me, and his world was not mine. The *Our* of the title did not include me.[7]

It was to these days of rapidly growing personal, racial, and cultural consciousness during his boyhood and youth in California that the writer referred from time to time in adulthood. This was a consciousness that endured throughout his life; a sense of awareness, he recalled, that began when he came to himself one day in the children's reading room of a Los Angeles library.[8] From this point forward, Arna pledged himself to learn all he could about his cultural past and to play his own part in setting the record straight. This vow created in him the impulse to write for young readers and, eventually, caused him to choose librarianship as a second career.

As if his parents' negative attitude toward the South and toward their cultural heritage had not been enough, it seemed to Arna Bontemps, while he was growing up in California, that even the schools were cooperating in the conspiracy to shelter him from his cultural past, to deny him his reading needs. He began to feel an overwhelming need to read about his own ancestors, for in all of his classes from kindergarten through college he was, with an occasional exception, the only person of color. Most of his teachers and classmates, he believed, would have been content, because of his physical features, to extend to him courtesies that foreigners enjoyed in this country. But young Arna would have no part of any such pretense, and became indignant over suggestions that he ignore or deny his heritage. He early grew sick of the myths and stereotypes to which he was subjected daily about "the Negro's incapacity."[9] He sensed that along some lines he was being miseducated, for he wrote:

When I was growing up my teachers, as well as others unaware of what they were doing, gave me to understand that the only meaningful history of the Negro in the United States (possibly even in the world) began with the Emancipation Proclamation of 1863. . . . I began to suspect that the colossal omissions they perpetuated were more than inadvertent. They were deliberate. Many may have been vindictive.[10]

Convinced that his teachers were not being truthful with him about African-Americans' role in America's history, Arna began to explore alternative avenues for learning the truth. Somewhat confused and bewildered, he began to pose race-related questions to his teachers and to other adults who should have been able to help him, but the responses he received were negative and ill-founded. His thirst for knowledge about the past and about his roots increased daily. The efforts of his parents, his teachers, and the authors of his textbooks to separate him from his past had, ironically, the opposite effect. While his reading tastes matured along expected lines, with literature and history remaining his favorite subjects, his taste for books about Africans and African Americans also increased. Before he entered high school Arna's taste in reading had graduated from juvenilia to a mature level of fiction. The novels of Charles Dickens, Willa Cather, Sinclair Lewis, and Joseph Hergesheimer became his fare.[11] By the time he entered college, the novels of Conrad had taken the place of these earlier favorites as he continually sought to slake his hunger for challenging reading materials.[12]

He said of his reading needs during the preadolescent and adolescent years and of the Los Angeles Public Library's failure to meet them: "On the adult shelves, I found little with which I could identify . . . so I knew it was not that books to nourish pride and create a sense of belonging had not been written, but that they had been scorned and neglected."[13] And on another occasion he explained, "the authors of the books treated me as if I didn't exist."[14]

But fortunately for this developing youth his "Uncle Buddy," with his folk tales and dialect poems, was still around, much to the dismay of Paul Bontemps.[15] Arna also had friends among his peer group who were growing up alongside him in the Furlough Track, a kind of transplanted version of "Soulville." Together these youths kept alive—by sharing the bits and pieces of African-American songs, sayings, beliefs, and customs picked up from parents and grandparents—an interest in their cultural heritage. Arna was not about to allow anything or anyone to steer him away from these refreshing paths of discovery. He continued to read and to ask questions during his journey into blackness. He read Phyllis Wheatley, George Moses Horton, and Frances Ellen Watkins Harper, but the narratives of Jupiter Hammon and Nat Turner, the orations of David Walker, Denmark Vesey, and Henry Highland Garnet were not made available to him.

It became clear during these years that Arna Bontemps would excel in whatever field of endeavor he chose. And there were others from "Mudtown," his contemporaries, who would also succeed, those whose parents had migrated from Texas, Louisiana, Arkansas, and Oklahoma. These young people, like their friend Arna Bontemps, did not allow Furlough's noisy railroad track, its one street lamp, its deep ruts in the streets, its high weeds, nor its makeshift verandas and outhouses to discourage them. Arna, along with his friends, had accepted the fact that their neighborhood had become a ghetto, the very kind of environment their parents had sought to escape in the South.[16] Scores of Furlough's families were sending their sons and daughters to high schools and colleges. Some of the boys would become prominent ministers, dentists, doctors, and one or two even became lawyers. The girls became nurses and teachers; all were from a community that did not have a single sidewalk. But these were not, as Arna would explain later, "the gaudiest talents among Furlough's kids. One bright-eyed youngster became in later years a trumpeter in Duke Ellington's first band [Arthur Whetsol]. Another, fighting under the ring name of Baby Joe Gans, came close to a welterweight championship of the world. Furlough folks knew him as Babe Slaughter. One grew up to play the title role in the sound-film version of *Uncle Tom's Cabin*, not to mention other movie parts. One went to U.C.L.A. and became an All-American end and track star [Woody Strode]. One became a writer of books."[17]

The year 1917 was auspicious for literature by African Americans. William Stanley Braithwaite was awarded the NAACP's Spingarn Medal for achievement as a writer-critic, and Claude McKay's sonnet "The Harlem Dancer" appeared in *The Seven Arts* under the pen name of Eli Edwards. This year in many ways was an anticipation of the Harlem Renaissance of the 1920s. In September 1917, not long after Paul Bontemps had been made supervisor of the S.D.A. school in Los Angeles, he enrolled his son Arna in a different high school. This was approximately one month prior to the youth's fifteenth birthday. The elder Bontemps thought it best he have a conference with his son. Still endeavoring to prohibit what he considered to be Buddy's unwholesome influence, Paul Bontemps felt that the white boarding school would be good for the boy. He cautioned " 'Now don't go up there acting colored.' "[18]

Arna was convinced that he carried out his father's wish, for years later he wrote, "he sometimes threatened to pull me out of school and let me scuffle for myself the minute I fell short in any one of several ways he indicated [a plight nearly as severe as Langston Hughes's father's opposition to his son's literary studies]. Before I finished college, I had begun to feel in some large and important areas I was being miseducated, and that perhaps I should have rebelled."[19] But Arna never forgot during these years the charms and hexes, ghost stories, minstrel talk, dialect stories, and slave and master stories that "Uncle Buddy" had imparted to his apt young grand-nephew. Arna's chief aim was to become a proud credit to his family and to his race.

Arna remained at the San Fernando Academy through the spring of 1920, several months before his eighteenth birthday. For the next twenty-three years, he was in and out of Adventist schools, first as a student and later as both teacher and principal.[20] His schoolmates, long after 1920, remembered that he often talked of his desire to become a writer. They have described him during these high school years as a reticent young man who had a remarkable facility with words.[21] Imagine an eleventh-grade class finishing a unit on poetry, and as a culminating writing assignment the teacher has asked the more than thirty students to write an original poem each. Heads are bent industriously over desks; brows are wrinkled and pencils are doodling. In the last seat of the third row a serious-faced Arna Bontemps is poring over his most recent effort. All around his desk lie wads of paper, what is left of rejected attempts. The teacher asks to hear the poems. Several students volunteer to read theirs, but shy Arna in his back seat eases his paper inside his notebook, and is only too glad to hear the dismissal bell. How would the other fellows, his teammates on the football team, react to his poem? He was trying hard during these days to be a regular guy.[22] They would certainly tease him if they knew he wrote poems at home every chance he got.

But Arna had a stubbornness to match his reserve. He refused to abandon his dream of becoming a writer, no matter what others thought. Poetry, until after the Great Depression, would remain his favorite medium. And it was at San Fernando Academy that he received at least some attention from the faculty, the kind that encouraged him to write. The first teacher to notice his writing was one of his tenth-grade instructors. She would write encouraging remarks on his papers, and she offered him special help. But this was about all the ''special help'' he received, for at this time he had not met a professional writer of any kind.[23]

Paul Bontemps had resisted his son's tendency to read and write more than the anxious father thought he should. Even during Arna's early boyhood, while his mother was alive, both parents had decided to restrict the number of books their son could check out of the library at one time. They considered it unhealthful for a young boy to become so utterly absorbed in books. But this was not the only source of Arna's conflict with his father, for despite their strong love for each other, their temperaments were so radically different that Paul and Arna could not avoid clashes of opinion. The elder Bontemps was capable of brusqueness. He was the masculine, vigorous construction worker who had suppressed his own youthful literary bent. His son, on the other hand, had inherited his mother's quiet, polished demeanor. He had also inherited her sense of the aesthetic. Not only did Arna reject his father's choice of vocation—bricklaying— but his perspective about almost everything was different from his father's. The elder man was a stern disciplinarian, quick-tempered and domineering. These sides of his personality had an abrasive effect on Arna's calm reserve. But Arna did inherit at least one trait from his father—his stubbornness. Sandra Carlton Alexander has summed up the tension between father and son: ''The clash . . . would resound within the walls of the Bontemps household again and again even after Arna had reached maturity.''[24]

After he himself became a father, Arna learned to appreciate the capacity for kindness and gentleness in this big bear of a man who was his father. But never did he stop regretting in his elder the behavior that he considered hard-headed and closed-minded. On the other hand, Arna remained proud of his mother's calm dignity and intense spiritual quality.[25] As a youth, Arna learned to eschew conflict in his dealings with others, and always prided himself on his tactfulness, on his ability to live peaceably with everyone. In a 1971 interview, responding to a question about his friendship with Langston Hughes, Bontemps pointed with pride to the fact that he and Langston never had a falling-out of any kind.[26] As a child and as a young man Arna Bontemps did not have unnecessary conflicts with others, a trait that characterized his relationships all of his days. It could be that his refusal to squabble was partially the cause of his conflict with his father, for the elder would have interpreted the younger's silence as contempt.

Paul Bontemps had decided that he would make a medical doctor of his only son, but Arna had decided that he would not be "made into" anything by anyone, believing that he should be free to choose his own career; and he had already decided what that career would be—he would write for a living. But in the second decade of this century, Paul Bontemps could not conceive of his son's earning a decent living with a pen. Paul loved his son intensely and was secretly proud of both his stubbornness and his academic ability, but did not fail to express his disapproval of the future writer's tendency to read large numbers of books. In later years Arna sometimes amused himself by recalling his father's early opposition to his literary pursuits, and in a speech before the Louisiana Education Association's library section he said that his father's "attitude toward moderation convinced him that reading for pleasure, like the taste of candy, was something that had to be curbed in a growing boy."[27] It is a miracle that this lack of understanding, this lack of acceptance on the part of his father and others where his interest in and love for books was concerned, did not have some lasting ill effect on this sensitive youth, for he said to the librarians in Louisiana: "I finally concluded that everybody was to some degree hostile to my reading needs."[28] Paul Bontemps's protestations never ceased and Arna Wendell Bontemps never ceased to ignore them. While still in high school, Arna decided he would live his life in an atmosphere of books, and he did so from that time until his death in 1973.[29]

After his adolescence had spent itself, Arna began to appreciate Paul Bontemps for the interest he exhibited in his son's development, despite their clash of opinions. The elder Bontemps never stopped trying to do what he thought was best for both is son and his daughter. It was certainly expensive to keep them in private schools, but Paul never failed to make necessary sacrifices so that he would be able to offer his children an excellent education, and so that he could keep his promise to their mother about his care of them. After all, to seek better educational opportunities for his children was the primary reason he had made the 1906 move to California. He was determined that his children would not be forced to attend mediocre schools.

Ione Morrison Rider has related an incident that lends insight into the character of the youthful Arna Bontemps. "The boy Arna wanted a car," she wrote. "Well, the father said reasonably, we could get a car. It would cost thus and so. We could not have a car and you go to college. . . . The boy decided to go to college and wait for the car."[30] This interest in owning a car coincided with the young Arna's developing interest in girls. He and his first cousin, Bennie Albans, frequently went on double dates, during their youth, in Bennie's car. Albans was the son of one of Arna's aunts, his mother's youngest sister Lourania, whom the writer always referred to as "Aunt Ludie."[31] In the twilight of his life Arna recalled: "I can remember when my cousin Bennie and I used to take her [Vesta, the girl Bennie married] and another girl riding in [his] roadster.

And that was a very elegant time in our lives."[32] And there were other girls during these youthful days in Furlough: Julia, the pretty daughter of the Mexican storekeeper, and the "even prettier" black girl who was named Alameda and whose features were "more Mexican than Julia's."[33]

One of the stalwart influences upon Arna Bontemps in his youth was the Black Church. His father's role as a shepherd of a congregation caused Arna and Ruby to attend church gatherings of all kinds more frequently than they would have otherwise. As a youth, Arna was loyal to the Church that had nurtured him. He attended worship and bible study religiously and sought to apply in his daily living the high principles of morality and the simplicity of lifestyle that were drilled into him at home and at school. Not only did he derive from the Church some of his attitudes about life, he also rejected what he considered were its unloving customs of legalism. Without a doubt, his attendance at the various services and functions of the two small black congregations in Furlough enriched his exposure to African-American culture. He enjoyed the hymns, but was especially moved by the spirituals and gospels. He never forgot that particular Sunday night when a quartet of college men from Tuskegee gave a concert of songs in one of these churches, reviving the audience's interest in the spirituals they had neglected since leaving the South.[34]

Arna had learned several spirituals and had read Booker T. Washington's *Up from Slavery* and W.E.B. Du Bois's *The Souls of Black Folk*.[35] Among his favorite books at this time were Milton's *Minor Poems*, Caesar's *Gallic Wars*, Meyer's *General History*, Bunyan's *Pilgrim's Progress*, and Goldsmith's *Vicar of Wakefield*. Yet it was through the church and its sermons, songs, and testimonies that another aspect of his early education was developed. This was still another vibrant link with the past. It was through the bright minds and talent he encountered at church that he was able to debunk many of the unfavorable myths he had heard about Negroes. It was during these days, too, that he saw "The Birth of a Nation" and other myth-making movies.[36] But his exposure at home, at school, and at church was broadened by his wide reading. Together these gave him what he needed to counter the disturbing influences of the mass media. But it was primarily his early church-related experiences that formed the spiritual and intellectual foundations for much of his later thought. This is particularly true with regard to the religious and meditative theme that first manifested itself in his poetry and subsequently in his prose.

Time passed and in May 1920 Arna graduated from San Fernando Academy where he had distinguished himself. He and his father had already agreed years before that he should go on to college after graduation, but what they did not agree upon was the choice of a college major. In the fall of 1920, about a month before his eighteenth birthday, Arna found himself in the freshman class at Pacific Union College at Angwin, in Napa County, California, still another Seventh-day Adventist school. Once more he found himself the only brown-skinned person in his classes.[37] His major was listed on paper as "Pre-Med" to satisfy his father. But as soon as an opportunity presented itself, Arna changed his major to English with a minor in history. He flourished in the environment of "plain living and high thinking" that P.U.C. offered. While obviously interested first in premedicine and then teaching, Arna kept in the back of his mind his dream of becoming a successful writer. Meanwhile he kept his hand in by writing a column called "Campus Notes" for a Los Angeles newspaper. He also worked on campus as a janitor, in the student work program as a reader, and in the print shop, thus helping his father to pay for his education.

Arna earned good grades in all subjects at P.U.C., and his inquisitive mind led him into new avenues of thought. But he had no time to waste, for the course of study was demanding. He once explained why such SDA schools as P.U.C. have excellent academic reputations and why these schools have been so popular among "ambitious Negroes." He wrote, "it has to do with the sheer reading and study that Adventism demands. . . . I still think that three or four of the P.U.C. teachers had more on the ball than almost any I've run into."[38] Arna responded well to the kind of rigid discipline he found at college, appreciating the challenges his professors provided. And when his freshman year had ended, he was more certain than before about his prospects as a writer.[39]

While interesting literary advancements were being made in Harlem by a small group of talented African-American writers during the first years of the twenties, Arna Bontemps was busy trying to earn his first academic degree. Consequently, he remained for a while oblivious to what Claude McKay, Jean Toomer, Jessie Fauset, Langston Hughes, and a few others were doing in "The Big Apple." But he did find time occasionally to bask in the success of other poets. Such was the case when in 1922 he discovered by reading *Harlem Shadows* the beginning of the "Awakening" that was to become "The New Negro Movement." Of this experience Bontemps later said:

I remember it well. I had been a summer school student at U.C.L.A. and picked up a copy of the McKay poems in the main public library on the way home. I had not seen a review or heard any mention of the book. . . . Naturally I had to borrow the book that very minute and read it on the yellow Pacific Electric streetcar that day and a second time that night, then begin telling everybody I knew about it. The response of my black friends was surprising.[40]

Eventually May 1923 rolled around and Arna Wendell Bontemps received the A.B. degree from Pacific Union College. He had accomplished this in only three years. Throughout college Arna went home during the summer months as he had done while in high school. Socializing with others of his race during vacation periods helped round out his education, especially where his roots were concerned. He had also kept up his interest in music by singing in the glee club during most of his time at P.U.C.[41]

Immediately after graduation, he began working full-time at the Los Angeles Post Office and haunting the reading room of the public library in his spare time. Then came that great day in midsummer 1924, only a little more than a year after receiving his diploma, when he received news that a poem of his would be published. The poem's title was ''Hope'' and it first appeared in the NAACP's *Crisis*. His friends were as delighted about his success as he had been about the success of Claude McKay two years earlier. The letter announcing the poem's acceptance had come from Jessie Fauset, the magazine's literary editor and a writer in her own right. The letter announced that the poem would be published in *Crisis's* August 1924 edition.[42]

The young poet could not conceal his delight and mentioned it to a cousin who was working alongside him at the post office. The cousin could not keep the secret either, so the word was out in no time.[43] Wallace Thurman, destined to become one of the key writers of the Harlem Renaissance, and who later got a job at the post office where Bontemps had worked, advised the young poet to move to New York where the literary action was. In a 1942 letter to Harold Jackman, who at that time had requested Bontemps's help in assembling biographical information on Thurman for *The Negro Caravan*, Bontemps explained that for a period of about three months he and ''Wally'' had worked on the same night shift at the Los Angeles Post Office, both as clerks, but without meeting each other and that it was after Bontemps had given up the job that he met and became acquainted with Thurman through mutual friends. Thurman, like Bontemps, had enrolled in a premedical course which he also quit when he found he liked writing better.[44] Arna heeded Wally's advice and set out with a determination to ''make it'' in the literary world. ''By July,'' he recalled, ''I had (a) received a copy of the August issue, which carried my poem, (b) resigned my job at the post office, and (c) packed my suitcase and bought a ticket to New York.''[45]

Once in New York City, Bontemps continued to send his writings, mostly poems at this time, to *Ladies' Home Journal*, *Collier's* and all of the American magazines that published poetry, just as he had done in California when he first graduated from college. He did not always achieve immediate success in these youthful efforts, for he said of those attempts that he would ''send things out . . . and they shot it back. . . . I didn't take that as being radical at that point.''[46] This persistence in sending his ''things'' to prospective publishers is evidence that by age twenty-one Arna Bontemps had a stable sense of self-worth and that his confidence in his own literary skill was increasing.

Chapter 5

Unique Role in the Renaissance

By 1924 Harlem had become the avowed capital of black America. Arna Bontemps, like so many other talented young "Negroes" in various parts of the United States, had set his sights on New York City years before his arrival. He had decided against teaching in California and had planned to go to New York where he could "dig and be dug in return," as Langston Hughes, who would become Bontemps's best friend, would say. As Bontemps himself later explained, he wanted to view the New York happenings "from a grandstand seat."

Arna first arrived in New York City in August 1924. There he found many young artists like himself, all living in Harlem. These young men and women had come from such cities as Cleveland, Topeka, Salt Lake City, and Eatonville, Florida. He had come from Los Angeles at age twenty-one, sixteen months out of college. Seeing Harlem for the first time was the thrill of his life. He had arrived, at last, at a place where he could immerse himself totally in African-American life and culture. His own curiosity about this culture and lore, of course, did not begin suddenly with this move to "The Big Apple." Long before he knew anything about New York and Harlem, and long before the phrase "New Negro Movement" had been coined, Arna Bontemps had been preparing to appreciate what he found upon his arrival in Harlem. As soon as he got off the train at Grand Central Station, he began at once to blend into the New York environment. He recalled that he began learning to ride the subways on his very first day in the city, for as soon as he could retrieve his luggage at the depot, he boarded a subway train and got off in Harlem at the 125th Street stop.[1]

At twenty-one, Arna was ecstatic about being in Harlem for the first time and about the prevailing mood in the city. He was fascinated by the sights and the sounds, and as soon as he could find a place to live, began drinking deeply of the city's cultural springs. Before he was there forty-eight hours, he had begun to partake of the kinds of activities he had come to New York to experience. The first performance he attended was Eugene O'Neill's *All God's Chillun Got Wings*, starring Paul Robeson.[2] A few days after he saw this performance, he purchased a balcony seat for a performance at the Colonial Theater on Columbus Circle and "surrendered all my senses," as he described his involvement, to the musical presentation titled *Chocolate Dandies*.[3] This work starred Eubie Blake and Noble Sissle, a song and dance partnership that had already become established through the musical *Shuffle Along*. Also one of the show's main attractions was tall, brown Josephine Baker, who at that time was on the verge of stardom.

Arna went around the city to performances of all kinds, in theaters, in night-clubs, and in churches; and of everything he saw and heard he made mental notes. On the day of his arrival in the city, he was carrying a sheaf of poems under his arm. During high school and college, poetry had been his favorite literary form, and remained so through most of the Harlem period. Consequently, he continued to try his hand at verse after he had secured a teaching job in Harlem.[4]

As soon as he made the decision to leave the Los Angeles Post Office to seek his fortune in New York City, he began taking advantage of his contacts in the Seventh-day Adventist Church. These led to his receiving an appointment at the denomination's Harlem Academy, their largest high school. He had made most of the arrangements that led to his first teaching position prior to leaving Los Angeles. He found a tiny apartment at Fifth and 129th Street, where from a window of one of the rooms he could see the "rooftops of Negrodom," trying all the while to believe his eyes. Arna realized that this city-within-a-city that everyone called Harlem was indeed a whole new world.[5] So he settled into his apartment and began enjoying this new life. This would remain his address in the city until his marriage two years later.

In *Personals*, his last volume of poetry, Bontemps has left a lyrical description of what Harlem of the twenties was like and of the effect it had on him during those days. He wrote: "In some places the autumn of 1924 may have been an unremarkable season. In Harlem it was like a foretaste of paradise. . . . What a city! What a world! And what a year for a colored boy to be leaving home for the first time! . . . full of golden hopes and romantic dreams, I had come all the way from Los Angeles . . . to hear the music of my taste, to see serious plays and, God willing, to become a writer."[6]

During the next seven years, even while holding a full-time job, the young, energetic apprentice writer was able to accomplish all of that and more besides. He realized from the beginning that he was only one among many talented, aspiring, young artists in Harlem, all striving to capture the peculiar flavor of black culture and to immortalize this culture in their poems, plays, paintings, and songs. Like the others among these heralds of this new cultural and aesthetic awakening, Arna Bontemps seized every opportunity to perfect his art. This is not to imply, though, that he restricted his friendships to the artists in the Harlem of the early twenties. On the contrary, he reveled in the reality that Harlem had become a heterogeneous mixture of blacks from every part of America and abroad. He formed friendships with migrants from the rural South who had recently arrived, and he also mingled with Africans, West Indians, and Puerto Ricans; a mixture of immigrants who shared a common plight and who created a new consciousness.

Arna basked in the collective awareness that would eventually express itself in a remarkable feeling of racial identity and solidarity. Speaking on this subject, he later observed:

Within a year or two we began to recognize ourselves as a "group" and we became a little self-conscious about our "significance." When we were not too busy having fun, we were shown off and exhibited and presented in scores of places, to all kinds of people. And we heard their sighs of wonder, amazement, sometimes admiration when it was whispered or announced that here was one of the "New Negroes."[7]

It was a good time for Arna Bontemps to be in Harlem and he knew it. He was determined to absorb all that Harlem of the "Strolling Twenties" had to offer. Not long after he arrived, even before he began his teaching schedule at Harlem Academy that fall, he had begun to show his sheaf of poems. More than one publisher expressed interest in this youthful work, some suggesting he add another twenty poems and publish them in an anthology. But he never got around to finishing this enlarged volume of poems during the Harlem years, for he was already engrossed in the creation of his first novel, *Chariot in the Sky*, which never got published.[8] Writing this novel, teaching at the Academy, and having fun with his friends did not leave as much time for writing as the young poet needed.

Despite all the demands on his time, however, he had been in New York only a short while before he had published more than a dozen poems in literary magazines. But where his literary productivity was involved, Arna had much in common with his contemporaries, for as a group the Harlem writers seemed to have more talent than time. He summed up their situation aptly when he wrote: "We were the first-born of the Dark Renaissance. We were not just struggling artists trying to find ourselves. No, there was something special about being young and a poet in the middle 'twenties.' "[9]

This was the primitive Harlem of wild parties and untamed youths dancing the Charleston and the Camel Walk up and down the streets, and Arna Bontemps was right there in their midst. He enjoyed the ballrooms and stages, the all-night whist games and bridge tournaments, the "houserent" parties, where everyone crowded in and danced with the lights off and purchased pigs' knuckles, which they ate and washed down with bathtub gin.[10] It was an age of joy, of primitive abandon. Everywhere the "link with the jungle" was discernible, and Arna was fascinated by it all.[11] With Countée Cullen, Langston Hughes, A'Lelia Walker, Harold Jackman, and a coterie of other, Bontemps frequented the little churches contained in abandoned stores and even in houses where he witnessed ecstasy in its purest form. There was no end to the hand-clapping, the swaying and moaning and shouting. This was living proof of the survival in America of an African culture, the culture Arna Bontemps as a youth had sought in books and that his father had sought to quell. This thought must have come to his mind: "Why has the Negro American kept his wildness in his play and his worship and lost it, ostensibly, in his art?"

So Bontemps and his contemporaries in Harlem banded together and decided to give to America a new aesthetic. Critics, of course, are still debating whether they succeeded. It is safe to say, though, that these new poets and the movement they initiated came close to repeating in this country what the Pre-Raphaelite Brotherhood had accomplished in England two generations earlier. Bontemps, for the duration of his life, was convinced that the insularity of the Harlem Renaissance kept its influence from spreading. He felt sure that a tiny shift in circumstances could have made all of the Harlem books best sellers and the plays box-office successes.[12]

For four decades and a portion of a fifth after the end of the Harlem Renaissance, Arna Bontemps was still alive and writing. He was also still making assessments of the Movement, and his thoughts and observations about this period are some of the most authentic, most valid commentary we have. His dating of the Harlem Renaissance is especially logical and still worthy of attention, despite recent, scholarship that has attempted to settle the question finally by beginning the period with the 1924 luncheon that Charles Spurgeon Johnson hosted in honor of these "New Negroes." The year 1924 is, admittedly, a convenient date, and I have used it in a recent publication on Zora Neale Hurston's *Jonah's Gourd Vine*, published in the first issue of *Forum*, the official organ of the Zora Neale Hurston Society that Ruthe Sheffey of Morgan State University founded several years ago. But Bontemps, one of the few Harlem poets who lived to view the age in retrospect, insisted on dating the Harlem Renaissance from 1921, the year in which Langston Hughes published his first poem, "The Negro Speaks of Rivers," in *Crisis*.[13]

The first manifestation that these intellectuals in New York were acquiring a distinct readiness for African-American artistic expression actually came during the preceding year, 1920. Things began to happen in the Harlem literary scene and they were happening among the very young. Bontemps, as late as 1972, saw the 1921 publication of Countée Cullen's poem "I Have a Rendezvous with Life," written in response to Allen Seeger's "I Have a Rendezvous with Death," as typical of the period.[14] Cullen's poem was published in the DeWitt Clinton literary magazine, *The Magpie*, and it shook New York because of its irony— a high school boy from the Harlem ghetto who was writing poetry. How could such optimism, everyone wondered, come from deep within a black ghetto?

Bontemps was impressed by the anomaly of this poem's optimism, for Seeger's poem had expressed the kind of pessimistic attitude toward war and toward life in general that characterized America's mood at the time, for America had not yet recovered from the effects of World War I. It was a mood that, in some ways, parallels the mood prevailing among protesters of America's involvement in Viet Nam four decades later. Arna considered Cullen's poem, and Hughes's, fitting openings to the Harlem era.[15] By 1921 a period of optimism was beginning and had become clearly recognizable by 1922. Arna had found on his arrival in New York that the American soldiers were still returning, and that many of the most popular shows involved World War I. It was a time when people were still shocked by the horrors of war. There was a kind of shadow over the land. He saw and discussed with his friends the long-running movies "The Big Parade" and "All Quiet on the Western Front." And on Broadway he saw "What Price Glory."

But New York had been fortunate; it had not experienced the kinds of rioting during 1919 that other large cities, including Chicago and Washington, had. Hence Bontemps and his literary friends were able to muster feelings of optimism. Garvey and Hughes were both optimistic during this period. The mood of "Rivers" reveals this optimism. Also in that year came Garvey's second conference held at Harlem's Liberty Hall. It was during this time that he named himself "Provisional President" of Africa. In the fall of that year (November 1921), the musical *Shuffle Along* premiered. This Broadway smash represented a most significant breakthrough for African-American artists, for it was written by black authors Flournoy Miller and Aubrey Lyles, and it used an all-black cast, composers, choreographers, and production crews. This postwar musical played to packed houses, despite the rundown condition of the 63rd Street Theater. Long after the show had closed, it left Arna Bontemps singing, along with the rest of the nation, Eubie Blake's "I'm Just Wild About Harry" and "Love Will Find a Way."[16]

Prior to Arna's arrival in Harlem, the 1922 musical *Running Wild* followed on the heels of *Shuffle Along*. Yet he, despite his tardy arrival, reaped with the other Harlem writers the benefits this production gave to the nation. It had popularized the "Charleston" and other steps the writer enjoyed during his Harlem years. Also in this year, Paul Robeson, talented Columbia University law student, made his theatrical debut in Mary Hart Wiborg's play, *Taboo*. Claude McKay's *Harlem Shadows* also appeared during this year. All of these literary developments were occurring while Arna was still in his last years of college.

By the end of 1922, there had been enough literary successes among the Harlem group to encourage the National Urban League to expand their newsletter into a magazine entitled *Opportunity*.[17] And during the following year (1923) Paul Robeson starred in two hits to vindicate his mediocre performance in *Taboo*. The first of these was O'Neill's *All God's Chillun Got Wings*, and it was followed by a revival of *The Emperor Jones*.[18] To keep the ball rolling, several other literary events occurred. Jean Toomer's *Cane* was published, and was followed by the American debut of Roland Hayes with the Boston Symphony. He was a sensational hit.[19] Also in 1923 came Jessie Fauset's novel *There Is Confusion*, and Walter White's novel *The Fire in the Flint*, although it was not published until 1924. This was the ready-made literary climate Arna Bontemps stepped into on the day of his arrival in New York.

Charles S. Johnson had hosted his auspicious luncheon in March 1924. Johnson had been especially drawn toward McKay and Toomer, both of whom had been acclaimed by major critics, and was perceptive enough to accurately interpret this new impulse of expansion as an impetus that could benefit a first-rate literary magazine such as his *Opportunity*; hence the origin of Opportunity's literary contests. The purpose of this luncheon held at New York's Civic Club was to honor and present to the public this new generation of writers. But Arna arrived too late to attend the luncheon, a fact he never stopped lamenting.[20] Hughes was not there either, for it came shortly after he had dropped out of Columbia and set out on his first sea voyage. Nor was Jean Toomer present at the luncheon. But the literary situations of both Toomer and Hughes were different from that of Arna Bontemps.

Hughes was already well-known by 1924, and Toomer's *Cane* had appeared the previous year, making him need no introduction to the literary powers of New York. On the other hand, if anyone could have profited from such a formal introduction, Arna Bontemps could have. Had he been present at the luncheon, his entire career no doubt would have gotten a boost equal to that the others in the group received, for Arna was as talented as any poet of the period, and more talented than some. Not only was his name absent from the proceedings of the luncheon published in the May 1924 edition of *Opportunity*, but he was also not represented in the anthology that Alain Locke published the following year.

Alain Locke attended the luncheon on enforced leave from Howard University.[21] He had been selected as mentor by a small coterie of Harlem writers who were known as the "Harlem Writers' Guild." His role as stimulator of these young writers did not go unnoticed by Charles S. Johnson, for Locke had always made a distinction between them and the older group: Du Bois, J. W. Johnson, Chesnutt, and others in their category. The second occurrence was that Locke was asked by the editors of *Survey Graphic* to edit a special issue of their magazine featuring the guests of honor at the luncheon. This was published in the spring of 1925 under the title *Harlem: Mecca of the New Negro*. It was such a success on the newsstands and in the libraries that Horace Liveright asked Locke to expand the magazine issue into a book for his publishing house, which became a kind of repository of the works of the Harlem writers.[22] Liveright could discern the importance of the Renaissance writers even more clearly than they themselves could at this time.

Carl Van Vechten had used his influence with Liveright to secure these benefits for Alain Locke. Van Vechten was a man of wide cultural interests and excellent literary contacts. But it was not until later that Bontemps met Van Vechten who, despite his ulterior motive for spending so much time with blacks—their portrayal in *Nigger Heaven*—could have given Bontemps's writing career the initial boost it needed. Because he missed the luncheon, and because his lifestyle was different from that shared by the other Harlem writers, Arna's career developed in relative isolation from the others in the Harlem group. A short time after Locke's first edition of *The New Negro* was published, he began work on the second edition, in which Bontemps's poem "The Day-Breakers" appeared. This was the first time a poem of his had appeared in a book; previously he had been published only in periodicals.

The real star of that 1924 luncheon had been Countée Cullen, who was only a junior in college and approximately one year younger than both Hughes and Bontemps. Cullen had read a few of his poems at the luncheon and had so impressed the literary world that his poems started appearing in rapid succession in major American magazines, most of which had never before carried a poem by a person of color.[23] One of the first of his poems to appear after the luncheon was "Yet Do I Marvel," carried by *Century* magazine. Near the end of the year (1924) "The Shroud of Color" appeared in *American Mercury*, the longest poem the magazine had ever published.

Before the end of the year, too, his first collection of poems was issued by Harper and Brothers and was an instant success. But no such literary boost came to Arna Bontemps, who by this time was finishing his first semester of teaching at Harlem Academy. Hughes had returned from Paris and the other ocean voyages described in his autobiography, *The Big Sea*. Bontemps would soon meet in person the young poet whose name he had first encountered upon receiving the August 1924 issue of *Crisis* that carried his own poem "Hope."

As Ferguson explains in her biography of Cullen, it was he who was largely responsible for Arna's introduction to Harlem society.[24] It was Cullen who arranged Bontemps's first meeting with Hughes. On the day of his arrival in Harlem, Arna learned that the 135th Street Library was walking distance from his apartment. One day at the checkout desk he met young Roberta Bosley, who was one of the student assistants there and who claimed to be a cousin to Countée. One of the circulation librarians there was the roommate of Ethel Ray Nance; her name was Regina Anderson, a person Arna had met through Roberta Bosley. This is his description of what happened on that day in August 1924:

After I found a room, I went out to see what Harlem was like, and walked up and down the street, down Lenox Avenue, and I was looking for the public library. I guess I was crazy like that . . . to start watching for the library. . . . And when I got there, there were a couple of very nice-looking girls sitting at the desk, colored girls. I had never seen that before, you know, in California. And I said, "I want to apply for a card," and started filling out the paper. And Roberta said, "Look here, haven't I seen your name someplace?" "Well, I don't know, you might have," I said. Then she went back and got a copy of *Crisis*, which was the one which contained my first poem. It was just out that month, you see. I'd had it from California but it was still the current issue. And she said, "I'd seen this poem, but I thought this was a woman, this Arna." And I told her, "Don't!" and went on to say that I hoped she wouldn't hold it against me; it was the name my mother gave me . . . apparently she didn't because about two weeks later I took her to a party.[25]

This party is one of several described by Blanche Ferguson in her biography of Cullen. It was actually a dance held at the Renaissance Casino, a new, attractive club where young Harlemites liked to congregate. Cullen thought this would be the ideal occasion for introducing his new friend, Arna Bontemps, to people in the city who had interests in common with him. Bontemps at first was a bit hesitant about accepting the invitation because he had not yet met a girl whom he could take to the dance. Countée was taking W.E.B. Du Bois's daughter Yolande whom he later married. So Countée arranged for Arna to take Roberta.[26] The party turned out to be a grand affair. A jazz band played, and Arna had an exceptionally good time. But no one present could hold a light to Cullen on the dance floor. ''Countée's dancing skill,'' says Ferguson, ''was the envy of his friends. Some of them maintained that the rhythm left over from his poetry went into his feet.''[27]

Langston Hughes did not return to New York until late November 1924, and it was shortly thereafter that Countée introduced him to Arna, the individual who would become his closest friend and correspondent until Hughes's death in 1967. When Langston's ship docked at New York, he had only one quarter to his name. Immediately he contacted Countée, who was elated that he was back and about the time of his arrival. To Cullen's way of thinking, Hughes could not have arrived at a better time, for on that very evening the NAACP was hosting a party and all the literary people, black and white, would be there. Assuring Langston that his reputation as a frequent contributor to the *Crisis* was all the invitation he needed, Countée exacted a promise from him to be there that night.[28]

At this party Cullen told Hughes about Arna Bontemps, one of the newest young writers in the city, and that he and Arna had become friends. A few days later Hughes was the guest of honor at another party, a much smaller gathering of friends who wanted to hear him read the poems he had written during his ocean voyages. The quiet young teacher named Arna Bontemps, who missed the NAACP party, was present at the smaller gathering; it was here that Countée introduced him to Langston, explaining that Arna was also a writer. He explained, too, how he had met Arna, who had arrived one day at the home of Countée's parents bearing a letter of introduction, and how as soon as the elder Cullen opened the door he yelled to his son, ''It's Langston Hughes.''[29] At the party Langston and Arna, both somewhat shy, both of medium height and olive-complexioned, greeted each other and shook hands, each half-apologizing to the other for having been the subject of a case of mistaken identity. Then Langston took Arna around to introduce him, and this is how an enduring friendship began.[30]

The next three years, 1925–1927, were relatively quiet for Arna Bontemps except for his marriage late in the summer of 1926 to Alberta Johnson, then a student of his at Harlem Academy, and the birth of their first child in 1927. There were other accomplishments, though, which Arna, in his characteristic manner, tended to play down. By 1927 he had abandoned his youthful dream of earning a living from his poems. Given the prevailing conditions with African Americans and their literary pursuits, Arna had been forced to view his poetry writing as a kind of avocation. But he did continue to compose poems and had a number of notable successes until the eve of the Great Depression. Arna found himself being invited more often than he had been formerly to read his poems, mostly to small audiences, and he won several prestigious poetry prizes. He had spent most of 1925 taking graduate courses at Columbia while teaching at the Academy. And there were the endless parties and literary soirées to attend.

His place of employment during the Renaissance years was located in the center of black Harlem. The Academy was on 127th Street off Seventh Avenue, and it was there in one of his English classes that he met Alberta Johnson. Miss Johnson had arrived in New York during the same year the poet-teacher had gone there to seek his fortune in literature. She had come to attend school. She had been born in 1906 in Du Pont, Georgia, a small town near Waycross, making her some four years younger than her teacher. Her parents, Edward and Phoebe Johnson, had both died when she was a very young child, and her grandmother, Lucy Wilson, had reared her in Waycross. Early in her childhood Alberta had become a Seventh-day Adventist and had attended the SDA school in Waycross until after the eighth grade, which was as far as many schools in the South went in those days. Desiring to continue her education, she went to Harlem Academy in New York to begin her ninth-grade year. She recalls that the education she got there was a good one, for the teachers gave their students the personal attention they needed. It was here that she met her husband. They were both freshmen in a sense, she in her first year of high school and he as beginning teacher.

Alberta Bontemps's memory of Arna Wendell Bontemps as he appeared to her in the fall of 1924 is a vivid one, and no doubt more reliable than any description of his youthful days anyone alive can provide, for Mrs. Bontemps's mind is not in the least impaired, and her most vivid memories are those of her husband and their life together. Her description reveals those subtle aspects of Arna's personality that distinguished him during his adult life. She reminisced:

Well, he was a very young, fine, dashing young teacher that all the girls were enamored of. And I happened to be in his class. He had told the class not to come into the room after he had begun teaching unless they knocked. And on the morning of this particular day, I had been detained by the principal. And, naturally, I was a little late getting to my class. So, I knocked and . . . went to my seat and sat down. And then he made a reference to the fact that I was late. In fact, he called my name: "Johnson, did I not tell you that when you were late to this class to knock?" and so I stood up and gave him back . . . what I thought about it; that I had followed his rules.[31]

Mrs. Bontemps recalls that the young "Mister Bontemps" taught with a great deal of humor in his classes, for many of the students were his own age. She recalls that on the morning of this, their first confrontation, he was more than a little amused, for though he had tried to keep a straight face, she could detect a "crinkle of a smile." It was then that she first became aware of what she described as the "dry, subtle sense of humor" that was one of her husband's most memorable traits, an aspect of his personality, as Sandra Alexander has noted, that "characterized him in the eyes of his associates."[32]

There had been little opportunity for Arna to actually date Alberta, for the girls of Harlem Academy were strictly supervised, most living in homes with SDA families whose religious fervor and moral standards met the expectations of church officials. Such was the case with the petite and pretty Alberta Johnson. Thus, as she recalls, this was his first notice of her as a person, and not as just another student in his class. She remembers thinking how handsome he was and that he dressed extraordinarily well for the economic period in which they found themselves. "That was the time when men wore caps," she reflected, "and he looked very handsome in a cap."[33] She recalls it was later in the school year when he again exhibited interest in her. At first they were all, the teachers included, just a group of young people socializing together.

One Saturday Arna and Alberta joined a group of students and teachers at the home of Alberta's friend and schoolmate, Ruth Watkins. On this particular Saturday Arna had asked Alberta to go with him to Mount Vernon to a gathering at the Watkins home. The gathering could hardly have been called a party, for it was on the Sabbath, and at this time Adventists were not supposed to sing secular songs of any kind, and certainly not on a Sabbath. But there was a player piano in the Watkins home and Arna decided to entertain the group by singing and pretending to strike the keys as the player did its job, antics his widow calls "going through the motions."[34] The gentleman suddenly turned toward his lady and began serenading her with his own rendition of Irving Berlin's "Always," a popular tune of the day. From that time on the courtship strengthened and on August 26, 1926, two years after the young poet's August 24th arrival in Harlem, he married his "Sweetie," a term of endearment he used throughout their life together. Mrs. Bontemps recalls that throughout their forty-seven years of marriage, "Always" remained their favorite song.[35]

In May 1927 a baby girl, the first child, was born and they named her Joan. And before another year had passed, the second child, a son Paul, was born (April 1928). Not long after his 1926 marriage, Arna had won the Alexander Pushkin Prize for the poem "Golgotha Is a Mountain." And during the following year he won the Pushkin Prize a second time, for "The Return." Later that year he won the *Crisis* Poetry Prize—the first presented—for "Nocturne at Bethesda."[36] This is a poem he mailed to Countée in October of 1926, not long after Charles S. Johnson had hired Cullen as *Opportunity's* assistant editor. The letter addressed "Dear Countée" explained: "Here is 'Nocturne.' There should be some excuse made for it. Personally I do not feel that it is finished. I hope to effect some changes in it in due time."[37] During Countée's two years with *Opportunity* (1926–1928), Arna was a frequent contributor of reviews and original poems to the magazine.[38] But Arna never had the time for revising his writing that many of his contemporaries had.

Despite his achievement alongside his contemporaries in the "New Negro Movement," and despite his involvement in most of their social gatherings, Arna was markedly different in personality and lifestyle from the others of "the group." His marriage to Alberta and the six children they had together, the last of whom was born in 1945 after Arna began his tenure at Fisk, produced a kind of quiet stability in his life that the other Harlem writers never experienced, not even Countée with his second wife, Ida. Alberta's role was always supportive, "standing in the shadows," caring for their children, while her illustrious husband followed his first loves, reading and writing.[39] Recently Mrs. Bontemps confided that the author married her because he knew she had no ambitions that would interfere with his writing.[40]

Writing in *The Big Sea*, Langston Hughes maintained that Arna was both the brilliant writer and the stable family man. He argued that this second dimension was a trait that marked him as a symbol of social stability in a group of some rather unstable literary associates.[41] Even more than a decade after Arna's death, his friends and associates have little doubt that it was his wife Alberta who encouraged the characteristic stability the writer exuded throughout their life together. But the facts of his life prove that Arna himself possessed more than his share of emotional strength and stability.

Aaron Douglas, the painter who arrived in Harlem early in 1925 not long after Bontemps, spoke of his colleague's uniqueness when set alongside the others in the Harlem group, admitting that he never went inside Arna's home in New York. Douglas said that he would go to the house when he wanted to take Arna out, and wait outside.[42] He recalled that Bontemps's background was of a religious kind, while Douglas and others of the group were more impish and less restrained. They would slip Arna out and take him to Rockville Center, or to Gwen Bennett's place, trying hard to get him back before dawn, but rarely did. Douglas, like Cullen and the other Harlem artists, liked to dance, but dancing was against Arna's religion.[43] But Arna did openly go to theaters and musicals, and Arna knew that Wallace Thurman, or "Wally," as he preferred to call him, thought of him and Alberta as rather bourgeois. This knowledge did not cause Arna any concern, nor did it alter his friendship with Douglas or Thurman.[44]

During the years between their first meeting in 1924 and the onset of the Great Depression in 1929, the Arna Bontemps–Langston Hughes friendship became firmly established, for the two men had more in common than it would at first appear. Hughes was more the hedonist, more the bohemian than Bontemps's upbringing and personal sense of decorum would allow him to imitate. All of his life Bontemps, as had Aaron Douglas, had striven to avoid the kind of insularity that characterized most of the Harlem group. And Langston, though less well-rounded than Bontemps, was not as narrow in his tastes and exposure as were most of the others. This willingness to adapt, to expand his interests, must have endeared ''Lang'' to Arna, strengthening the friendship as the years passed.

Arna remained adamant in his belief that there was something ''wrong'' with the young artists of the Harlem years, for they were, in his estimation, too reluctant to get out and do other things besides reading poetry and going to plays. But compared to the narrow interests of young people today, these artists of the ''twenties'' were following other, more interesting pursuits.[45] As early as his high school and college years, Arna had maintained an interest in music, but he broadened his circle of friends to include those interested in athletics, religion, and politics. He had learned, long before he left California, to cultivate friendships with all types of people, for he realized that he was not likely to find a single individual who could share all of his interests.[46]

His mind was vast, and he was, with his many interests, a true Renaissance figure, one who found in Langston Hughes his intellectual twin. Although not as versatile as Arna, Langston certainly admired versatility in whomever he found it. Countée Cullen, on the other hand, was not at all versatile. He was all literature, but Arna was tolerant of this trait in his friend. Arna was also delighted to find that Langston had other interests besides literature. He and Langston often attended sporting events together during the Harlem years. And while Hughes did not seem to know as much about the technicalities of the various games as did Bontemps, he certainly knew how to enjoy them.[47]

During their nearly forty-three years of friendship, Hughes and Bontemps never had a falling out of any kind. They were able always to express their differences of opinion whenever these occurred, but were more apt to think alike on most issues than to differ.[48] Their friendship was explainable more on the level of their similar backgrounds and complementary temperaments than on any similarity in their personal lives. Both had educated parents; both had fathers who opposed the son's choice of a literary career; both were excellent students, although the parochial college from which Bontemps graduated was certainly different from Hughes's Columbia, and the Lincoln University that became his alma mater. Both men were strong individualists, and while they sometimes placed emphasis on opposite issues, these differences were never great enough to produce conflict or tension in their relationship. Both were lovers of peace, lovers of harmony, and avoiders of strife of all kinds.[49]

Because he was so versatile and had interests in many subjects, Arna did not allow married life to prevent him from taking full advantage of this marvelous time to be young, black, and a poet in Harlem. He maintained contacts with all of the young transplants who with him became the Harlem literati. He had been on hand when in the spring of 1926, a few months before his marriage, Langston's first book, *The Weary Blues*, came off the press, carrying an introduction by Carl Van Vechten. It was the follow-up to Hughes's sharing the third-place *Opportunity* prize with Cullen in the spring of 1925.[50] Bontemps also witnessed in 1926 the meteoric rise of Van Vechten's *Nigger Heaven*, which went on to become the most successful novel of the decade. Bontemps witnessed the swarms of white patrons it brought into Harlem's nightclubs to see the "New Negroes."[51] It took Van Vechten, a white man, to discover "the Negro" for the literary world, a fact that Bontemps could not help resenting, as did most of the other Harlem writers. And in *Heaven*'s wake, a long succession of plays appeared, all centering around "Negro" themes and casts, a brand-new development, and Arna Bontemps was on hand to enjoy and evaluate each new production.

There were other artists who were inspired by their darker-skinned counterparts. In 1926 George Gershwin met W. C. Handy and heard his "St. Louis Blues," and was inspired as a result to compose "Rhapsody in Blue." Bontemps witnessed the introduction of jazz into the mainstream of society during these eventful times. In 1927 two other white artists, Julia Peterson and DuBose Heyward, who had together written *Porgy*, started writing about "primitive blacks." Bontemps stood by with the other African-American artists, astounded, as white artists began literally to possess the Harlem Renaissance. This caused a bitterness to creep over Bontemps that would haunt him during the remainder of his life, for he rarely spoke of the Harlem Renaissance during his mature years without lamenting the extent to which he and other "New Negroes" were exploited.[52] These white writers received the front-page publicity and promotion that had been denied the non-white artists who inspired their works.

This was the story of 1927, so that by 1928 Bontemps and the others in the Harlem group began to feel disenchantment with the New York that had inspired them only a few years earlier. Bontemps felt, as did most of the others, that he had been "elbowed out."[53] And he was to resent for the rest of his days Van Vechten and others who had picked up what the Harlem group had started, cheapened it, and made it commercial.[54] In short Arna Bontemps, toward the end of the Renaissance, had begun to feel used. During 1927 Locke had written a piece about these circumstances for *Opportunity* before it suspended operation during the fall of that year.[55] And in 1928 Rudolph "Bud" Fisher, the writer-physician of the Harlem group, wrote one of the most successful works of the decade, his novel *The Walls of Jericho*, a satire of those who had exploited African-American artists under the guise of praising them. This thematically successful work taught some poignant lessons to all concerned about how to demolish the walls of class and race.

The year 1928 found Arna busy writing a novel of his own. The one he had written earlier, *Chariot in the Clouds*, had not succeeded in finding a publisher, hence he was trying to salvage this work by rewriting an earlier version. Meanwhile, Wallace Thurman was writing his successful novel *The Blacker the Berry*, although it was not published until 1929. McKay's *Home to Harlem* was published in 1928, his first book since *Harlem Shadows*. It became a roaring success, though it received mixed reviews from the African-American press. So offended were the Harlem literati by *Home to Harlem*'s untimely revival of the Primitivism theme, that *Crisis* held a symposium to analyze such controversial works as *Nigger Heaven* and *Home to Harlem*. But Bontemps, in retrospect, considered the symposium a failure, for he recalled a particular irony of the occasion: Most of the people called upon to express opinions about what kinds of materials non-white writers should use were themselves white writers.[56]

On April 9, 1928 Bontemps had taken part in one of the most outstanding social affairs of the decade, the wedding of Nina Yolande Du Bois and Countée Cullen. There were sixteen bridesmaids with Harold Jackman as best man and Bontemps and fourteen others serving as groomsmen.[57]

But the Great Depression came, and though the stock market crash did not affect the almost penniless Harlem writers as rapidly and in the same ways it affected the whites in New York City, Bontemps and his friends, as early as the winter of 1928, had begun to sense the end of that era when "Harlem was in Vogue." The insularity of the dark Renaissance had begun to be torn down against the wills of those who had enjoyed it. To Bontemps and his contemporaries who created it, the Harlem Renaissance had been not so much an economic venture as an artistic awareness, an artistic expression. Bontemps's apprentice period was nearing its end, and he had benefited from the Harlem experience.

As a young man of twenty-one he had come to the city seeking information about his culture, his history. In New York he had found this knowledge. He had come seeking a deeper understanding of self; this he had gleaned during his first five years in New York. At twenty-six he was ready for the arduous journey toward satisfying his lifelong ambition of becoming a professional writer. By the end of 1927, about the time he decided to try his hand at a novel, he had seen the handwriting on the wall—his chances of making a living writing poetry were slim.

Without personal contacts it was difficult to get poems placed in such magazines as *Scribner's*, *Harper's*, and *Atlantic*. Arna soon learned that trying to get one's poems judged by the editors of these larger organs was a slow process hardly worth the five dollars earned per poem, the going rate in the late twenties.[58] Although his job at Harlem Academy kept food on the table—he had even served briefly as the principal after "Professor Moran," the previous principal, left the school—Arna also had set his sights on earning some money from his literary endeavors, money that could enhance the quality of his family's life and secure the future of his children.

But he was to experience one disappointment after another during the decade. His disenchantment with poetry had surfaced as early as April 1927 when he was quoted in *Crisis* as saying that poetry is immoral, his implied reason for quitting poetry. Scholars have tended to ignore this uncharacteristic remark, but it is fortunate that Ann Allen Shockley broached the subject in her interview of Bontemps eleven months before his sudden death. As it turned out, this entire expressed attitude had been tongue-in-cheek, as I had suspected all along, a device not at all uncharacteristic of Arna Bontemps. In true Bontempsian style he explained the remark by saying he was just trying to be "crazy," that it had not been meant to be taken seriously. The true reason, of course, that he gave up poetry was that he needed to make a living.[59]

By the end of the twenties James Weldon Johnson had contacted Bontemps about including some of his poems in an anthology the elder poet was planning to revise. And Bontemps, still in his twenties, had by this time demonstrated that he could compete with the best of his contemporaries. Besides publishing ''Dogwoods at the Spring'' and several others of his poems in various issues of the school paper and in literary magazines at Pacific Union College, he had also placed poems in an impressive list of periodicals: *Crisis, Opportunity, Fire, The Commonweal, The World Tomorrow, The Carolina Magazine*, and in various reprints.[60] He had also been represented in several anthologies.[61]

But the frequent literary prizes Arna Bontemps had won during the Harlem Renaissance had not been enough to make a name for him as a poet. Competition was tremendous. Consequently, he made a painful decision before the decade ended—he would abandon poetry, his first mistress, and try to effect a lasting liaison with prose. Arna Bontemps's literary efforts during the Renaissance, primarily because of the demands of the roles he played as husband, father, and teacher, placed him at a disadvantage alongside his writer friends. He was somewhat overshadowed by the greater Harlem lights. Although his literary contributions and publishing efforts remained steady during the Harlem years, Arna Bontemps was not able during this period to match the productivity of a Cullen or a Hughes. He did, however, make his presence felt, and in retrospect his uniqueness shines more brightly than it ever shone during the Harlem decade.

Bontemps's birthplace, Ninth and Winn Streets, Alexandria, Louisiana. (Courtesy Kirkland Jones.)

Arna Bontemps, c. 1939. (Moorland-Spingarn Research Center, Howard University; The Rose McClendon Memorial Collection of Photographs of Celebrated Negroes by Carl Van Vechten.)

Old library building, Fisk University, 1986. (Courtesy Kirkland Jones.)

Arna Bontemps and Langston Hughes, c. 1950. (Photo by Harold Stovall; Moorland-Spingarn Research Center, Howard University.)

Memorial Chapel at Fisk University, 1986. Place of Bontemps's funeral in 1973. (Courtesy Kirkland Jones.)

Exterior, Memorial Chapel, Fisk University, 1986. (Courtesy Kirkland Jones.)

Arna Bontemps and writer Roy Hill, c. 1971, in Atlanta. (Courtesy Roy L. Hill.)

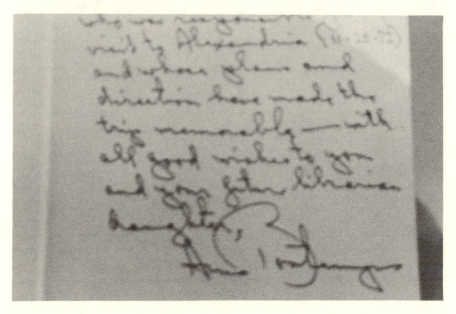

Bontemps's autograph in a copy of *Young Booker* presented to Audrey Nabors Jackson in November 1972 at Alexandria. (Courtesy Kirkland Jones.)

(*Left to right*) Mr. McGraw, Arna's playmate at Alexandria; (*center*) tour guide; (*right*) Kirkland Jones, February 1986. (Courtesy Kirkland Jones.)

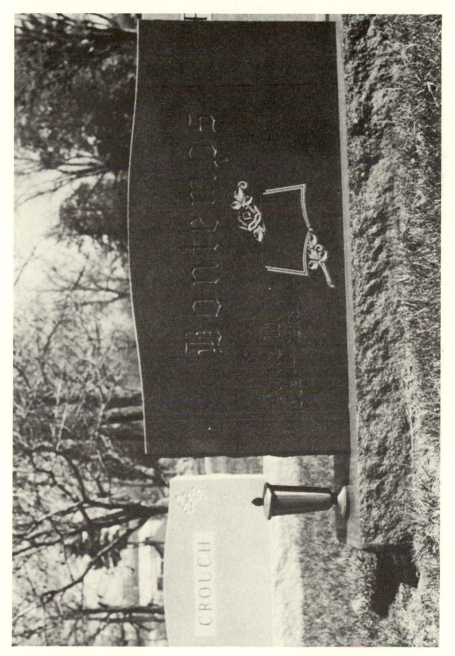

Grave marker, Greenwood Cemetery, Nashville, 1986. (Courtesy Kirkland Jones.)

Arna Bontemps Museum, Third Street, Alexandria, Louisiana. (Courtesy Bobbie Williams, Beaumont Independent School District.)

Chapter 6

The Depression Period

By the end of the 1920s Arna Bontemps and his contemporaries could look back on the period as a difficult though inspiring time. The years 1920–1930 were trying for the African American no matter where in this country he found himself. Bontemps, in his numerous writings and speeches about the first half of this century in America, has chronicled the injustices and exploitation he and his darker brothers and sisters suffered in this land of their birth. His writings and speeches on the Harlem Renaissance remind the researcher that the atmosphere of the times, even in Harlem, was oppressive. Bontemps and his contemporaries in the Harlem group had continued to produce first-rate literary works, many of which have become more important and influential than even their creators had dreamed. But he, like most of the others in the group, received meager financial rewards for his efforts. Like his friend Countée Cullen, Arna understood the paradox of making ''a poet black'' and bidding him to sing.

By the onset of the Depression in 1929, Bontemps had begun to recover from the shock and disappointment of having his fledgling novel, *Chariot in the Sky*, rejected by publishers and was hard at work on its successor, *God Sends Sunday*. An examination of this work marks it as more memoir than novel. *Chariot*'s dialogue and description, page after page, do not jibe, and the work exhibits other youthful crudities as well.[1] Its most significant feature is the nostalgia theme, the topic that was to yield Bontemps's best works during his mature years. Based on Arna's childhood, ''Uncle Buddy'' appears in a not-very-fictionalized version. It is precisely this autobiographical element, however, that would have made it sparkle.

It is unfortunate that Bontemps's publishers did not encourage him in this effort, for with a minimum of polishing and revising, this novel could have become a success. But in some ways the work was a failure, and Bontemps was the first to admit its poor reception. In fact, the real reason it failed has been articulated by the author himself. "The white publishers weren't ready," he said, "for that kind of novel."[2] Perhaps these publishers felt America would not buy yet another of these childhood stories, for the market was glutted with stories of white boys and white girls in their search for maturity.

Bontemps had come to the realization that with a wife and two children to support, writing, for him, would have to become an avocation instead of a sole career. He knew that he would write, indeed had to write. Hence it was during the end of the 1920s and the beginning of the 1930s that he began to develop writing habits that would stand him in good stead for the remainder of his long and fruitful career. During his first two years in Harlem, 1924–1926, he wrote at night. But after his marriage, he found that he and Alberta needed some uninterrupted time together during the evening hours. Furthermore he learned during the earliest days of his marriage, after he and Alberta had moved out to the Pelham Bay area, that after he had written poetry all night he went to his classes the next day sleepy-eyed and unalert.[3]

But Bontemps did not let the job at Harlem Academy or the roles of husband and father stop him from writing. He had always liked to sleep late into the morning hours, but he knew that something would have to be sacrificed if he were to write at all.[4] He decided, then, that he would have to resist the urge to sleep late. Getting up at five or six in the morning was a real fight at first, but after trying it a few times, he discovered he wrote well during these hours and that getting up early caused him to feel better during the day and that, as a result, he never "lost the zing."[5] At night he would go to bed and sleep. So this became a habit that he practiced during his years in Huntsville, Alabama, so that by the end of the Depression and during the Chicago years, it had become his daily routine.[6]

Arna did not, as many writers do, make rough drafts of his works before writing the final copy. In fact, he seldom wrote more than one draft, a practice he attributed to the conditions under which he was forced to write. This was true of his poems and his prose as well.[7] He explained to Ann Shockley: "I believe if I had been free to, and had all of my time for writing, I would have made a half dozen copies [versions] of everything as Langston did, and as Richard Wright always did. . . . But I always had a job and . . . responsibilities, and . . . a family. . . . I couldn't neglect my job, so I had to budget my time."[8]

The result was that he would do a great deal of thinking about what he was going to write during the day, making sketchy notes. When he got a chance to write, he almost always knew what he was going to say beforehand. In other words, he was composing as he went about his other duties. Hence there was very little difference between his published works and what he wrote the first time. His method of mental composition and his actual output, despite his many other obligations, are evidence that Arna Bontemps was a natural, the kind of born writer one finds in the most successful of the Harlem group and in many who emerged in the wake of the Renaissance; such personages as Richard Wright and Chester Himes, authors who also wrote in spite of limitations placed upon them.

For the African-American writers, the national disaster did not begin the moment the stock market crashed in 1929. The Great Depression came upon this "talented tenth" not like an earthquake but more like quicksand. At first, it was something happening only on Wall Street,[9] but it arrived in Harlem by 1930. Early in this year, Arna began to sense that it would not be feasible for him to remain in New York, for the Depression had killed the kinds of publishing opportunities he and his contemporaries had enjoyed. Although he had not by 1930 received as much recognition for his literary accomplishments as had Hughes and Cullen, his artistic success rivaled that of his two friends, a remarkable achievement when one considers that Hughes was a confirmed bachelor and that Cullen, though married, had no small children underfoot. Though Cullen did have a job in the public schools of New York, it is clear that both he and Hughes had more uninterrupted time to devote to literature than did Bontemps.

The "strolling twenties" had not been an easy time, but the hard times the Depression brought in the 1930s made the 1920s seem easy by comparison. The one bright spot for black artists during these first years after 1929 was Marc Connelly's musical *Green Pastures*, which opened on Broadway in February 1930.[10] Connelly, a white writer, had taken Roark Bradford's *Ol' Man Adam an' His Chillun*, a collection of short stories, and constructed from it an entertaining folk drama. It ran for 557 performances at the Mansfield Theater, went on an extensive road tour, and then returned to Broadway for a five-year run.[11]

But this play did far more for the African-American actor and musician than it did for the writer. In an unpublished, undated manuscript found in Bontemps's papers at the George Arendts Research Library at Syracuse University, he wrote that with the arrival of the Depression, circumstances rendered him jobless and introduced him to a brand-new interest, the craft of the private press. Bontemps began to read books and brochures on the subject and decided to try for a piece of the pie.

A result of this involvement was the first book printed on his own private press. He chose the setting of the well-known English essay, "The Roadmender," by Michael Fairless as the basis for his first effort. The end result of these labors was a series of small, experimental keepsakes produced in editions of from one to fifty. These sold well; consequently, the activity continued for about eight years, well into the Chicago period. Even Bontemps himself could hardly believe how busy he kept during these years. But these publishing activities eventually gave way to other interests, other pursuits, for the writer's youthful dreams of fame and fortune, of becoming a firm like Wayland Williams or even Stone and Kimball, had vanished into limbo. But it was fun for Arna while it lasted.

The Depression even killed the frequent and fancy string of social gatherings of A'lelia Walker's "Dark Tower." Arna, from its opening in 1928, after A'lelia's mother, Madam C. J. Walker, died, was a regular patron. He was there to watch as A'lelia turned her impressive mansion into a club room where she hosted receptions, dinners, and parties for the literati. In fact, it was largely in honor of the young literary set, Arna believed, that the "Dark Tower" had been established.[12] He had grown accustomed to attending all kinds of functions there, but these "attractive little gatherings," as he described them, did not continue very long.[13] By the spring of 1931 the club's founder had died suddenly, but she had grown tired of her experiment before her death, for the club's high prices, even for the rich clientele it catered to, proved impractical during these Depression years.[14]

By 1931 the Depression had brought to an end what Bontemps called in more than one of his writings "the dream world of Renaissance Harlem." The artists of the group had begun to scatter; one by one they were returning to their hometowns and going to other, less logical places. Bontemps observed that the "New Negroes" appeared in places as far apart as Eatonville, Florida, and Martha's Vineyard; Atlantic City, New Jersey, and Carmel-by-the-Sea, California. Some grew haggard and confused. A few eventually secured jobs with the cultural projects of the W.P.A. (Works Projects Administration), a program in which the writer would eventually participate.[15] By the end of the 1930–31 school term Arna knew that he, too, would have to go wherever he could find employment, for financial straits had caused Harlem Academy to close its doors. This was sad news for Bontemps and his family. "Professor" Moran and others of the faculty would be going to Huntsville, Alabama, to work at Oakwood Junior College, an institution that seemed to have no serious money problems.

It was fortunate for Arna and his dependents, Alberta, Joan, and Paul, that his first novel *God Sends Sunday* had come off the press a few months before it was time for them to move, providing a small amount of cash to help carry them through the summer months, or until Arna could find another job and earn his first paycheck. Reviews of the novel had begun to appear and these were encouraging. Critics praised the novel's "color," its use of dialect, its swift movement, its economy and power. One of the earliest reviews to come out was in the *New York Times*, setting the tone for others that followed. The unsigned article in the Book Review section commented:

This first novel by a young Louisiana Negro, already known as a poet, plows deeply into a rich soil of Negro personality, turning up a gay pageant of pagan color or ripping out the very roots of native poetry in the common speech of a most spontaneous race. The vivid picturesqueness of expression leaps out with the natural freshness of childish naiveté rather than with the burnt-cork brilliance of a minstrel show. Arna Bontemps has caught the lightheartedness and the soft melancholy of the Negro race with such a perfect natural grace that it is only on a second reading that one begins to realize the gem-like qualities of the recorded conversation and the artistic economy in the vividly intense pictures of common life in the Negro quarters.[16]

Three days after this first review appeared, the *New York Sun* said the novel's author "spins a tale that should last a long time," and the reviewer went on to praise the dignity of the protagonist, Lil'Augie. And within another four days, the book section of the *New York Herald Tribune* praised the novel's "sober discretion" and went on to say "there is something of Porgy in the tale of Little Augie, but more of Vachel Lindsay's 'broncho that would not be broken of dancing.' "[17] This type of friendly review continued well into 1932.[18]

The poet turned novelist was having no little success. But the novel did not sell, for 1931 was not a good year for novels, as Bontemps himself explained.[19] He admitted that the novel was inspired by his "Uncle Buddy," "the little brown man" from Arna's childhood, "who came to live with us in the West."[20] As a small boy, Arna had not recognized the great-uncle as a possible character for fiction, but had been impressed by the almost Homeric wanderings of this quaint old man, and by his stories of goblins, "haints," and "hoo-doo." The writer explained, though, that this uncle imparted a new quality to his "own small world of fruit trees, poultry houses and spring wagons. Telling his dreams at the breakfast table, reciting strange poetry as we dug in the potato patch, recalling bright experiences from his past as we walked to the grocery store, he gradually admitted us to his own wonderful universe."[21]

No doubt the greatest irony surrounding *Sunday*'s publication is that as the novel was coming off the press, its author lost his "Uncle Buddy." Buddy, who had received an autographed copy of the work, went out celebrating, and returning home on foot, was hit and killed by a car. Equally ironic is that Arna's father Paul rejected the novel for religious reasons. And the novel was rejected, too, by W.E.B. Du Bois for secular reasons. The writer discusses Du Bois's review of *Sunday* in a recorded conversation with Margaret Perry.[22] Du Bois's taste in literature, of course, was decidedly Victorian, causing him to view *Sunday* as "low-life" literature.

In *Sunday* Bontemps told the story of the rise of Little Augie, a tiny jockey, who won notoriety for his "luck" during the 1890s. Augie, son of a slave mother, lost his luck and became a penniless wanderer. But through his resourcefulness, Augie succeeded despite setbacks. By 1931 there were no more African-American jockeys, but this did not seem odd to Bontemps, whose antiquarian interests had always run high, nor was it an oddity in the Harlem Renaissance, for the period generally recommended the past.[23] By the time *Sunday* was published Bontemps had already established himself as a poet, and the book's style is that of the poet-novelist with its rhythmic language, bordering at times on the grandiose. But the characters are real, never maudlin. Dialogue is emotion-charged yet economic, a blend its author had not achieved in *Chariot*. But here that vivid, terse brand of speech so peculiar to Louisiana creoles and that makes Ernest Gaines's fiction effective, is the wry ingredient that imparts excellence to that of Bontemps.

After the publication of *Sunday*, critics hailed Bontemps as one of the most important writers "of his race," and they recognized the authentic rendering of the "Negro Language" as his most outstanding talent. Hence, if Bontemps considered the work a failure, it is probably because it did not sell. Perhaps it is safe to say at this point that the novel's positive features outweighed its negative ones, and that as first novels go, it held much promise. Throughout the novel, life "in the quarter" was vividly and economically depicted and supported by faithful dialogue. Contrary to what one might expect of a novel set in the 1890s, *Sunday* did not degenerate into a minstrel show. However, Bontemps and Cullen did write a play based on the novel, which they called—at first—*God Sends Sunday*. They finished it in 1932; its exciting history will be discussed in a later chapter.

During the twenties Bontemps had won handsome sums through his poetry prizes, two of them for one hundred dollars each and one for seventy-five dollars.[24] But there would be no more such instant supplements to his income. The Depression continued to rage, and Arna and Alberta found themselves in the late summer of 1931 scheming to make ends meet. He had done his job well during his seven years as a teacher at the defunct Harlem Academy, and his contact with "Professor" Moran had landed him a new job at another Adventist school, the historic Oakwood College, then a junior college that had been established in 1896 in Madison County (Huntsville), Alabama.[25]

The problem that Arna and Alberta faced was the expense of moving so far away and his working a full month before receiving a paycheck. Besides, Joan and Paul were both scheduled to start public school around this time. But Arna was not alone in feeling the pinch of the Depression, for economic hard times had caught up with first one and then another of the "New Negroes," causing them to experience difficulties. Langston Hughes recalled his own trying times in *I Wonder as I Wander*, the second of his autobiographies in which he wrote of the effects of the Great Depression: "I had just lost my patron. Scholarships, fellowships and literary prizes were scarce. I had already gotten several awards that were not to be had a second time. Jobs were very hard to find. The W.P.A. had not yet come into being. If I were to live and write at all, since I did not know how to do anything else, I had to make a living from writing itself. So, of necessity, I began to turn poetry into bread."[26]

Arna, though, was fortunate in that he did not know how to do something besides writing for a living. He had demonstrated already that he could teach. Consequently, before the end of August 1931, Arna, Alberta, Joan, and Paul found themselves enduring the suffocating heat and humidity of Huntsville, trying furiously to get settled into their new residence before classes began in early September. As soon as he had rested a bit from the trip South and the labors of unpacking and arranging the family's meager belongings, Arna began to seek ways of producing literature in the insufferable Alabama heat. He solved this dilemma by writing outside on the shady side of their rented house, armed with bath towel and fly-swatter, while Alberta did her best to encourage him by sending pitchers of ice water and lemonade via the children. But if the summers were extremely hot, the Bontempses were to find that the Alabama winters were cold and damp. Hence settling into their new home and becoming adjusted took time.

Their house was in almost deplorable physical condition, but it was not without a particular charm that appealed to the writer. But the teaching load at Oakwood was heavy. Nevertheless, Arna managed during this period to keep up his correspondence with Langston and Countée. In early October, not long after his first semester at Oakwood had started, he mailed a penny postal card to Cullen care of the Salem Methodist Episcopal Church of New York City with his own new address on the reverse side. The message read: "Will write as soon as I get settled. At present have no place to rest my typewriter. This is a good place for writing *if* [underlined twice] I am not worked too hard. The place was originally a slave plantation. I live in the ruined 'old mansion' and have found it haunted with ghosts."[27]

The family had not been in Alabama long before its head began raising the eyebrows of citizens, white and black. An able-bodied young black man with a growing family who read for a hobby created more than a little suspicion. During this period Arna borrowed many books by mail, a habit that was considered queer and that attracted unfavorable attention. "Folks" simply could not understand why the professor had so much typing to do. Why was he not working an extra job, or planting a vegetable garden to help feed those children of his? After all, the Depression was going on. Already Arna had begun doing the research and outline for *Black Thunder*, his second published novel, and the feeling in the community of Huntsville was, "How many books could a man read in one lifetime anyway? We laughed together at the questions," he explained, "but I realized they were not satisfied with my joking answers. How could I tell them about Gabriel's adventure in such an atmosphere?"[28]

It was by no means a good time to be in northern Alabama, for it was the time of the Scottsboro Trials. Arna wanted to attend the trials, but the administration at Oakwood had advised him to stay as far away from the issue as possible. He and Alberta discussed the matter and decided against getting involved, for they were not transients as most of the spectators were; they could not have simply gone away if violence had erupted.[29] But I cannot help feeling sorry that Arna was denied this experience, for he certainly would have gotten a novel from the Scottsboro drama.

By late October 1931, before Arna had been on the job at Oakwood two full months, he had already begun to regret the move South, especially in the ultra-conservative environment of an Adventist school, a negative climate exacerbated by Alabama Jim Crow laws and mores. The correspondence he had begun with Cullen almost a month earlier (early September) was to continue well beyond his three-year tenure at Oakwood. Nearly every letter to Countée during this period contained a greeting or message to be passed on to Harold Jackman who, like Cullen, had remained in New York City. In these letters Bontemps usually included some bit of information or descriptive remark about the sociopolitical climate in Huntsville or about the working conditions at the junior college. The earliest of these letters reveals that Cullen had already engaged Bontemps's services as back-up writer and consultant to the play version of Cullen's newest novel, *One Way to Heaven*. Bontemps, as a favor to Cullen, had also agreed to read the final proofs of the novel, which had not been released. In this same letter, Arna could not resist the need to voice to his trusted friend his utter disappointment with his new job. He wrote:

This is perhaps the world's worst school. But it is at the same time perhaps the most picturesque school in the South. I live in the old ruined mansion that was the great house when Oakwood was a plantation. In those days Andrew Jackson was a frequent visitor and sat at the fireplace that now warms my toes. There are slave huts on the outskirts of the place, and on the adjoining plantation they say there are still slaves who do not know that they are free. At any rate, I hear their rising bell every morning at 3:30 A.M. It is the same bell that has been used more than one hundred years. The campus of the school itself is almost perfection to my taste. There are dozens of trees: magnolias, oaks, walnuts, etc. And they are still filled with hosts of blue birds and squirrels. You cannot imagine how well suited these are to each other. I mean in color. There is a rose arbor in the center of the circle and flower beds along the edges. And even now, with the green going fast, I frequently find myself walking on air, almost madly exhilarated [sic]. You must come down and spend some time. Maybe things will be best in the spring. But anytime you come I think you will enjoy the trip. You will find that you have a reputation here and that the hospitality of the folks will be gratifying. . . . No buildings, few teachers, no vision and no learning. But many of the students are fine. They had cooked up a strike that was getting to a flower just as I was getting settled. I admired them for it. . . . a general shake-up is possible.[30]

Arna was homesick already for Harlem and for the company of his friends. There was virtually no one on the faculty at Oakwood with whom he could communicate about literature and writing. To ease the boredom, he was planning his first trip to Nashville, his first excursion of any kind since arriving at Huntsville.[31] He had a "superb trip" to Nashville, where he visited James Weldon Johnson, Charles S. Johnson, Arthur Schomburg, and several others of his friends on the faculty at Fisk.[32] But at Oakwood, Bontemps's sympathy for the student strike had placed him on a list of suspects before the ink was cold on his first year's contract.

Before year's end, he had been reprimanded by the administration and felt it time to start sending his resume to other places. With the Depression now in full bloom, the summer program at Oakwood had been canceled, and even its principal, J. L. Moran, had fled to his home in New York to spend the summer months. Arna decided, however, to remain at Huntsville for at least another year, for Alberta had announced that they were expecting again.

By November 1931 Cullen and Bontemps had begun a relationship with their new literary agent, Leah Salisbury, one that was to continue long after Cullen's death and until after the play version of *God Sends Sunday*, under the title *St. Louis Woman*, had been produced at home and abroad. Before the end of June 1932, Arna left Huntsville for a "jaunt Eastward" that would include New York. He drove his secondhand Model A Ford that he described as a "rattletrap."[33]

During the previous March, he had finished his assigned portions of *Heaven*, the play which he and Cullen had agreed to call *Easy Ridin'*. But there were still no definite production plans by the time he left Huntsville for the East Coast.[34] By the following fall, news had come from Nella Larsen's husband that her "ofay novel" had been accepted by a publisher. This was exciting news to Arna and he hoped the venture would succeed, for its success, an all-white book written by a black female novelist, "would further liberate the Negro novelist," he believed.[35] By December 1932 Langston had informed Arna of his plans to stop at Huntsville for a visit during his upcoming lecture tour, a visit that almost cost Arna his job and that bore on his eventual decision to leave Oakwood.[36] "Lang" had written some fairly incendiary poems and essays condemning the treatment of the victims of the Scottsboro scandal, and Arna himself had gotten involved with the world's unrest by speaking out on the subjects of Ghandi and the Scottsboro trials.

But his biggest sin, as far as Huntsville's influential whites and the black powers at the college were concerned, was his association with Hughes and other "outside agitators" who had vented their rage and outrage on these subjects. The school's head, only a short time before the birth of Bontemps's third child, had called him in and demanded that he publicly burn his small library, which the administration considered to be too race-conscious and provocative for the good of the school. This was the principal's idea of sufficient penance for the author's past sins. Arna's collection of books included *The Souls of Black Folk*, *The Blacker the Berry*, *My Bondage and My Freedom*, *Harlem Shadows*, *Black Majesty*, and the *Autobiography of an Ex-Colored Man*. To burn his books, of course, was unthinkable, but considering his family, he swallowed his pride and tried to overlook the wound to his sense of personal dignity that the suggestion had caused.[37]

Poppy, his third child and second daughter, was born on January 3, 1933, and though the father was elated, he was faced with still another financial worry, the hospital bill for mother and child he had promised to pay by the end of January.[38] Just prior to Poppy's birth, he and Countée had finished their first truly collaborative effort, the first dramatic version of *Sunday*, which they would later name *St. Louis Woman*. Arna was embarrassed and somewhat taken aback when a few days after the birth of his new daughter he received a letter from a Mr. Pierce of Harcourt suggesting that the firm was considering engaging Mercer Cook and Sterling Brown to write an entirely new dramatic version of *Sunday*.[39]

This had arisen while Arna was complaining about his purse, that his "money sources" were nearly dry. Meanwhile, things at the school and in the city of Huntsville were extremely tense, for Huntsville is near Decatur with Scottsboro at the midway point between them. In the midst of these tensions, Arna, to satisfy his publishers, was furiously rewriting the juvenile story *Shine Boy* in hopes of putting some money into his rapidly dwindling accounts.[40] By the end of the 1932–33 term his headache, caused by conflicts with the school's officials, had intensified. He wrote to Cullen: "I am not at all sure what the summer holds for me yet. There may be a trip to N.Y. There may be a move to California for the winter (If I fail to land a job here; they are cutting the faculty in half, and I am not a favored one, afraid that I am looked upon with suspicion by these rural souls)."[41] Meanwhile, Arna was grateful to receive newspaper clippings and other literary news from New York that arrived in almost every letter from Cullen, for it helped make his repressive environment bearable.

As things turned out, Bontemps remained at Oakwood for another term, the 1933–34 school year, and this, to the relief of the entire family, would be his last. He had never intended to stay at Oakwood for the duration of his college-teaching career, for he recalled: "Not knowing where else to turn, I wandered into Northern Alabama on the promise of employment as a teacher, and hopefully to wait out the bad-times, but at least to get my bearings."[42] Instead of waiting out the bad times, he found at Huntsville that bad times were waiting for him; but amid repeated, humiliating requests that he burn his books, Bontemps continued to write. A fortunate development had appeared soon after his move to Alabama.

Hughes, recently returned from Haiti, had written to suggest that he and Bontemps collaborate on a book for children. The jaunt to Haiti had provided Langston with a delightful story, but the story needed Arna's firsthand knowledge of children and his vivid imagery and lilting prose. Arna liked the idea, so using his own children as sounding boards, he and Hughes created *Popo and Fifina: Children of Haiti*, first published by Macmillan in 1932. The book's popularity was phenomenal, and it has since been translated into many foreign languages.[43] Early in the 1930s an involvement with children's subjects crept into Arna Bontemps's second literary period.[44]

The first play version of *Sunday* was written by Bontemps and Cullen and produced under the same title in 1934 at Cleveland's Karamu Playhouse by the Gilpin Players. (This play is not to be confused with a later version, *St. Louis Woman*.) Bontemps had won the *Opportunity* literary award in 1932 for his best, most frequently anthologized short story, "A Summer Tragedy," a work that was to be published posthumously as part of his own anthology of short stories, *The Old South*.

"Summer" remained to the Bontemps canon what "Sonny's Blues" has become to Baldwin's short fiction efforts—outstanding—and it remained the short story of which Arna was proudest. It unfolds the story of Jeff and Jennie Patton, both reminiscent of the frail old couple who slept in the abandoned treehouse of the author's boyhood on Furlough Track. Driven and deprived by the deadend structure of the sharecropping system, this aged husband and wife team are eventually driven to a joint suicide revealed in an especially effective surprise ending. It is an excellent testimony to Bontemps's ability to deal with emotional subjects without descending into melodrama. It is a touching requiem for Jeff and Jennie, who have together harvested forty-five cotton crops for Major Stevenson on Greenbriar Plantation. Jeff has had one paralytic stroke and fears another, for Jennie, who is blind and in poor health, depends solely on him.

Their children have all died. Concluding that some life situations are worse than death, they get into their wheezing old Ford and carry out a carefully engineered joint suicide.

Bontemps had begun to study his own children's reading habits as soon as they learned to read.[45] Hence during this period in the thirties, he was able to observe the speech patterns of his own children and work toward the simplification of the dialect he employed in his books for children. In the fall of 1933 he had another children's book accepted for publication.[46] It was titled *You Can't Pet a Possum* and was issued by William Morrow early in 1934. The story is about Shine Boy, an eight-year-old Alabama lad, and his devotion to Butch, his yellow hound. The book was an immediate success because of its appealing theme and the uniqueness of its "rendering of Negro life and speech for children."[47]

The Huntsville experience had taken an enormous toll on the sensitive writer. Those three years in the South had not been peaceful. He could not forget that just three miles from Huntsville the Scottsboro boys were being held at Decatur. Throughout Northern Alabama racial turmoil and Jim Crow indignities were rampant. This area Bontemps had earlier defined as a "green eden" had lost all of its former appeal. The tension of this environment had created stress within the Bontemps household. And, as if this were not enough, Arna and Alberta both felt rejected by the denomination they had loved and supported since childhood. Arna wrote that the tension became difficult to bear when he and his family began to sense "quaint hostilities" directed at them by members of the Adventist community.[48]

Despite the strict tenets and rigid dogma of this fundamentalist sect, it seemed to Arna that the Adventists had never quite understood the principle of brotherly love as Christ taught it. He had had enough of explaining to officials the kinds and quantities of books that came constantly through the mails. He had had one too many of his bohemian writer friends either insulted or leered at whenever they stopped at his residence or his campus office as they went to and from Decatur during the Scottsboro trials. And worst of all, the Huntsville residents and campus officials reacted even less kindly to his best friend Langston, who could raise their ire with no effort at all, no doubt because his writings departed too radically from their denominational standard of "uplift literature."[49] It seemed that whatever Arna did, whomever he associated with, was considered "questionable" by the elders of this sect. His oldest child has summed up the situation better than anyone thus far: "Maybe they considered that he wasn't a good enough Seventh-day Adventist," quipped Joan Bontemps Williams.[50]

But one encouraging development helped to keep the writer's psyche intact. Early in 1934 *New Challenge* had purchased his short story, "Barrel Staves," and published it that spring.[51] It is the story of Skeeter Gordon, a young, married teenager who has been exiled from Harlem to the Bronx after his chocolate-colored wife evicts him. A comic treatment of the exile-and-return motif, it is a lighthearted piece that the author designed to appeal to both juvenile and adult readers. The story's dialect slows the reader a bit at first, but as a whole the story is entertaining. Coming out when it did, it served to keep Bontemps's hand in the young-reader market while he was planning to write another novel, one its publishers would eventually name *Black Thunder*. At this juncture came two of his most polished poems, "A Note of Humility" and "Southern Mansion."

By the time school closed in May 1934, Arna had submitted his resignation, probably under duress, to the top official at Oakwood College.[52] As soon as he had evaluated final exams and submitted final grade reports, he packed his wife and three children with everything they owned into his "rattletrap" Ford and headed for California. It turned out to be a trip he would never forget and which his widow still remembers. When asked to comment on the trip from Huntsville to Los Angeles, Alberta Bontemps laughed pleasantly and exclaimed, "Oooh, brother! That was a ride."[53] Continuing her description she explained:

We were packed into this Ford, and we had Joan and Paul, and Poppy, as a baby. And we had everything we owned in that car. And he had to do all the driving, and we had to find places to stay, through friends and by word of mouth, because we could not stop then for rest or food. And he would always have to make a certain stop, so many miles to a certain place where we could stop and have rest. . . . Then we got to the border. If you had an Alabama license on your car, you were searched more thoroughly than . . . if you'd come from Michigan, or some other place, because Alabama was hot and they were afraid of the boll weevil getting into California. And they were going to see to it that you had nothing that had cotton—a pillow, or anything. . . . I look back on it now and wonder how we did it. And he was so tired. When we got to Coolidge Dam there was no place to pull over to rest, no shoulders or anything. And during this particular stretch of driving, he was so tired [emphasis]. Finally we came near the Coolidge Dam and there was a little place you could pull over and stop. And we stopped. And everybody just fell over on each other . . . sleeping. And I woke up. He was outside the car with the flashlight, looking around the car. And I yelled to him and asked what was he doing. And he said, "I'm looking to see if the wheels are not over the cliff." But he was asleep. He was walking in his sleep. Then . . . we arrived at the father's house in Watts.[54]

This was early summer 1934, and Bontemps spent the remainder of that summer writing. Circumstances forced him, Alberta, and the children to live for a time with his father and stepmother until he finished *Thunder*. These were not easy times for anyone in that household, for having five extra people on an extended visit cramped Paul Bontemps's customary lifestyle, and he did not mind voicing his objections. But because he had no money coming in—the trip from Alabama had been long, hot, and expensive—Arna swallowed his pride, primarily for the children's sakes.

The two older children, Joan and Paul, still recall that year in California with grandfather Paul and his second wife as their most difficult time as a family. The entire family was crowded into the small extra bedroom at 10310 Weigand Avenue in Los Angeles. With no transportation, it was a boring time indeed for Alberta and the children, for upon arrival, Arna had sold the car so that he would be able to buy food for the summer. He would have no one saying he did not feed his family. Having no space for his typewriter, he wrote *Thunder* in longhand on top of a folded-down sewing machine.[55] He spent much time and energy during these days flagellating himself for not having been more provident. And he recalled that though his father and stepmother seemed to bear up fairly well under the strain of their presence, "it was inevitable that old frictions between father and son would surface again," especially since the elder Bontemps's tendency to reproach his son for his seeming lack of resourcefulness still went unchecked. The elder man, it seemed, could not resist making occasional remarks about "young people with bright prospects making shipwreck of their lives."[56]

As though the family did not have trouble enough, sickness invaded their ranks. Not long after their arrival in California Joan developed asthma, and Paul had pneumonia twice during the year. Arna's pride was wounded, but he continued to write, relying upon his inner strength in combination with the discipline and drive that had always characterized him, to complete the task he had laid out for himself. Recalling those days, Mrs. Bontemps said of her husband's ability to endure the strain: "They were tough times, but they were not too much for Arna. He was a quiet, deep person, and he was very spiritual. He never displayed his religion on the outside much, but deep down, he was religious."[57] Remembering these trying times in Watts, Arna was to reflect: "I could have loved the place under different circumstances, but as matters stood there was no way to disguise the fact that our luck had run out."[58]

Arna worked so hard during these days that he became immune even to criticism.[59] He had decided after his first visit to Fisk that this novel would be a slave narrative, for while visiting, he discovered that Fisk's collection of these antebellum narratives was the largest he had seen anywhere of a form that had been neglected since before the Civil War ended.

By spring 1935, *Black Thunder* was finished, though Beacon Press did not publish it until 1936. The book came out with an excellent introduction by the author and received glowing reviews. In the year of its publication, Richard Wright praised it as the only novel of its kind that dealt forthrightly with the Negro's historical and revolutionary traditions.[60] A historical novel, *Thunder* is the fictionalized story of the "Gabriel Insurrection" that occurred in 1880 in Henrico County, Virginia, near Richmond. The book's hero is Gabriel Prosser, an insurrectionist, modeled after the traditional "bad nigger" stereotype, a type that Bontemps returned to in his third novel (*Drums at Dusk*, also a historical novel, which was published in 1939). As in *Sunday*, Bontemps's use of dialogue and dialect was exceptionally accurate in *Thunder*. The plot was engaging and the narration economical. Although the slave revolt portrayed failed, Bontemps succeeded in showing, contrary to the propaganda of many non-black writers of the post-Reconstruction and pre–Harlem Renaissance periods, that African Americans as a whole did not accept injustice lying down.

Following available court records from the actual case, he depicts Gabriel as a mischievous slave who is subjected to cruel and excessive punishment and who, because of his desire to escape these conditions, plans a rebellion for which he gains support from free blacks, slaves, and a few whites. Gabriel's intention is to take over the arsenal at Richmond, confiscate the weapons, and seize the town. Some of Bontemps's best descriptive prose is devoted to the passage depicting the failure of the uprising, produced by torrential rains and a last-minute betrayal. The rebellion is suppressed at the novel's midpoint with the remainder of the story devoted to the capture and punishment of the perpetrators of the insurrection.

In addition to Wright's review, other reviewers also appreciated the novel's valid view of history. Critics described the novel as "good and powerful," "truer than most history," and "a sort of prose spiritual"; all agreed that the narrative was movingly rendered. Such an achievement was indeed remarkable when one considers the uncongenial circumstances under which the novelist wrote the work.

Arna did not wait for the publishers to release *Thunder* before making plans to leave Watts. As soon as Beacon accepted the book, he received a large enough advance on royalties to move his family to the Midwest. On the day he received the check he began packing their belongings and moved, a few days later, to the "Windy City," for he had been offered a job with still another S.D.A. school, Chicago's Shiloh Academy, where he would serve as principal until 1938. He had sought several college positions, all of which he considered to be more "worthwhile" than the kind of job he took. His chief desire was to find something that would allow him to reside in New Orleans. Hence during the months after he left Huntsville, he began to seek employment at Dillard-University and also had some correspondence with Howard University. But the lack of a graduate degree of any kind kept him from securing employment at the more prestigious schools.[61]

The writer's most difficult years had been 1930 to 1936. But even an ill wind blows some good. In rural Alabama he had been able to immerse himself in African-American folk culture for the first time since his boyhood, when he vicariously experienced this culture through the stories of "Uncle Buddy." In Alabama the exposure had been firsthand. He mingled with the natives, quickly making friends with them, and they began to take him to church services and other public gatherings where he was able to amass a wealth of folk materials that would become the raw ingredients of his fiction. The most memorable of these experiences occurred on his first visit to a primitive Baptist church in Huntsville, where he witnessed both footwashing and benchwalking in a single evening. The footwashing ceremony, with the savage dancing of its participants, and the sheer ecstasy of the benchwalker, were to appear as artistically woven episodes in the fabric of several of Bontemps's short stories created during the 1930s, although most of these stories were not published until much later. Typical of these is "Rock, Church, Rock," first published in 1942, and "Let the Church Roll On," published posthumously in 1973.[62]

In May 1935, while Arna and Alberta were packing up to move to Chicago, he published in *New Challenge* again; this time a children's work titled "Dang Little Squirt," the appealing story of Manuel and his uncle Eligio, who in the story's climax goes to jail after an exciting altercation with a baton-wielding policeman.[63] The story's use of Mexican-American dialect is flawless. And there are several other appealing short stories from this period. Included in this group are the juvenile stories "The Frizzly Chicken," "Bubber Joins the Band," "The Devil Is a Conjurer," and "Lonesome Boy, Silver Trumpet."[64] It is significant that each of these stories depicts one or more children growing up in a rural setting. While he was writing *Thunder*, Arna had continued to write stories for children and juveniles. He began to experiment with formulas and devices that he believed would improve the quality of children's literature, for he had not forgotten the dearth of good children's books by which his own childhood had been blighted.

He hoped to add a few stories that would help counteract the unpleasant traditions and associations of such stories as *Little Black Sambo* and *Epaminandos*. He was convinced that he had something better to offer America's children, and he felt that African-American children and youths deserved to have reading materials on their historical past, materials that were carefully researched and thoroughly documented. He knew, though, that not all of them would pursue their past in Africa and America as persistently as he had while growing up in California.

When Arna broke ties with Oakwood College and moved to California, he was less than six months away from his thirty-third birthday. Already he had three growing children, and he remained convinced that it was only through reading that they would be able to grow intellectually and psychologically. He shared this conviction with Langston Hughes, prompting them to try their hands at another jointly written juvenile book; the result was *Bon-Bon Buddy* (c. 1935). All things considered, the Huntsville and Watts experiences had been good for Arna Bontemps's career as a novelist and writer of books for children and teenagers.

Chapter 7

The Chicago Period

By the late spring of 1935, as soon as Joan and Paul had finished the 1934–35 school term in Los Angeles, Arna moved his family to Chicago, settling into apartment 1-A at 731 East 50th Place, the address from which most of his correspondence was written over the next eight years. The apartment was situated in the heart of Chicago's famed "South Side," a ghetto that already had become a dangerous place to live, and which, Arna and Alberta learned at once, was far from a wholesome environment for raising a family. But any quarters would have seemed pleasant after a year in his father's spare bedroom, for the only pleasant thing about the year they spent in California had been the weather, which in January 1935 Arna described as "positively grand."[1] In his haste to leave Watts, he apparently neglected to send his literary agent a forwarding address, for as late as the third week of September, Leah Salisbury wrote to Cullen inquiring of Bontemps's whereabouts. She had written to Arna at the Weigand Avenue address in Los Angeles during the summer while Countée was abroad, and received word from the latter that Arna was no longer there. Salisbury was not given a forwarding address by the Paul Bontempses.[2]

Arna and Alberta knew before they were in Chicago a month that they would not stay there any longer than it took for him to complete a graduate degree. In New York, between 1926 and 1931, Arna had taken scattered post-baccalaureate courses at New York City College and New York University, and at Columbia. But he had not put in enough sequential study at either school to satisfy residence requirements for a graduate degree. He had a taste of college-level teaching and knew that with a degree from a school as prestigious as Chicago he would have no trouble securing one of the "worthwhile" college positions he had sought. Thus by the fall of 1935 he had matriculated in the University of Chicago's Graduate School pursuing the Ph.D. in English, but he would stop just short of preliminaries to enter the Graduate School of Library Science in 1942. Meanwhile, his family experienced two increases in rapid succession after their arrival in Chicago. On December 16, 1936 their third daughter, Camille, was born, and approximately two years later, came Constance, the fifth child and fourth daughter.[3]

On January 28, 1936 *Black Thunder* came off the Macmillan press, only a short time after Cullen's play *Medea* was published. Moreover, in January Arna executed a contract with Langston Hughes through the office of the American Dramatists Guild of New York to serve as his collaborator on the play, *When the Jack Hollers*[4] a work Bontemps and Hughes had originally titled *Careless Love*.

Arna and Alberta were revolted by the violence in the streets of Chicago's South Side where they lived. No week passed without the occurrence of some kind of violent crime right under their noses: armed robberies, purse snatchings, muggings, burglaries. Their apartment was burglarized twice, putting them on the verge of despair. On one of these occasions a trunk was stolen from their basement that contained Alberta's wedding dress, an heirloom she was saving for her daughters, and several scrapbooks Arna had compiled of clippings, photographs, and other documentation of the Harlem Renaissance. He lamented this loss to Cullen in a 1945 letter written from Fisk University (Syracuse Papers), and I am sure he lost valuable artifacts, knowing his penchant for collecting.

On arriving in Chicago, Arna and Alberta had been shocked to find garbage scattered everywhere, for Los Angeles was a clean city. Years later Arna summed up the situation in these words: "We had fled from the jungle of Alabama's Scottsboro area to the jungle of Chicago's crime-ridden South Side, and one was as terrifying as the other."[5] Political corruption in Chicago was deeply entrenched and the prevalence of racial restrictions made it clear that the Jim Crow they had hoped to leave behind in Alabama was dogging their days in Chicago. The schools in the city were segregated, and Arna tried to transfer his children to an integrated school that was more accessible to their residence than was the Jim Crow school his children were attending. But the arrangement fell through when he was quoted an outrageous fee for the privilege of transferring.

One situation that made the Chicago years bearable, at least for Arna if not for the entire family, was the thriving literary scene Chicago afforded. Soon after his arrival, he began to meet other writers of all ages and colors and of both sexes. He attended the round of lectures, parties, and dramatic productions patronized by the circle of writers with whom he associated. From these contacts he received encouragement in his literary endeavors. He was also encouraged by Chicago's large number of wealthy patrons of literature and the arts.

Consequently Arna found himself, only weeks after his arrival in Chicago, in the midst of a literary and cultural awakening that, in some ways, promised to become as influential as the Harlem Renaissance had been. He observed a "second awakening," less gaudy but closer to realities around him.[6] The various cultural projects of the W.P.A. had hired a number of writers, black and white; but for the most part the African Americans among them were not the ones who had been associated with the Harlem Awakening. Such well-known writers as Hughes, Cullen, and Hurston had picked up enough momentum by the time the Depression hit to make the ride out of the bad times on their own. And those like Bontemps, Sterling Brown, and a few others, including painter Aaron Douglas, had secure teaching posts or other jobs and were serving as supervisors, consultants, and editors for the W.P.A. projects. But a decade had elapsed since the zenith of the Harlem Movement, and another group of seedy-looking young writers haunted the public libraries in Chicago and produced literature of various kinds.[7]

Perhaps the most talented in all the W.P.A. groups were those who did brief stints on the Illinois Writer's Project, a fact that is not at all surprising, considering Chicago's reputation as a melting pot of literary talent during the first half of this century. A list of successful writers who had gotten their starts there includes Carl Sandburg, Ernest Hemingway, James T. Farrell, Harriet Monroe, Ben Hecht, Edgar Lee Masters, and Robert Morse Lovett. Later came Vachel Lindsey, Theodore Dreiser, Floyd Dell, and Carl Van Vechten. These and others had established a tradition worthy of emulation, and many were still in Chicago when the W.P.A. began to select some of the younger writers for the Illinois Project.

One of the first of these Depression-bred writers to be selected was Richard Wright. During those days Margaret Walker worked closely with Wright at the Erie Street offices of the Illinois Writer's Project. And many of the performing artists like Katherine Dunham, those who lost their jobs when the Federal Theater Project was killed by its foes, were picked up by the Writer's Project. Dunham became a supervisor of a related project, and one of the writers who worked with her was Frank Yerby.[8] In addition to these, there was a whole string of writers, some of whom came to the Project after Dunham and Yerby had left: Willard Motley, Nelson Algren, George V. Martin, Stuart Engstrand, and Jack Conroy, editor of the *Anvil* and author of the novel *The Disinherited*. Soon after joining the W.P.A. work force, Conroy entered what turned into a long, amiable period of literary collaboration with Bontemps.[9]

Although Bontemps knew before he had been on the job at Chicago's Shiloh Academy a year that his stay would be brief, he managed to tough it out as principal there until the end of the 1937–38 school term. At the end of his third year he resigned his position, for some of the same "quaint hostilities" that had made him and his family miserable in Huntsville were not long in appearing in Chicago. Somehow, he had not expected to find in such an enlightened city the intense fundamentalist hostilities he soon began to encounter at Shiloh. Arna was far too active in Chicago's literary circle to suit the school's officials; this they considered "the Devil's work." And the question of book burning came up again. Bontemps's widow summed up the situation this way: "And then it happened again at Shiloh Academy. . . . He said again that they weren't too happy with his involvement with literature."[10] So the final confrontation with the officials of Shiloh Academy in 1938 made it plain to Arna that he would have to make what he later called a "clean break" with the denomination he considered too rigidly dogmatic for one of his literary talent and taste.[11]

This he did in his characteristically quiet manner; without announcement, without fanfare. Before submitting his resignation, he had already secured a job with the Federal Writer's Project, then housed in the old Rosenwald mansion. Perhaps Arna's resourcefulness would have pleased his father, but his break with the Adventists certainly did not. Nevertheless Arna continued to provide for his family, even though his yearly salary at the Academy never exceeded $1,800. He was to say later of this period to a developing writer at Atlanta University that he had a "little brown wife and some little brown babies" and that his "little brown wife and little brown babies ate food."[12]

Meanwhile Arna looked to Alberta for encouragement, and to the clan of Chicago writers who had adopted him for intellectual stimulation. And he had certainly stayed busy with scheduled literary projects. By late spring of 1936 he and Cullen had finished the first version of the play *St. Louis Woman*, their adaptation from Bontemps's first published novel. *When the Jack Hollers*, a play Bontemps wrote jointly with Hughes, opened in late April at the Gilpin Theater, while a play that Hughes did alone, a farce called *Little Ham*, was concurrently running in Cleveland. Bontemps read as usual every major newspaper he could get his hands on to keep up with the literary and theatrical news, and Cullen kept him supplied with news of New York. Bontemps confessed, too, during this time, that he spent most of his energy trying to devise schemes that would take him to New York for a visit.[13]

But late April 1936 brought about one of the highlights of Bontemps's Chicago period, a reception held in his honor at the Lincoln Center. The affair was sponsored by the Chicago Chapter of the National Negro Congress and featured a symposium on *Black Thunder*. The list of speakers included Frank Hayes, *Chicago Daily News*; Metz Lochard, the *Chicago Defender*; Frank Marshall Davis, Associated Negro Press; Thyra Edwards, prominent social worker-lecturer; Samuel Stratton, Negro Life and History Group; and Dr. Harold M. Kingsley.[14] At this time Arna was seeking a Guggenheim Foundation grant in creative writing, a stipend he was not successful in obtaining until more than a decade later (1949). But he knew he needed free time to write and regretted that the success of *Thunder* had failed to carry enough weight with the Foundation.[15]

The year 1937 was not as productive for Arna as 1936 had been in terms of completed literary projects. He did, however, reach back into the Depression period and find a character he had created during his Alabama days. In 1937 Houghton Mifflin published a revised version of this original tale under the title *Sad-Faced Boy*, a juvenile novel. Its hero, J. P. Morgan, is a mischievous black boy whose shaved head is a kind of trademark. J. P.'s only outstanding experience has been the daily grazing of his herd near his family's home, until one day he and his three cousins, Slumber, Rags, and Willie, wander off to Harlem to seek their fame and fortune as musicians. But these country bumpkins return home in a mild state of disgrace after an encounter with a roving band of ghetto gangsters who rob them of their shoes.

In this story Arna's experimentation with children's themes and formulas had paid off. In 1938, after he had begun working with the Writer's Project, two significant career developments occurred. He met and forged a friendship with Jack Conroy during this year, and won the first of his Rosenwald Fund fellowships for creative writing, allowing him to travel and conduct research in the Caribbean until 1939.[16]

On the 1938 Rosenwald Fund application he listed the ages of his four children as ten, nine, four, and two; and stated his chief employment ambition in these words: "I hope to find a position [in] a first rate Negro college or university. I want to continue teaching as well as writing."[17] As references he listed three heavyweights: Benjamin Brawley, Head, Department of English at Howard; Charles S. Johnson of Fisk's Department of Sociology; and James Weldon Johnson, who had for some years held a chair in creative writing at Fisk. Bontemps's proposal to the Foundation was to write, by the end of the fellowship period, at least one children's short story with a tropical setting. He wanted to gather materials in the West Indies, Mexico, and Central America that would allow him to continue to create stories with special appeal to young readers. He was particularly interested in investigating the ancient history of the shorelines of the countries and islands. His other aim was to gather materials for a second historical novel treating the decade prior to the span of years of *Black Thunder*, a work he would publish in 1939 under the title *Drums at Dusk*.

Bontemps's cherished friend and literary collaborator, Jack Conroy, has described how it all started in 1938:

It was in the Erie Street offices of the project that I first met Arna Bontemps. I knew of his novels, *God Sends Sunday* and *Black Thunder*, as well as his poetry. We had a mutual friend in Langston Hughes, who always spoke admiringly and affectionately of Arna when we'd meet. . . . The Rosenwald Foundation was sponsoring *The Negro in Illinois* venture and had donated space in the mansion once occupied by philanthropist Julius Rosenwald.[18]

Bontemps and Conroy had this one-time bedroom as an upstairs office, where each day their field workers, most of whom were writers, came to their co-supervisors to report their research findings. Some conducted interviews, while others searched the files of newspapers and other periodicals, old and current. Bontemps had instructed them to copy any item relating to "Negroes." The result was the construction of a comprehensive social history of African Americans and of prevailing white attitudes toward them. Although some of the material collected was trivial, most of it was significant.

One field worker, for example, given the task of assembling the history of the NAACP in Chicago, unearthed important information about the mistreatment of "Negroes" by the legal system, citing the famous Loretto case as one of the many examples. And a study of Black Muslim cults was another area that yielded some important documentation. But as Conroy has reported, this "inside" information was never used in the projected multivolume *Negro in Illinois*, the work for which it was intended.[19] The project, however, turned out well for both Conroy and Bontemps, for they were able to use the materials gathered during the late thirties in their history of African-American migration titled *They Seek a City* (reissued by Hill and Wang in 1966 as a revised version titled *Anyplace but Here*).

Conroy recalled that during this period Bontemps occasionally received a letter addressed to "Miss" Arna Bontemps, at which time the recipient goodnaturedly explained that the feminine ending of his first name had "often elicited such a salutation."[20] But what Conroy remembers most about Arna during these days at the project is the encouragement he gave to other writers and actors. Canada Lee visited the project and reported that Arna's advice during the Harlem period had helped him through a difficult time. And there was Fenton Johnson, the morose, aging poet whose career was boosted by Arna's encouragement and by the inclusion of several of his poems in the Bontemps–Hughes anthology, *The Poetry of the Negro*. One of Arna's most admirable traits was his untiring effort to aid other writers, for he knew the heartache of rejection slips. Conroy recalls that Arna "tried persistently to find publication for the works of writers he considered unjustly neglected."[21]

Between July 4 and September 2, 1938, *Cavalcade of the Negro Theater* was produced during the American Negro Exposition at the Chicago Coliseum. Langston and Arna, chaired the Exposition, with one of its stars, Etta Moten, assisting with music. Since Bontemps was the historian of the group, and since the stage presentation portrayed the history of African-American theater from pre–Civil War days to the modern swing era, he did most of the actual writing. The production had a large cast of stars with supporting actors from among the membership of the Federal Theater in Chicago.[22]

One of the major features of the Exposition was "Tropics after Dark," a theatrical piece the collaborators had centered around the offbeat native rituals of Haiti and other islands in the Caribbean. The exotic setting lent itself to the play's treatment of voodoo practices.[23] On the day the show played to its last house, September 2, 1938, Arna left Brooklyn, New York's, Pier 5 for Haiti aboard the steamer "S. S. Cottica."[24] He remained in Haiti for the rest of the month. By mid-October he had put the finishing touches on *Drums at Dusk*, his new novel, and had written to Cullen sending him some of the poems of Christian Werleigh, National Poet of Haiti, who had befriended Arna during his Haitian hiatus.

The lecture circuit that year was demanding for both Arna and Langston. Late November found both poets in the Watts district of Los Angeles as guests of the Fillipa Polia Foundation.[25] And during the second week of December Bontemps was presented in a public program as guest lecturer by Chicago's Plymouth

Congregational Church, where Horace A. White was pastor.[26] The week in Los Angeles of sunny days and ninety-degree temperatures was a pleasant respite for Arna from the wintry December gusts of Chicago. But though the California climate left him limp and uninclined to work, as soon as he returned home he dashed off a letter to Cullen requesting that Cullen consent to some changes in the script of *St. Louis Woman* that the Los Angeles Federal Theater wanted to hire Hughes to write. Gradually "The Woman" was beginning to receive recognition, and Bontemps was elated. Cullen, who had just finished helping Edward Waters Turpin to write a dramatization of the latter's *These Low Grounds*, wrote the following reply:

I have just received your letter with its good news that there is a possibility that the Federal Theater in Los Angeles may do . . . *Woman*. Perhaps Langston can do something with it, and I certainly have no objections to any revisions that may be made so long as the play is produced. But I don't understand why you were not asked to do the revising. I am not at all willing to relinquish any share in the play to Langston. If he works on it and is paid by the project out there, his remuneration should end there. Leah Salisbury thinks the same. . . . I have an unshaken faith that [the play] . . . will go on sometime, and when it does it will not do us much good if our royalties have to be shared four or five ways. The play is from your book, and maybe you should have the final say, but I have been working with the play and trying so hard to get someone to take it that I cannot give my consent to anyone's having a share in a commercial production of the play, . . . nor in the movie rights.[27]

If sharing royalties with "Lang" would not have bothered Arna, he was disappointed by news about "The Woman" which he received a day or so after Christmas 1938—the production Orson Welles was planning for the new year had been dropped. The good news was that Ione Rider's biographical article on Bontemps had already come out in the January–February issue of *Horn Book*.

Arna spent a significant portion of New Year's Day 1939 writing letters of inquiry to some of the black colleges in the South. He still did not have the master's degree in hand, but felt more than ever the need to get his family out of Chicago. His dream of moving to New Orleans, the port where his French great-grandfather had docked a century before, was still very much alive, hence he still had hopes of landing a job at Dillard University. Besides Dillard, he wrote to Atlanta University; LeMoyne College in Memphis; Lincoln University in Pennsylvania; Langston's alma mater; and Talladega College. But their replies were noncommittal. He felt that college officials at the Southern universities where he had applied, most of which were private and church-supported, would consider the year he had just finished on a Rosenwald grant sufficient, and that the hope of finishing his M.A. by the nebulous projected dates of "this summer or fall" would land him the college job he had desired for many years.[28] But Arna had not been consistent in his pursuit of an advanced degree, failing, because of his employment and writing schedules with the duties of fatherhood thrown in, to satisfy some of his professors, as grade reports in the "Syracuse Papers" suggest.

Meanwhile the Federal Theater in Los Angeles had proven, much to the delight of both its authors, that it meant business about its planned production of *St. Louis Woman*, but Bontemps and Cullen, as well as their agent Leah Salisbury, remained nonplussed about the efforts of Hughes and others to horn in on their already meager royalties. Arna was determined to avoid a quarrel with his friend and others who seemed increasingly determined to inject themselves into the play as proprietors. Consequently, in typical Bontempsian style, he left most of the wrangling up to Salisbury, Cullen, and Harcourt.[29] But Arna could not gain money for losing it, since Harcourt was insisting through his agent that he receive no royalty payments on "The Woman" until he had repaid the balance on a cash advance the publisher had granted him on *God Sends Sunday*, the play's parent work. He still owed the company $325.60.[30]

News came that the Gilpin Players were planning a short run (April 28–May 3) of *When the Jack Hollers*, Hughes's and Bontemps's collaborative folk comedy about black sharecroppers and the Ku Klux Klan in the Mississippi Delta. The cast was to include such names as William Johnson, who had won critical acclaim in 1920 for the title role of "Emperor Jones" while still a student at Kansas State College, along with a star-studded cast that included Louise Apple and Hazel Walker, and more than a dozen others. The Gilpin group did produce the play but not until 1940 when they staged it at their favorite theater, Cleveland's Karamu Playhouse (where six years earlier they had presented *God Sends Sunday*, the first of several dramatizations Bontemps and Cullen made of the novel by that name).[31]

An introduction to Bontemps's third novel, *Drums at Dusk*, published in March 1939 by Macmillan, was to be aired May 6 of that year, on Chicago's "Know Your Authors" program. Ethel Reid Winser, director of the program, had acquired radio rights to the novel. This program, devoted to new books, featured a brief interview with the author at the opening of the broadcast. In this newest book, Bontemps had written of the participation of French colonials under d'Etaing in the siege of Savannah near the close of the eighteenth century. The novel portrays a colonial society of white planters and their white wives and sable concubines. This theme of "love across the color line" is combined with the themes of "escape and revolt" and "race and protest" to produce an exciting plot in which half a million slaves are bent on getting revenge on their cruel owners. This was an ambitious work indeed, but the writer handled successfully the complex social and racial materials.

Dusk received some favorable reviews at home and abroad, but on the whole it fared worse with critics than did Bontemps's previous two novels, for most critics expected another *Black Thunder*. Some reviewers objected to the seemingly excessive burden the author placed on the reader's "romantic imagination."[32] The author's aim had been to take advantage of the drama inherent in this historical event while calling attention to a significant occurrence nearly forgotten by historians, probably for no other reason than it did not influence the outcome of the war. And the resulting story about the "Negro uprising" in Haiti occurring during the course of the French Revolution does have merit. *Dusk* recounts the events and conditions that heralded the successful Haitian revolt led by Toussaint L'Ouverture in 1791. Its hero is a young Frenchman who sympathizes with the plight of the blacks and who, with the help of his black friend Toussaint, escapes the terror of the revolting slaves, taking with him to safety the girl he loves.

Bontemps's preoccupation with the tortured past of the African American dates back to his own childhood, hence his concern with slavery-related settings in each of his three historical novels: *Black Thunder*, *Drums at Dusk*, and *Chariot in the Sky*. In fact, he told an audience that his interest in slave insurrections had been born during his grammar-school days in California. To a gathering at the 1936 reception held in his honor, the writer recounted that while still a youngster he had "wondered why slaves never fought for freedom." He went on to say that only later did he learn of the many attempts at insurrection during the antebellum period.[33] Throughout his school days and young adulthood, Bontemps had continued to dig for detailed accounts of this aspect of black history. During the radio interview he confided his real reason for choosing a Caribbean setting for his second novel (*Thunder*): "My interest in Haiti—the colonial Haiti, the rich French colony—sprang originally, not so much from books like *Black Majesty* and *The Magic Isle* as from the knowledge that Alexander Dumas, an early favorite of mine, had his roots there."[34]

Bontemps's Syracuse Papers contain three unfinished versions of *Drums at Dusk*, evidence that this second historical venture proved more difficult to bring to fruition than he had anticipated. These original manuscripts reveal that the author changed the novel's title at least three times before settling on the title it now bears. The first title he chose was *The Scourge*, and later he named the manuscript *The Troubled Island*. Once it was put into final form, though, he had no trouble finding a publisher, probably a benefit derived from his previous literary successes. Macmillan not only published the novel in the United States in the spring of 1939, but in 1940 they also published it in England.[35]

Dusk had actually been completed before the check from the Rosenwald Fund arrived, hence its author did not actually engage in extensive on-location research in Haiti preparing to write this novel, as he had done while researching *Black Thunder*. In fact, he explained his procedure in this portion of a 1939 interview:

Winser (Interviewer): Mr. Bontemps you must have spent quite some time on this island to be able to write about it so well.

Bontemps (laughs): On the contrary, Miss Winser, I have been very much amused because the Haitian scholars were rather hard to convince that I had written the book . . . before I arrived there.

Winser: Did you have any trouble proving it?

Bontemps: I had the manuscript with me. . . . You see, I had intended to rewrite it after

I got there. . . . I was surprised to find I had only two trees to change to make the landscape correct.[36]

Dusk would have been, without a doubt, an even stronger novel had Bontemps created enough of a Haitian atmosphere for the reader. His accurate memory of Haiti did stand him in good stead where the history of the island is concerned, but my assessment accords, at least this much, with that of Alexander, who objects to an absence of the atmosphere of Haiti in the novel, for she has observed: "if Bontemps succeeds in capturing the big picture, he fails here in recreating the smaller units of human experience."[37] Bontemps would have done well to make the Haitian visit and then finish the novel. But the old problem of financial woes did not always allow him the luxury of following established procedures in his writing. Hence the weaknesses that mar this otherwise acceptable novel.

The 1940s crept in with Arna calmly going about his various duties at the Federal Writer's Project and working on his private writing whenever he could. Again in 1940 he began the year by contacting colleges in the South, initiating an exchange of letters with college administrators that continued through the last month of the year. He thought it strange that none of the college presidents whom he contacted, even as late as midsummer, were sure about openings for the following fall. Most expressed interest in his personality and literary accomplishments, but nearly all wanted to know the "minimum salary" he would accept. Meanwhile he and Conroy decided to act on their plans to collaborate on stories for the juvenile market. Conroy's first assignment with the Project lent itself to this kind of writing, for it included collecting and putting on paper a group of industrial folk tales gathered among factory workers in Illinois. He found that the majority of these yarns fell into the category of the tall tale. Bontemps began to examine these at Conroy's request, identifying the ones he thought would make good children's stories, for he had already published several books of his own for children and at least one in collaboration with Langston Hughes.

By the end of April he had finished a new manuscript which during the previous February he had been commissioned to write by the National Tuberculosis Association, an article the association decided to issue as a pamphlet designed to educate the public about the disease. Arna accepted this project purely because he needed money. Dr. Cameron St. Guild, the Director of the "Negro Program," was especially impressed with several of Bontemps's newest slants and liked several of his proposed titles for publication, particularly "The Low-Down on T. B." and "Beating the Bugs." The finished work was issued during the summer as a nine-page pamphlet titled *The Low Down on Tuberculosis*.[38]

Fall found the writer as busy as ever and a bit let down that he had not returned to New York since leaving the city in August 1931. He was missing, too, the frequent letters from Cullen. A brief hiatus in their exchange of letters had been brought on by Cullen's marriage earlier in the year to his second wife Ida, the one who proved to be everything he had sought in Yolande Du Bois but did not find. In mid-November Arna, wanting to congratulate Cullen on his latest book, decided the newlyweds had had enough uninterrupted time together and said in a letter to his friend:

My belated, but no less resounding congratulations on your new wife. I shall look forward to greeting her and you together if I'm lucky enough to get to New York this winter. In the same breath let me say that I'm enchanted not only by *The Last Zoo*, but also by the suggestion that I helped to urge along its creation. . . . I was worried when you let season after season pass without adding to your cards in the catalogue. . . . You have more than justified the long silence. There isn't much to be said about . . . *Zoo*—it is simply a small classic . . . original and worthy of an important poet. I also liked very much the illustrations. Sebree's style is perfectly suited to the theme. . . . For a long time I had wondered what became of the young painter I met one night at Anthony Hill's house, down the street from me here. Now I understand. . . . I have a hunch that there are a good many books for children, books abounding in fancy, that could use his style of illustration. Ben Abramson . . . tells me that Harper's are very high on the book and are pushing it. . . . Well, one favorable result has followed your marriage already. Hunh? . . .[39]

During the same November, the play *Jubilee*, a collaborative effort of Hughes and Bontemps, was announced by the *New York Times* under "New Scripts."[40] And by December 1 Arna did manage to escape the "Windy City" for a few days, this time not to New York but to Hollywood where both he and Hughes had been invited by the public schools to read some of their poems and children's stories.[41]

In January 1942 Harper published Arna's anthology of Negro poetry for children and teenagers under the title *Golden Slippers*.[42] He saw this book as an answer to a widespread plea among teachers and librarians for a collection of poems that could be used by children and adults as well. In the resulting anthology he included all the favorites—Dunbar, Johnson, McKay, Braithwaite, Hughes, and Cullen—and he also introduced a number of new names, including Robert Davis, Richard V. Durham, Dorothy Vine Johnson, and Josephine Copeland. He included some of the best poems of Fenton Johnson, Frank Marshall Davis, Georgia Douglass Johnson, Mary Effie Lee Newsome, Helene Johnson, Wesley Cartwright, and Marcus Christian. The anthology also contained a long poem, one of the newest by Melvin B. Tolson, whose "Dark Symphony" had attracted rave reviews a short while before and had been praised by *Atlantic Monthly*. Arna also introduced a half dozen of his buddy Lang's poems that had not been previously anthologized. The anthology's array of literary talent impressed critics, for this was a timely work that broke new ground by including the best of the traditional lyrics and ballads along with an impressive number of recent compositions.

While demonstrating his acumen as an editor-compiler, Bontemps was also careful to let the anthology prove that poetry has been a part of the African-American heritage longer than had been generally thought, and he spotlighted the poetic talents of writers like W. C. Handy and James Bland, men whose musical genius had obscured their poetic talents. *Slippers* was illustrated by twenty-two line drawings and included an appendix and lively biographical sketches of the contributors. Arna designed the book's format to make it useable and to make it sell. The book did create one embarrassment for its author: Melvin Tolson's name was misspelled throughout, a faux pas for which he apologized profusely to Tolson, and which Tolson merely laughed off.[43]

As early as 1941 Bontemps had finished the first version of his editing of *Father of the Blues*, W. C. Handy's autobiography, a labor that would create the most embarrassing situation of Bontemps's literary career and for which he received little more than ingratitude from Handy. Arna had actually done most of the writing from notes provided by Handy. The book was copyrighted in 1941 by Macmillan. The chain of events following Handy's dissatisfaction with Bontemps's efforts—I found at Syracuse a copy of a suit filed against Bontemps by Handy—left Bontemps with hurt feelings and with his sense of fairness violated. Bontemps wrote very little on the incident except a restrained reply to Handy; the dissatisfaction had been all on one side—Handy's.

Handy knew little about literary collaboration and even less about publishing, and was offended over Bontemps's wording in several places. Bontemps's desire was to make the book appealing to readers, and it is pitiable that Handy was too naive to appreciate these special effects. At any rate the estimation the press gave of the Handy–Bontemps fiasco was equivocal, for on the morning after the writer's death a news organ published this statement: "Bontemps regarded his association with W. C. Handy as a highlight of his career."[44]

Still needing to supplement his income after finishing the Handy book, Bontemps wrote to Marshall Field III, applying for a staff job on Field's newest paper, *The Chicago Sunday Sun*, suggesting that he become the writer on "Negro subjects," following the example of *The New York World* and *The New York Herald Tribune*. He closed the letter with the following postscript: "You might want to know that I am a masculine writer, despite the uncertain first name."[45]

A few weeks later Bontemps received a letter from his old friend and fellow writer, Harold Jackman, acknowledging the receipt of several books Bontemps had sent to him care of Aaron Douglas. Jackman was impressed with *Golden Slippers* and complimented its author on the book's organization, and was sure that its selections should appeal to young readers.[46] The radio version of *Jubilee* had just come out and M. B. Tolson, who caught it by accident while visiting in Kansas City, was thrilled by the experience. He promptly wrote to Bontemps on his return to his post at Wiley College, describing the many favorable comments he had heard about the play from "both blacks and whites."[47] Before the year ended, Arna had become a literary columnist for Marshall Field's paper and had received the first in a series of letters from Carl Van Vechten asking him to contribute some of his original manuscripts to the James Weldon Johnson Collection at Yale and telling him of his longstanding desire to photograph him in color. Bontemps replied positively to both requests.[48] Van Vechten's response was prompt and enthusiastic.[49]

By 1941 the collaborative efforts of Bontemps and Conroy on literature for children began to bear fruit. The first of their children's books was issued by Houghton Mifflin and was titled *The Fast Sooner Hound*. The collaborating authors based the plot on one of Conroy's tall tales about a "Mangy, unprepossessing hound" that he had heard in the Wabash Railway shops in his hometown, Moberly, Missouri.[50] This mangy cur "didn't look like much, but . . . could run so fast . . . he'd leave the fastest trains . . . behind."[51]

This book became a best-seller for children, and as recently as 1974 its sales were still "galloping along at a pretty fast clip," to quote one of its authors.[52] It still appears on most library lists of recommended books for children. The original story was titled "The Boomer Fireman and His Fast Sooner Hound."[53] The book was written after a suggestion from Harwick Moseley of Houghton that the tale would make a fine juvenile book. Conroy admits he was inclined to dismiss the whole idea, but Bontemps read the tale and agreed with Moseley. Conroy reports the following results: "I told him I'd never written a juvenile and wouldn't know how to go about it. 'Why not tackle it together,' Arna suggested. And so we did. The original tale might be considered too robustious both in language and situation for kiddies, and Arna helped in gentling it a bit (but not much!). Some purists objected to the bad grammar and the outrageous behavior involved, but they were in the minority."[54] By the time they collaborated on their next juvenile book, Bontemps had already moved to Nashville while Conroy remained in Chicago.

In February 1942 Bontemps simultaneously applied for readmission to the Graduate Library School of the University of Chicago and for a graduate fellowship.[55] He had been in and out of Chicago's Graduate School since 1936. At the same time that he was readmitted to the library school, the Rosenwald Fund gave him a second grant, this time to pursue the "Negro in Illinois Project" in Chicago. Consequently on May 29, 1942 he resigned his job with the Federal Works Agency. On a memorandum form addressed to Jacob Scher he wrote that his resignation as Assistant Project Technician would be effective June 1, 1942. In a personal note included after his signature he wrote, "I have thoroughly enjoyed my work, and all personal contacts have been consistently harmonious. My interest in the unfinished book [*Negro in Illinois*] will continue. In fact, I plan to spend the 18th and 19th of June checking up on the outstanding chapters."[56]

Before the end of June Arna had, at long last, arrived in New York City for a brief visit, an act he was to repeat during the following summer en route to Nashville. While there, he saw Carl Van Vechten and as many others of his old friends from the Renaissance as he could. After his return, he received the first letter from Van Vechten in which the latter addressed him by his first name. Van Vechten was still trying to get Bontemps to help him garner materials for the Yale collection, for Arna had already been instrumental in Van Vechten's securing a number of manuscripts and photographs in the Chicago area, which he had mailed to Van Vechten. In a letter Van Vechten brought his friend up to date on the success of his collecting efforts. By this time Van Vechten had received Richard Wright's manuscript titled "Twelve Thousand Black Americans," and fifty manuscript poems by Countée Cullen; almost as many letters in longhand from James Weldon Johnson to Anne Spencer; and the original manuscript of Langston Hughes's "Mulatto."[57]

By fall 1942 Bontemps was hard at work on his library science degree. It was fortunate that some of the graduate coursework he had already completed at Chicago was applicable to the degree program of the Graduate Library School. Christmas came and went, and as he usually did at Christmas, Arna mailed books to a few friends. That year one of the books he sent out was Zora Neale Hurston's *Dust Tracks on a Road*. This he mailed to a former colleague from his days as a teacher at Oakwood College.[58] During the spring of 1943 he took final exams in his last required courses for the library degree, and during early summer sat for the comprehensives. He had planned to spend a few weeks at Yaddo, the writer's colony, before summer's end, but had to scrap these plans to report to Fisk University, where he had been hired the previous March as Head Librarian.

Thomas Elsa Jones, Fisk's president, had hired him several months before he was scheduled to finish the graduate degree, for Jones was interested in the prestige of having an established writer on the faculty at Fisk. Jones agreed to allow Bontemps as much leeway as he possibly could to pursue his writing while holding down the library position.[59] Arna had received a rapid succession of letters from Jones ordering him to come down and straighten out problems with staffing that the acting librarian, Frances Yocom, was having difficulty solving, or probably did not wish to solve, for the tone of her several letters during this period to her new boss reveal a hint of sour grapes.

After a brief stay on the campus in June, long enough to meet his staff, assess the library's holdings, and make arrangements for housing in one of Fisk's faculty residences, Bontemps went back to Chicago where he attended a workshop to which Jones ordered him to apply—the 1943 Summer Workshop in General Education sponsored by the American Council on Education of Chicago. Arna and Alberta with the children were scheduled to leave Chicago for Nashville on August 30. By this time, two of the Bontemps children were of high-school age. Joan had turned sixteen and Paul was fifteen and, to his father's delight, had secured a part-time job with a Chicago optical company.[60] Arna, meanwhile, was saying his goodbyes. He had established a number of friendships during his more than eight years in Chicago, and these friends were not willing to let him leave without a proper sendoff. His correspondence reveals that the round of parties lasted several weeks.

During his brief stay at Fisk in late June and early July, Bontemps had become excited about moving to Nashville and working at Fisk. He could not have joined the Fisk faculty at a more auspicious time, for Fisk was in its heyday then, enjoying a period of prosperity and academic excellence that was to last into the 1960s, not to mention the thriving social life the campus provided. Arna had been impressed by most of what he saw there. He was surprised to find a big summer school in session, and spoke to several of the classes on his initial visit. Soon after his arrival on campus, he decided that the former "Allison House" would come closer than would any of the other available campus residences to satisfying his family's needs. On the last day of June he wrote hastily to his family in his sprawling hand:

Dear Alberta and babies!

There has been no time for letters. Instead, I am sending this carbon copy of my note to the supt. of buildings and grounds. *Please save it*. At least it will give you an idea of what the house needs. It *could* be a comfortable house—if they will do *all* that is needed. In all other ways things are coming along quite well. The campus is beautiful now—especially around the library. And the kindergarten . . . Constance will attend . . . has tricycles for all the children. . . . Pearl High is beautiful. The course is good, too, except that Joan and Paul may have to take Spanish instead of French III. . . . Maybe they and I can work on French together privately. Pearl High has a capacity of 1,200 students. . . . The building beats DuSable! It is four blocks from our house. . . . The church is the same distance in another direction. I have accomplished my errands and will try to get a train after the crowded weekend and holiday (5th). . . . am staying in the faculty club and eating in the students' dining hall . . . meals are .65 each, but they are remarkably good. Best of any school I know! . . .

Ever, Arna.[61]

Chapter 8

Career at Fisk University

By March 1943, when the board of trustees at Fisk University approved the appointment of Arna Bontemps as head librarian, he had already established himself as a writer with an impressive number of poems, novels, and children's books to his credit, plus numerous articles and reviews. Thomas Elsa Jones had been impressed with these writing credits long before he sent Bontemps a wire requesting that he come at once to the campus for a visit.[1] The writer also had compiled by this time a good work record. From 1924–31 he taught at Harlem Academy, a private secondary school; from 1931–34 he taught at Oakwood Junior College of Huntsville, Alabama, like Harlem Academy, a Seventh-day Adventist institution.

After that he spent a year as a freelance writer in California at his father's home in Watts, and between 1935 and 1938 he returned to private schoolteaching at another Adventist high school, Shiloh Academy of Chicago, this time as principal. After he left Shiloh, Bontemps spent several years as an editorial supervisor on the Illinois Writer's Project, during which time he finished residency and language requirements toward the Ph.D. in English at the University of Chicago, a course of study he never finished. In 1938–39 he used a Rosenwald Fellowship for creative writing and travel in the Caribbean. When this ended, he returned to his job on the Writer's Project and shortly thereafter enrolled in Chicago's Graduate School of Library Science, for which study he had received an additional Rosenwald stipend. And in 1942 he received a third Rosenwald grant, this time to pursue the Negro in Illinois project in Chicago, after the Federal Project had been terminated.

Since his graduation from Pacific Union College in 1923 and the brief stint at the Los Angeles Post Office, Arna had lived mostly in New York and Chicago, with these two periods separated by a brief interval spent in Alabama and another hiatus spent writing in Los Angeles. By July 1, 1943, he had begun his actual duties as Head Librarian at Fisk and continued his active, participatory affiliation in a number of writers' guilds and professional organizations. His poems had appeared in many magazines and anthologies, and his list of awards and prizes included the *Crisis* Poetry Prize in 1926; the Alexander Pushkin Poetry Prize twice, in 1926 and 1927, and the *Opportunity* Short Story Prize for 1932. He had been listed in *Who's Who in America*, *Who's Who in the East*, and *Who's Who in the Western Hemisphere*. His list of published novels included *God Sends Sunday* (Harcourt, Brace, 1931); *Black Thunder* (Macmillan, 1936); *Drums at Dusk* (Macmillan, 1939).

For children and youths he had published *Popo and Fifina*, with Langston Hughes (Macmillan, 1932); *You Can't Pet a Possum* (Morrow, 1934); *Sad-Faced Boy* (Houghton Mifflin, 1937); *Golden Slippers*, an anthology of poems (Harper, 1941); *Fast Sooner Hound* with Jack Conroy (Houghton Mifflin, 1942); and nearly a dozen short stories for juveniles and adults. Secondary works on Bontemps's writings included biographical sketches and a critical evaluation in *Horn Book* of January–February 1939. He had also ghostwritten W. C. Handy's autobiography, *Father of the Blues*.

Arna's formal postbaccalaureate study had consisted of one summer (1924) at the University of California at Los Angeles; two summers at Columbia University (1925, 1926); and scattered courses in languages, creative writing, and other areas at City College of New York and New York University between 1925 and 1931. He had completed residence requirements for the Ph.D. in English at the University of Chicago, excluding the comprehensive examinations and the dissertation.[2]

He had maintained over the years informal association with a number of the nation's top libraries, including the public libraries of Los Angeles, New York, and Chicago. On several occasions he had been invited to speak to the librarians of the Los Angeles Public Library System through the efforts of Helen English, Director of Branches, a person with whom Arna had established a friendship while still a teenager in Los Angeles. On at least one occasion he had been brought to Los Angeles from Chicago by the public schools. In Chicago he had maintained a similar involvement with libraries and librarians, including participation in a series of symposia and broadcasts sponsored by the Chicago Public Library. He had also served for several years on various committees of the Hall Branch Library of Chicago. Also during the Chicago period, he was invited to New York at the suggestion of Ernestine Rose of the 135th Street Branch as a possible curator for the Schomburg Collection (spring 1942).

During the same week of his summons to Fisk for an interview, the writer was commissioned by the American Library Association to compile a bibliography on "Color and Democracy" for use in all American Libraries.[3] Moreover, he had already submitted to the *Gazette*, a publication of the Yale University Library, a portion of his master's thesis entitled "The James Weldon Johnson Memorial Collection of Arts and Letters," a lengthy essay issued during his second month on the Fisk faculty.[4] And before he moved his family from Chicago to Nashville in late August of 1943, he had already entered an agreement with a major library association to publish a revised version of his master's thesis, which came out during the following summer under the title "Special Collections of Negroana."[5]

At forty, then, Arna Wendell Bontemps was quite a catch for Fisk University, with or without the terminal degree. He was happy to be on a regular salary once more, for his family needed this kind of security. He was even happier to be working on the same faculty with his friends Charles Spurgeon Johnson and Aaron Douglas, his next-door neighbor at Nashville, and with poet Robert Hayden and musicologist John W. Work. James Weldon Johnson, who had done much to keep alive Arna's interest in Fisk after his first visit to the campus during the Huntsville period, was no longer there. He had died in a tragic automobile accident in 1938, not long after Bontemps joined the staff of Chicago's Federal Writers' Project.

But even with the dean of the black poets gone, Fisk was a haven for the younger writer. Here was a chance to put behind him forever the kinds of difficulties he had experienced while trying to work in SDA schools. And the environment at Fisk would help to ease the writer's disappointment in another area, for he had not found the Harlem he had hoped to discover when he visited New York in 1942–43. Gone were most of the persons who had made Harlem famous during the 1920s and early 1930s. Some had moved to neighborhoods bordering on Harlem, and others were living in Westchester County. Gone were the cabarets and rent parties, and in their places Arna had discovered prowling boys, evil-eyed criminals, and outlandish cults. Expressing his consternation at what he found he wrote: "What in God's name had happened? To me there seemed only one explanation. No matter what else one might see there, Harlem remained what it had always been in essence, a black ghetto and slum, a clot in the American bloodstream. And the fruit of compulsory group segregation based on race. The children born there in the beautiful years of the middle 'Twenties' had grown up to be muggers and cultists."[6]

Arna was happy he had moved his family from Harlem when he did and that they would have the inspiration and cultural exposure of living on the Fisk campus. He knew by the time he moved to Nashville in 1943 that the promise of turning Harlem into a cultural mecca for African Americans, as he and other writers of the Renaissance had hoped to realize, had become an impossible dream.[7] But the young writer-librarian found at Fisk the cultural and intellectual stimulation he required, as well as a sufficient amount of emotional solace. He was, at long last, in an environment where his craving for cultural identity and roots could be satisfied. Here he would find the same kind of refuge that had caused James Weldon Johnson, Charles Spurgeon Johnson, and others of his friends and colleagues to remain at Fisk, for salaries there had never been competitive, and certainly were not during Bontemps's tenure. But these scholars were satisfied by the other benefits the Fisk milieu offered them and their families.

Arna's second return to the South was in nearly every aspect different from his first return more than a decade earlier. In Huntsville, the contact with his roots had been more primitive, more rustic, than anything he would encounter at Nashville. In 1931 he had needed calm and serenity, the kind of restful environment the Alabama countryside and the warm, simple hospitality of its inhabitants provided. He had retained fond memories of his earlier days in the Deep South, despite the indignities he and his family had suffered at the hands of Adventists and white supremacists during his three years at Oakwood Junior College. He had a deep affection for the Old South, including his native Louisiana. But in 1943 he needed a different kind of oasis, one that provided a wholesome setting for his five children and a stimulating academic ambience for himself, one that would afford some opportunity to write. He also needed a work situation that would allow him to settle down and enjoy life for a change. All this and more he found at Fisk. He sensed that Fisk would provide just enough isolation for him to think and to write, and that it would also provide a kind of economic and social security that he, Alberta, and the children had never known together.

Though the library was drafty and frequently without steam heat during the winter months, there was little at Fisk to trouble this creative artist, and he found much there to stimulate him as a writer and teacher. For a number of years, he and Alberta had been concerned that they would not be able to provide the right kind of intellectual climate for their children and simultaneously make financial ends meet. The Fisk setting provided some relief from this kind of anxiety, although it seems that Arna never had quite enough money, for salaries were small at Fisk and he rarely made large sums from his literary efforts. And Nashville in the forties was relatively free of racial tensions, especially when compared to Huntsville between 1931 and 1934. While World War II was raging abroad and its effects were felt everywhere, the Fisk campus was a protective shield from much that was negative or hostile. Too, its situation in southeastern Tennessee made it more accessible to New York than Huntsville, Los Angeles, or Chicago had been.

If the Chicago years had been prolific for Bontemps, they were not to be compared to his lengthy, productive tenure at Fisk. He had long been convinced that the South offered unmistakable advantages as an abode for a person of his temperament.[8] He would remain grateful to his friend, mentor, and colleague, Charles S. Johnson, formerly of *Opportunity* fame and then the Academic Dean at Fisk, for approaching him about the job and for recommending to Thomas Elsa Jones that he find a place on the Fisk faculty for him. After Johnson brought Bontemps to the attention of Jones, who needed a librarian, Jones contacted the young writer. This was not Jones's first contact with Bontemps, however, for in 1938, just after James Weldon Johnson was killed, Jones had tried to persuade the writer to succeed Johnson as Professor of Creative Writing. Fisk had lost a triumvirate of librarians in succession: Louis Shores, then Carl White, and Neal Van Busen, who had been run over and killed by a truck in Michigan.

Charles Spurgeon Johnson, a Ph.D. and productive scholar in sociology, had been known as the "entrepreneur" of the Harlem movement, primarily because of his persistent efforts while editor of *Opportunity* to secure publishing opportunities for talented young Harlem writers. A few years later, Johnson would succeed Jones as President of Fisk, a position he held from 1947 until 1956.[9] And for Arna Bontemps, time on the job would prove the position at Fisk was tailor-made to match his cultural background and literary interests. In an unpublished manuscript, the writer explained why he had accepted Jones's offer of employment: "Dreaming of a beachcomber's island complete with mango trees and a thatched hut, perhaps, I hit upon what I hoped might turn out to be a kind of prose equivalent: the campus of a Negro college in Tennessee."[10]

Of course, not everyone agreed with the writer's decision to accept the job at Fisk. Several of his fellow writers felt that to confine himself to a librarian's post on the campus of a small, minority college, one with an emphasis on social events and a heavy load of teaching assignments and committee work for its faculty, was the wrong decision for any creative artist to make. One of the skeptics among his colleagues was historian Lawrence D. Reddick, who later became Curator of Harlem's Schomburg Collection of Black Literature.

Reddick wrote: "One of my former teachers at Fisk said to me in his offhanded fashion that he was bringing Arna there to be the University Librarian. I had my doubts that the job and the man would fit; but they did. He not only knew what was inside books . . . but became as popular with librarians and library users as he had been for years with writers and readers."[11] The years at Fisk turned out to be the most agreeable and productive of Arna's life, and his record there proves the decision to accept Fisk's offer as Chief Librarian had been wise.

The faculty and student body at Fisk, during September and October 1943, received the poet warmly, with all the usual amenities, as it did for Lillian Welch Voorhees, of longtime Fisk dramatics fame, who along with several others, joined the faculty at the same time Bontemps did. To help the Fisk community to appreciate this new campus personality, *The Herald*, a Fisk-published magazine, featured the writer in its October issue. And Bontemps's joining the faculty did not go unnoticed by the city of Nashville nor by academicians elsewhere. Before he had been there a month, letters began pouring in, asking him to serve as a panelist or library consultant, or inquiring of his views about literature for children and about creative writing in general.[12] He found time to answer each of these letters, sometimes writing as much as two full typewritten pages. His tone was always complimentary and encouraging.

But during these first days at Fisk, Arna still did not have his library degree in hand, and to ensure graduation by the end of the fall quarter (December 1943), there were a few loose ends he needed to snip. In a letter from C. B. Jaeckel, Dean of the University of Chicago's Graduate Library School, written two days after Bontemps's fortieth birthday, his mentor reminded him that at the time of his comprehensive examination he had agreed to make designated additions to a paper written to remove an "I" he had received in "Education 341," a course taught by a Mr. Russell. Jaeckel instructed Bontemps to finish the revisions at once and return them to his office, for Russell was not in residence during fall quarter 1943.[13] Arna had been too busy attending to the immediate needs of Fisk's library and making long-range plans for its improvement to think about improving a paper for an education course. He did, however, manage to submit the revisions on time, for at the end of the quarter he received the M.A. degree.

Arna was ecstatic about his new job at Fisk. He wrote to his old friend, Harold Jackman, explaining the extent of his involvement in the job: "My work here gets more exciting as it goes along. I am enjoying it a great deal. We don't have a collection of the sort you are starting at Atlanta or the one at Yale, but I'll try to work out some other ideas—of which you will hear more anon."[14]

Arna's office was located then in what Fiskites currently refer to as "the old library," the Erastus Milo Cravath Building, the kind of stately, Neo-Gothic structure found on so many of the campuses of older American universities. This office, by fall 1943, was one of the busiest places on campus. Professor Bontemps conducted frequent meetings with the library staff, overseeing changes in the cataloguing system and making improvements as needed, for Fisk's library had operated under an acting librarian for longer than usual, the result of Thomas Jones's not having taken enough time to find the right person to fill the vacancy left by Neal Van Busen. The new job was no less arduous than it was exciting. Bontemps flourished on the steady diet of athletic contests the Fisk and Tennessee State teams offered, for he had never lost his love of sports, and Fisk and State offered some of the most exciting football and basketball schedules to be found anywhere in the country. Recently, Fisk has suspended its football program, but this did not occur until after the death of Arna Bontemps. Bontemps would have taken the news of suspended athletics as hard as did most of the alumni.

Not all of the poet's excitement was the result of the Fisk situation. Some of it came from new developments in his writing career. While he was revising his M.A. thesis, a copy of the latest edition of *St. Louis Woman* had arrived from the publishers. This was a revised version of the play he and Cullen had submitted earlier in the year.[15] Arna's hope in the play's future was suddenly renewed, for he thought the revisions were the best he and his collaborator had made—they had made several changes in the play since its first draft. All he and Cullen needed now was for someone to produce this new version. Of course, wartime difficulties and other setbacks made success for the play long in coming. Cullen had written lyrics for ten songs to be performed as part of "The Woman," and both he and Bontemps were hoping for a hit or two out of the group. Arna's own favorites were "Mean, Mean, Mean," "Money Talking," "In the Beginning," and "I'm Little but I'm Loud." Neither author had yet heard the music for these lyrics.[16]

Bontemps began to receive numerous professional and social invitations, some of which represented definite boosts to his career as a writer. And now that he was associated with Fisk, it seemed easier for old friends and relatives, some of whom he had nearly lost contact with, to reach him there. One distant relative he had never met took the liberty of writing to him in response to a message he had sent to Lincoln University (in Missouri), where this cousin was teaching in the Department of English.[17] This relative was Leslie Morgan Collins, nephew of Arna's godmother, Ida Hines who, the letter revealed, was still alive and residing at 1330 Eighth Street, Alexandria, Louisiana, literally a stone's throw from the house at Ninth and Winn Streets where Arna had been born forty years earlier. The structure still stands (1988), though it is badly in need of restoration.

Collins is the younger brother of Samuel Collins, the person who became the second husband of Vesta Albins, widow of Arna's first Cousin Bennie, and she is the "female relative" Arna would see during his last trip to Louisiana in the fall of 1972. The contact with Leslie Collins proved auspicious for both men, for two years later, at Bontemps's urging, Collins joined the faculty at Fisk where he still teaches (1991), and where these two cousins remained friends and colleagues from that time until Bontemps's sudden death in 1973. The letter from Collins enabled Bontemps to reestablish contact with his "Aunt Idoo," his own mother's closest friend. This contact would later supply an important link with the Alexandria of his birth and early childhood.

On 17 December 1943 Arna Wendell Bontemps was awarded the Master of Library Science degree at the 250th convocation of the University of Chicago. The ceremony was held in the campus' Rockefeller Memorial Chapel, and Arna was one of the more than two hundred students, graduates and undergraduates, to receive degrees.[18] Congratulations were in order; these came from all over the United States, and several major newspapers carried announcements of the poet's newest achievement.[19] From this point on, with sheepskin in hand, he was able to devote more time to writing and to building up the Fisk archives than he had been able to during his first quarter on the faculty. Meanwhile, he continued to teach regular classes in creative writing and occasional courses in literature.

Not long after Arna started working at Fisk, he began corresponding with Carl Van Vechten about the possibility of Fisk's obtaining the George Gershwin Collection, the first acquisition in the huge "Negro Collection" built by Bontemps during his more than two decades as Chief Librarian. In early January 1944, Van Vechten wrote Bontemps from New York concerning the room where the Gershwin Collection would be housed. In an earlier letter, Bontemps had offered the "old periodical room" for the papers, a location that did not sound suitable to the grandiose tastes of Van Vechten. In this letter to Bontemps, Van Vechten dictated what would have to be done with the contents of the room and how the room must then be prepared to receive the collection. There were other conditions and stipulations, too, that Van Vechten wanted Bontemps to meet before he would part with the collection. This, and other letters in the Syracuse Papers, reveal an attitude on Van Vechten's part that would eventually try Bontemps's patience to the point of destroying their friendship, a relationship that would grow stronger before meeting a sudden death.[20]

It is ostensible that the "browsing room" "Carlo" had demanded Fisk provide for the papers was perceived by the donor as a kind of shrine—to what or to whom it is not entirely clear—instead of a reading room in a college library. An almost daily exchange of letters between Bontemps and Van Vechten began, a chain of correspondence that would continue until mid-November of 1949, when the friendship came to an abrupt end. Before the friendship cooled, Van Vechten had grown so accustomed to the daily letters from Bontemps that he mildly upbraided the latter whenever he missed a day.[21]

In the course of this correspondence, Arna began to hear from his white Bontemps relatives, most of whom were living in various parts of the northern United States. The first such letter he received was from a male Bontemps residing in Peoria, Illinois, who also had a son named Alex Bontemps and who descended from the same Alexandre Bontemps as Arna had. This cousin had written to him after seeing one of his books. Not long afterward he received a letter from a Mrs. Ellis, whose maiden name was Bontemps and who had also seen some mention of his books. Arna's reply to her was a warm, two-page letter in which he explained his roots, and he sent to her under separate cover an autographed copy of *Popo and Fifina* for her children. From this time until he retired from Fisk, he periodically corresponded with these and other members of the Bontemps clan, most of whom he described as "white creoles."[22]

One wonders how, with a house full of active youngsters and a library staff of nine full-time persons, plus a group of student assistants to supervise, Bontemps managed to keep up with his correspondence as he did and still complete his scheduled writing projects. In the letter to Mrs. Ellis, he gave a clue to his established writing habits. He wrote: "I have little enough time for concentrated writing. But I try to do a little everyday, and I comfort myself by saying that if I write just a page (or perhaps a sentence) a day the book will eventually be written. If by doing so I can come to know all the people named Bontemps, I'll feel rewarded!"[23]

Bontemps sensed that Van Vechten was ready by March 1944 to turn over the Gershwin Collection to Fisk University provided, of course, that Fisk was ready to meet the attached conditions. The collection, owned and assembled by Van Vechten, consisted of books on music, published scores, manuscripts, letters, photographs, phonograph records, scrapbooks, and miscellaneous materials. The first condition Van Vechten attached was that the name of the collection be the one he himself had chosen—"The George Gershwin Memorial Collection of Music and Musical Literature, Founded by Carl Van Vechten."[24] In addition the prospective donor attached a dozen other stipulations including the proviso that he be able to withdraw the collection at any time Fisk failed to live up to its end of the agreement.[25] This was a large gift to the library, one which Bontemps considered worthy of humoring the eccentric Van Vechten, and worthy of the chunk of his time the gift was consuming.

May 1944 was a busy month for Arna. It marked his first convocation as a Fisk faculty member and the close of his first term as Librarian, and he was enjoying a feeling of accomplishment. He entered an agreement with the Association of Childhood Education when the organization asked him to submit one of his children's stories for its journal. This involvement with the association was to continue for more than a decade and it did much to promote the author's books and stories for children and juveniles.

But he was also frustrated because *St. Louis Woman* was not having the success his children's works were experiencing. "The Woman" still was not being staged by drama companies, although several directors and companies had expressed interest in the play.[26] Meanwhile, publisher Will Cook was reviving his interest in financing a musical version of the play, an idea he had conceived as early as Arna's Huntsville period but dropped before it could come to fruition.[27]

A bit of good news came with the publication of the short fictional piece "Rock Church Rock" as a chapter in an anthology edited by Frederick John Towner and titled *Out of the Midwest: A Collection of Present-Day Writing* (McGraw-Hill, 1944). This piece, closer in form and content to the fictionalized folk tale than to any other genre, fits the "Midwest" of the anthology's title only in the sense that Bontemps wrote it during the latter part of the Chicago period. It comes straight out of the Huntsville years when its author visited the primitive black churches in the region. The tale is decidedly Southern, as is nearly everything else that has come from the Bontemps pen. Typical of his earlier prose, "Rock Church Rock" has become one of the author's most frequently anthologized short pieces.

By midsummer 1944 Bontemps and Conroy were hard at work on a documentary book on the Negro migration that they wrote jointly, a work that grew out of research findings assembled with the aid of the field workers they supervised during their years as co-administrators for the Illinois Writer's Project. A significant portion of Bontemps's correspondence from August through December 1944 consists of letters to his friend and collaborator.

Both Arna and Jack were on schedule with their assigned portions of the manuscript and the former was gleeful, for he could visualize completion of this significant project. By the end of July Arna had finished both the prologue and the Harlem chapter, but was dissatisfied with what he had written about Harlem. This kind of factual book required an objective approach, but his first draft of the chapter turned out to be a nostalgic piece about his own seven years in Harlem.[28] This he decided to publish elsewhere and to rewrite the Harlem chapter entirely.

He was proud, though, of what he had done with the prologue. He began by discussing the first black men who came to the South, that "green Eden" where they were fugitives and wanderers. He went on to tell that the first migrants were runaway slaves and how blacks kept going North after slavery ended. Next came a discussion of the little communities these migrants formed under the generic title "Mudtown," the type found in so many Northern cities in which the migrants congregated. After speaking of all the Mudtowns, he went on to depict the one he knew best—the Furlough Track on the edge of Los Angeles. He described how it turned out its musicians and prizefighters, along with its professionals: teachers, lawyers, dentists, and physicians. The collaborating authors wanted to illustrate the place this kind of community—the generic Mudtown—occupied in the lives of the uprooted Southerners who settled there. It was also their intent to tell the story of some of the people who came to Mudtown in such a way that the reader would understand the migratory impulse as personal experience, an experience that had deep meaning for most Americans. The second chapter took up Du Sable and the earliest migrants.[29]

The completed work was published as *They Seek a City* and besides the prologue had eighteen chapters and an epilogue titled "Anyplace But Here," the name used for the book when it was revised and reissued during the 1960s. But as was their practice, Conroy and Bontemps were working on more than one literary project. They were writing another children's book first titled *Slappy Hooper*, but which Houghton Mifflin issued more descriptively as *Slappy Hooper, the Wonderful Sign Painter*. Both *They Seek a City* and *Slappy Hooper* were published in 1945, while Bontemps and Conroy were hoping the wartime paper shortage would not delay its release.

When the fall term opened at Fisk in 1945, Arna was feeling the strain of overwork. In a letter written from New York's Hotel Theresa, his favorite stopping place in the city for more than a decade, he complained to Conroy that he had worked too hard and was experiencing difficulty resting, for running the library was a constant burden, one he carried with him wherever he went, even during vacations and holidays. To add to this encumbrance, he was summoned by Federal authorities, who wanted to make sure he was not a communist. It was primarily his association with Langston Hughes, who for some time had been under the government's close scrutiny—at one time government investigators had a way of showing up wherever Hughes was lecturing—that had brought about this turn of affairs. But after one round of questioning Bontemps was exonerated, for he had never associated with Marxists in any way, unlike several of his prominent contemporaries among the African-American writers.[30]

Encouraging news came from Annie L. W. McPheeters, Librarian of the Auburn Branch of Atlanta's Carnegie Library, who wrote to the author to let him know that her library had assembled an "Arna Bontemps Collection," consisting of all of his books for children and juveniles (a project started by the Alpha Epsilon Chapter of Phi Delta Kappa Sorority); a collection they planned to add to periodically. This was certainly a well-deserved honor for him. And another honor came during the following month. At the annual conference of the North Carolina Negro Library Association, held at Greensboro's Bennett College in late October, Bontemps was the keynote banquet speaker. His speech was titled "Adventures in Authorship." The conference theme for that year was "The Library and the Post-War World."[31]

At this juncture the author sold a piece to *The American Scholar* about the Harlem poets of 1924, the year of his arrival in New York. He titled it "The Two Harlems," but could not enjoy the success of publication nor the money earned for the old problem of others trying to usurp his and Cullen's monetary rights to *St. Louis Woman*. Leah Salisbury, it seemed, had not safeguarded their interests as she should have. Both authors had left instructions with her that any printed version should acknowledge that the play was based on Arna's first published novel, but much to his alarm, the newest version of the play had deleted any reference to that fact.[32]

The following portion of a letter from Bontemps to Cullen reveals distinct aspects of the Bontemps personality (his extreme sensitivity and his abhorrence of injustice); it also reveals that he had inherited at least some of his father's spleen and all of his obstinacy:

I have just written Leah . . . a long and somewhat discouraged letter. Neither its mood nor its content related to you in any way, but I do hope you will labor with the lady if you get a chance. The thing that provoked the gloomy item was a wire from L. S. Saturday morning bemoaning the "complications" of Harcourt . . . owning drama rights and seeking at the same time to pick up my contract with them. As you know, I'm about as jealous of . . . GOD SENDS SUNDAY as I am of my children, and I always get unhappy when they are the objects of too friendly gestures, or of hostile ones. I have never . . . understood L. S.'s concern about Harcourt's ownership of the GSS drama rights. . . . What bothers me is that while you and I have practically never failed to see eye to eye . . . Leah . . . seldom communicates with me except to ask for my contract with Harcourt . . . I don't see where the contract concerns her at all. . . . I do wish you would ask Leah to avoid the subject in her communications with me. It makes me physically ill. . . . As a matter of fact, her wire has rendered me completely incapable of doing the outline I had intended to prepare over the weekend.[33]

Arna's creole blood had burst into a near blaze. But I suspect that at least some of his wrath was rhetorical, especially the part about his being rendered incapable of writing, for it seems a bit out of the Bontemps character.

Arna spent the weeks between December 1 and 20, 1944 in New York supervising Edward Gross's production of "The Woman," but was at home in Nashville to spend Christmas with Alberta and the children, a holiday spent writing, as was his wont.[34] His sense of humor had returned, for he sent a card to Countée and Ida showing a very dark cherub, wearing a diaper, a small pair of angel's wings, and a miniature halo, complemented by a full head of pickaninny plaits. The happy black angel swung on a broken-down version of the pearly gates. On the page opposite this likeness Arna wrote only one word— Hallelujah! This card he inscribed in his own hand, "Arna and Alberta."[35]

The author was feeling the money pinch as usual, but this time more sharply than he had felt it since joining the Fisk faculty. He needed to raise enough money to send his two oldest children to college in January 1945—but this was a problem he had expected because they had both entered the first grade at the same time. The new year found him also feeling optimistic about "The Woman," at least more so than he had felt in recent months. Toward the end of 1944 Edward Gross, producer of the play *Chicken Every Sunday*, had entered a contract with him and Cullen and all other concerned parties to produce the play. Arna had taken a break from his work on *They Seek a City* to travel to New York about "The Woman."

To date, the play had suffered many setbacks, despite numerous attempts to put it on Broadway. Concerning this problem, he wrote the following complaint to Cullen: "Of course, I don't need to tell you the theater is very uncertain and that the plans to produce can be abandoned as lightly as they have been made. This *has* happened to "St. Louis Woman" two or three times before. The only difference now is that times are better for shows, but that may prove nothing."[36] This uncertainty surrounding the play helped to land Cullen in a New York hospital, leaving much of the burden of altering the script on Bontemps's shoulders.[37]

But during most of 1945 Arna was too busy to brood. His papers at Syracuse show that his involvement in campus life at Fisk had increased and the Fisk papers bear this out even more clearly. He was holding the chair or membership on every academic committee at Fisk, a level of participation that would increase. While he was having trouble from his efforts to place *St. Louis Woman* before American theater audiences, he was also preparing another manuscript that was published before the year's end. Its title is *We Have Tommorow*, a history text documenting the lives and contributions of such contemporary African Americans as Ralph Bunche, Hazel Scott, and several other illustrious people. This work is best classified as a juvenile book for want of a more descriptive designation, and, like several of Bontemps's books, it was published by Houghton Mifflin.

This is a significant work in the Bontemps canon, for it marks the beginning of a new genre for him. He found that he had neglected to write for black adolescents. As a father of five, expecting a sixth, he certainly understood the needs of this important though vulnerable segment of the population. He had long believed that the future of African Americans rested in the youths of America. Understanding that they needed worthy role models to emulate, he targeted this book to youngsters between the ages of fourteen and seventeen. He was convinced that the history of black America, past and present, afforded more than enough acceptable role models, hence the book's cross-section of famous blacks in politics, education, science, the arts, and athletics.[38] The book opened the door to a number of biographies he would write over the years for this age group, most falling within his middle years at Fisk.

The writer was delighted when in the spring of 1945 the Fisk Stagecrafters produced Cullen's play *Byword for Evil* in the campus theater. Bontemps was present on opening night and wrote the next day this ecstatic description to Cullen: "Here are a couple of programs of . . . the production of *Byword*. . . . Let me tell you how much I enjoyed the prologue and epilogue, both of which were new to me. They contained some . . . beautiful passages. Dramatically, too, they are perhaps the best parts of the play. I was transported."[39] In the same letter he reported to his collaborator that trouble was about to surface again for the both of them. W. C. Handy had written Bontemps an irate letter expressing his displeasure at their use of the phrase "St. Louis Woman," assuming it was from his "St. Louis Blues." Handy had erroneously concluded that the play was a dramatization of his song and that their use of the phrase would deprive him of the opportunity to sell his song to the stage or the movies.[40]

By April 1945 Edward Gross had already spent many weeks in Hollywood trying to promote the production of the play. He had decided it could be done only as a musical. While there, he had gotten the team of Harold Arlen and Johnny Mercer interested in writing the musical script. Arlen would do the lyrics; Mercer would produce the musical score. Apparently unaware that Bontemps and Cullen, both teaching for a living, could not easily take off in the middle of a school term for an extended stay on the West Coast, Gross wired Leah Salisbury that he needed both writers in Hollywood at once where they would need to remain at least four weeks. He offered to pay their railroad fares and seventy-five dollars per week in expenses.[41]

Bontemps agreed to go to California without Cullen under the suggested terms if he could receive the funds in advance, for he had traveled to New York about this play using out-of-pocket funds. He proposed that the trip take place in May, for the spring quarter at Fisk would have ended and he and Alberta were expecting their sixth child in June. Meanwhile, the two option checks he had received from Gross could not have arrived at a better time.[42]

On his return from California, Bontemps wrote this update to Cullen, who did not make the trip:

The work goes along very satisfactorily and the hopes of all concerned are very high for ST. LOUIS WOMAN. Arlen and Mercer and Ayres are friendly and intelligent people, and I . . . believe an excellent show will result from their efforts combined with ours. The show will be a "play with music" rather than a conventional "musical." It will come nearer to the Porgy and Bess technique than to any other I know, and there will be no songs or music unrelated to the theme. . . . And we all hope that another "Stormy Weather" or "Blues in the Night" will show up.

I have written two completely new scenes thus far and am now working on a third. . . . The kinds of things which the musical emphasis makes necessary.[43]

In this same letter Arna reported that Schuyler Watts, well-known producer and drama critic of *Tomorrow* magazine, had written and called him from New York about the forthcoming *We Have Tomorrow*, of which Watts had read an announcement.

Cullen was beginning to show signs of nervous strain as Bontemps had earlier. The two writers spent much of their May 1945 correspondence in a series of friendly yet firm wranglings over compensation for "The Woman," each jealously guarding what he perceived to be his rights and monetary dues.[44] Bontemps found himself equally engrossed in a literary proposal by Schuyler Watts.

On June 2, New York's *Amsterdam News* carried an article announcing that Arna Bontemps had been commissioned to write a creole musical play for Broadway. The play's theme and setting were right down Arna's alley, for he had long nourished a growing interest in the antique, and Louisiana had remained his favorite subject for writing. This musical was to deal with authentic creole material in its New Orleans locale prior to the Civil War. The production would be designed for a mixed cast of whites and blacks.[45] Watts had chosen Bontemps to write the script because he considered him a good writer, one who by this time was a recognized authority on authentic creole materials. He also chose Bontemps because he was "cosmic" in his objectivity and had achieved a detached style, a remarkable quality in a writer. With a touch of the Bontemps imagination Watts was sure the musical would be "great."[46]

The title of the finished drama was simply *Creole*, but it was never published nor produced and still exists among the Bontemps manuscripts not available for publication at Syracuse University. Bontemps stated that Watts had planned to produce the play and that he delivered the completed work to Watts. But he never heard from Watts again. Bontemps had noticed a change in Watts's personality and suspected that he had suffered some kind of breakdown shortly after receiving the completed manuscript.[47]

Bontemps had drawn the background material for the play's content from familiar sources, the kinds of creole stories he had heard his grandmother and grand-uncle tell about Louisiana. Much later, in 1964, when he was retiring from the Fisk Library post, Bontemps would write to Philip Butcher, Chair of the Division of Humanities at Morgan State University, who was then collecting creole materials for a literary project of his own. Bontemps's letter provided Butcher with a description of *Creole*'s content: "My grandparents and other ancestors were all mixed up in it."[48] In the same category with *Creole* is another unpublished manuscript, undated, among the Syracuse Papers. It is a play written in collaboration with Schuyler Watts titled *Careless Love*, which Bontemps and Hughes revised and issued under the recycled title *When the Jack Hollers*.

Then Arna Alexander Bontemps was born, the sixth and last child of Arna Wendell and Alberta Bontemps and their second son. Bontemps's oldest child recalled recently that "Alex" was born on June 13, 1945, a date she remembers well, for he was born at the time of her graduation from Nashville's Pearl High School.[49] A few days after the birth, the proud father received a congratulatory telegram from Langston Hughes that also mentioned a new film script Owen Dodson had published.[50] But Arna Sr., who always enjoyed births, weddings, and other family celebrations, could not enjoy the birth of his new son without having to cope with still another problem derived from "The Woman." Before young Alex was a month old, the Freddie Washington attack on the play stirred up a bitter controversy that primarily involved Washington, Countée Cullen, and Walter White, but Bontemps, as co-author, could not escape the dispute, despite his tendency to shun conflicts of all kinds. Washington was the nearly white actress who was sister to Isabel Washington, the first wife of Adam Clayton Powell. Walter White, whom the partisan Bontemps described as self-promoting and just plain nasty, had instigated this literary feud.[51]

Cullen, like Bontemps, was not quarrelsome, but White forced the squabble with Cullen, throwing his weight around in a manner that hurt the sensitive Cullen severely, a wound from which he never recovered. At White's suggestion Freddie Washington, ostensibly as big a selfseeker as White, wrote an article in her theater column for *P.M.*, one of New York's black newspapers, in which she thoroughly condemned *St. Louis Woman*. The article touched off the quarrel by criticizing the play for showing African Americans in what she and White considered a bad light. This attack, probably spurred by professional jealousy, had come at the worst of times, when the play was just getting off the ground. The truth of the matter was that Freddie Washington had coveted the role of Della, the "St. Louis Woman" of the play and who, failing to land the role for herself, had subsequently tried to win it for her sister.[52]

The whole incident went on for several months with Cullen's friends joining him against White and Washington. Much later, Bontemps would explain to one of his many interviewers that the quarrel had either hastened or brought on Cullen's death.[53] Cullen stopped communicating with Washington from this time until he died about six months later.[54] Bontemps had tried to soothe Cullen's wounded feelings, but without much success. The controversy over "The Woman" died down in early September, several months before Cullen's death, when White's daughter Jane signed a contract to play the leading role in *Strange Fruit*, a role that retains many of the so-called negative impressions about African Americans to which White and Washington had objected in the character of Della of the Bontemps-Cullen opus.[55]

At the height of the squabble Cullen had read scenes from the play at Walter White's apartment, where the latter had invited many persons from the New York literary circle. This is evidence that Cullen and White had tried to patch up their literary quarrel. Just prior to Cullen's reading, Bontemps, still seeking to console him and concerned about his friend under these strained conditions, sent him a special delivery that began "Courage to you and chin up . . . on this important night."[56] Arna also wired reminders of the scheduled reading to Aaron Douglas and his wife Alta, who were spending the summer break in New York, and to Dorothy Peterson and several others of his and Cullen's mutual friends.

The Pittsburgh Courier was one of the few newspapers that checked out the allegations against *St. Louis Woman* prior to its production. This paper had consulted Bontemps and others on the issue and afterwards wrote an article designed to discredit ill-founded assessments inspired by the Freddie Washington attack. The *Courier* article helped to increase the play's popularity at a time when it needed a boost.[57] The "green-eyed monster" had tried to kill the play but had failed. In November 1945, "VJ Day" found Arna on an evening train bound for New York where he would meet with Countée and other interested parties in preparation for the play's premiere.[58]

Later that month, Arna returned to Nashville where his correspondence had stacked up: Van Vechten, still collecting Johnsonia for Yale, letters concerning proposals for an unnamed new Bontemps book, and numerous other items needing attention. But Arna spent quiet Thanksgiving and Christmas holidays at home, catching up on as much writing and editing as he could. On January 9, Countée Cullen died.[59] The funeral was held at Harlem's historic Salem Methodist Church, where Cullen's father Frederick had been pastor. Arna, along with Harold Jackman, Owen Dodson, and five others of Cullen's male friends, served as pallbearers. As soon as the funeral was over, *Poet* magazine commissioned Bontemps to write a feature on Cullen for its section titled "Fotoscope," a piece that came out in the January 26 edition. In this special memorial article on Countée, Arna praised the fallen poet for his brave acceptance of death, citing several of the late writer's poems.[60]

The death of one of its authors attracted much favorable attention to *St. Louis Woman*, and requests for articles signed by Bontemps began to flow in from all over the United States, most wanting a story on how he and Cullen had come to write the play together.[61] The play had been scheduled for a March 30 opening at New York's Martin Beck Theater on West 45th Street. Earlier that month Bontemps had traveled to Philadelphia to direct a radio version of the script aired on the "Presidential Family Hour," a Sunday afternoon broadcast.[62]

The play did open on schedule, with Bontemps receiving opening-night congratulatory wires from several of his friends—Carl and Fania Van Vechten, Langston Hughes, Leah Salisbury, and Pearl Bailey, also a member of the cast. The play's run, however, was a disappointment, for it closed after a month. Shortly thereafter it went on a successful road tour. Bontemps had suggested the following names to producer Edward Gross as possibilities for the leading role, "Della": Lena Horne, Muriel Smith, Nina McKinney, Freddie Washington, Isabel Washington, and Hilda Sims. Lena Horne, scared away by the Freddie-Washington–Walter White controversy, decided she did not want the part. As a result, Ruby Hill got the role.[63]

The play and its all-black cast received mixed reviews, with most critics arguing that though the work was in the same genre as *Porgy and Bess*, it was neither a Porgy nor a Bess. The play's story centers around the passion of Little Augie, a "colored" jockey, for a sinful brown-skinned girl he wins away from bad Biglow Brown, a saloonkeeper. Biglow fights to keep his woman, and in Augie's timid quest for revenge he shoots and kills Biglow, who calls down curses on the jockey as breath leaves his body. Harold Nicholas played Little Augie and his brother Fayard played Barney, a character as diminutive in size as Augie. Rex Ingraham, who had played the Emperor Jones and De Lawd in *Green Pastures*, played Biglow.

The songs and lyrics of Arlen and Mercer were hits, the most successful of which was "Come Rain or Come Shine," a sultry number with a hint of the mournful that so often characterizes the boogie-woogie-blues of the era, strongly reminiscent of "Stormy Weather," a song that had been immortalized a short time earlier by Lena Horne. And the dancing and singing of Pearl Bailey, then a new discovery, drew raves.[64]

When the road show began in May 1946, Arna Alexander Bontemps was nearly a year old, and it dawned on the doting father that he had been so busy with "The Woman" that he had neglected to choose godparents for his namesake, an oversight his Louisiana-Catholic-Creole forebears would not have understood. One of the writer's best friends from the Chicago Renaissance years, Frank Wade, who visited in the Bontemps home and who thought "Arna Junior" was the most wonderful thing he had seen in many years, was named the child's godfather.[65]

But Arna was back to literary business in no time, for there were arrangements to be made with Cullen's widow concerning her inherited share of the play. As a result of these negotiations, a lengthy and amiable correspondence developed between Ida Cullen and Arna Bontemps. She and Alberta Bontemps had formed a friendship from their first meeting, a mutual good will that continued until Mrs. Cullen's death in May 1986. Additionally, contracts came from Paris for both Ida and Arna to sign preliminary to a scheduled production of the play in France.[66] This marked the beginning of an accelerated rate of published reviews and articles that Bontemps would continue for nearly two decades. The first article from this period was "Harlem Renaissance."[67]

The remainder of 1946 and all of 1947–48 were especially busy times at Fisk for the writer. His schedule of speaking engagements was exceptionally heavy with speeches at Memphis's LeMoyne College for Omega Psi Phi and for numerous other organized groups, including school librarians in Tennessee and neighboring states. Amid these events, Arna had to cope with the Handy controversy over the "St. Louis Woman" title, a disagreement that persisted and that would eventually result in Handy's filing a suit against Bontemps and other interested parties.[68] The suit was eventually dropped by Handy.

In 1947 Arna found himself adjusting to a new president. His old friend and mentor Charles S. Johnson, had become Thomas Elsa Jones's successor and Fisk's sixth chief executive. Johnson, a scholar par excellence and a true patron of letters and the arts, had always shown a special interest in Bontemps's career and would become his strongest ally during the span of years 1947–1956. All along, Johnson had shared Bontemps's interest in preserving African-American culture, and as much as he could judiciously carry out, Johnson continued his entrepreneurship of the Harlem writers through his support of Bontemps.

Fisk was at its zenith and so was Bontemps's literary productivity, though critics and anthologists continued during this period to slight him, possibly because they tended to think of him as more of a librarian than a writer. Yet no one could dispute, by this period, that Bontemps's true vocation was writing. Members of his family still remember that when he was not teaching a class or working at the library, he could be found somewhere deeply involved in a book— either one he was reading or a manuscript of his own he was preparing for publication. Alberta Bontemps's only rival in their forty-seven years of marriage was not another woman, she would agree, but his writing.

In December 1947 Arna Wendell Bontemps, along with two other "Dogs," as Greek probates are traditionally called in the black fraternal organizations, was initiated into historic Omega Psi Phi fraternity. John W. Work had been largely responsible for the writer's decision to pledge.[69] Before this pledge period ended, Arna moved his family to new quarters, this time to a different faculty house located at 1611 Meharry Boulevard. The author spent the last days of 1947 preparing *The Story of the Negro* for Alfred Knopf, a book he had completed the bulk of the previous summer with funds from a Carnegie Foundation research grant to Fisk that encouraged faculty research and development.[70] The work was published early in 1948, with a revised edition in 1955. Bontemps had been awarded this grant by a jury of his peers, Fisk's "Committee on the Improvement of Teaching."[71] Research for the book had been carried out in part at W.E.B. Du Bois's New York office where, while residing at Yaddo, the writers' colony near Saratoga Springs, Bontemps commuted each weekday.[72]

The Spring quarter 1949 was a busy time for the writer, for he was preparing to spend a portion of the 1949–50 school year away from his duties as Librarian to take advantage of a study grant from the John Simon Guggenheim Foundation. With the grant he finished research for his forthcoming book, *Chariot in the Sky*. It was around this time that he was elected to P.E.N., an international writers' organization that had fewer than half a dozen African Americans as members.

The period was also filled with a lengthy sequence of speaking engagements and saw an increase in Arna's African-American consciousness through Omega Psi Phi, especially with its national high school essay contest. Before Bontemps took leave, *Phylon* asked him to write a profile of Carl Van Vechten for an upcoming issue of this historic quarterly's treatment of race and culture. Simultaneously he entered into a contract with Carl Murphy of *Afro-American*, a newspaper that allowed him to publish a serial version of *Story of the Negro*.[73]

Despite the demands on his energy reserves during most of the period from 1947 to 1950, Bontemps's health remained good. In fact he had always enjoyed good health, spending only one brief visit in a hospital throughout his life, this during his mature years. But he did have an annoying psychosomatic knee that flared up once in 1946 during rehearsals of *St. Louis Woman*. It was the same knee he had reinjured some fourteen years earlier, during the Harlem period.[74] The theater people tended to get hysterical, and their behavior, coupled with having to make all of the changes the directors requested without Cullen's assistance, nearly proved too much for Bontemps. A couple of times during the rehearsal period he had the good sense to board a plane and return to Nashville for a few days.[75]

Late in 1949 he finished for Roe-Peterson a little supplementary reader in their "Real People" series. Another important literary project was completed that year as well, the poetry collection that he edited jointly with Hughes, entitled *The Poetry of the Negro, 1746–1949, An Anthology*. It was issued by Doubleday. This was, to date, the most auspicious publication of Bontemps's tenure at Fisk. It was considered by critics to be the most comprehensive anthology of African-American poetry yet assembled, even surpassing James Weldon Johnson's 1922 work, *The Book of American Negro Poetry*.

This volume would be reissued in 1963 in an expanded edition titled *American Negro Poetry*, a revision of which was issued posthumously in 1974, the year following Bontemps's death. It also came out in 1972 in a revised version that bore the original title. A few critics said the volume lacked the "unity" and "special charm" found in some of the more selective anthologies. Most, however, praised the collection as a representation of the best poems by and about "the Negro." The book was not long in taking its place alongside other standard collections. Divided into three sections—Negro Poets of the U.S.A., Tributary poems by Non-Negroes, and Poetry of the Caribbean—the anthology included adequate biographical notes and indexes. Its best feature is its documentation of the development of black talent at home and abroad. The anthology is a tribute to the poetic backgrounds of both Hughes and Bontemps, and it highlights Bontemps's resourcefulness as a trained editor-librarian.

The golden years, a period that began with Bontemps's appointment as Chief Librarian at Fisk, continued throughout his tenure in that position. He had indeed found at Fisk the right amount of isolation from the distractions all around him, that measure of isolation the writer needs; and he had also found the security he needed—the support and society of his friends and a good environment for his family. By 1950, conditions for African Americans were beginning to hold some promise of freedom, but freedom had not been attained to any large degree. African Americans were still, during the years from 1950 to 1964, a harassed lot, but Fisk continued to provide a refuge for Arna Bontemps and the other writers on its faculty.

Bontemps's second period at Fisk saw the passing of the monumental Supreme Court decision of 1954; it also included the unrest of a decade later when African Americans realized that ten years after this decision had legally outlawed segregation and discrimination, it had not produced in reality many favorable changes for the black masses, nor for the members of the "Talented Tenth," to whose ranks Bontemps belonged. Arna relied upon the shelter of the Fisk setting during these middle years even more than he had in the past.

These years were the most productive of the poet's life, for he was achieving more of the kind of balance between his teaching and writing careers he had always sought. His involvement in campus affairs increased as he assumed the directorship of the Exchange Student Program, and as his name became known to virtually every college and high school librarian in the country. And during these years, elementary school librarians were equally well-acquainted with him because of his excellent contributions to the field of children's literature.[76] While continuing to write and to encourage other creative artists, Arna lectured to groups of writers, teachers, librarians, and students throughout the country. And toward the latter part of this period, critics began to recognize the vastness of his contribution to arts and letters. It was during this period, too, that he began to reap some financial rewards from his literary works, for several of his books were reissued and sold well.

Though Arna experienced few problems during his Fisk tenure, not everything at the "Harvard of the South" was to his liking. Fisk never had enough money to support the kind of ambitious program it was running and had run traditionally. Arna met with one frustration after another during his years of building Fisk's "Negro Collection," a research center which, even at the end of his career, he considered his finest accomplishment. One of the situations that caused his heart to carry its "winter and its gall" was the break with Carl Van Vechten. Arna regretted the loss of this friendship, which had its roots in the Harlem Renaissance, not only because Van Vechten along with Hughes was among the few remaining Harlem artists with whom he had kept close contact—Zora Hurston was alive for most of this period but living in relative isolation. Most of all Arna regretted "Carlo's" betrayal, for he had believed that he could trust him. The rift occurred when Van Vechten ran afoul of Arna's stubborn streak. By 1954 Arna had taken about as much of Van Vechten's impulsive behavior as he could. At least twice during their lengthy correspondence—they wrote to each other almost daily from 1939 to 1954—Bontemps had found it necessary to ask him to stop his daily flow of letters and his coy demands for daily responses. These requests the author of *Nigger Heaven* ignored and had become miffed over them on more than one occasion.

Van Vechten lost all patience when he found out Bontemps had been entertained by mutual friends in New York who had not invited him.[77] He then became upset over Arna's manner of handling aspects of the gift to Fisk, mainly the housing and labeling of the items in the Gershwin Collection. Van Vechten then committed the impardonable offense of writing a letter of reprimand, not to Arna, but to the President of Fisk University, Bontemps's friend Charles S. Johnson.[78] For this betrayal Arna never forgave "Carlo."

Though Arna was inclined to avoid discussing the matter, he was confronted by questions about the break again and again during the remainder of his life, as recorded interviews and portions of his correspondence reveal, for nearly every librarian in the country had heard at least one version of this quarrel. And even after Arna went to Yale at the end of the 1960s to teach in the Afro-American Studies Department and to serve as adviser to the Danforth Fellows, and where he was named Curator of the James Weldon Johnson Collection, questions arose about the Van Vechten–Bontemps estrangement, for Van Vechten had founded the Johnson Collection.

Most of the nation's librarians and archivists could appreciate the tragedy of this failed friendship because of the accompanying loss of opportunity for Fisk University and for scholarship in general. That friendship had been productive for the Fisk Library and for the Yale Collection, and their colleagues had hoped for more of the same from the meeting of these two fine minds. Typical of the feeling among librarians and scholars is a recent assessment given me by Donald Gallup, former Curator of the Collection of American Literature at Yale's Beinecke Library. Gallup wrote how sorry he was that Arna's relationship with "Carlo" did not continue cordially to the end. Unsure of the cause of the difficulty between them, Gallup gathered it had arisen out of what Van Vechten considered "unsatisfactory handling" of the books he had donated during Bontemps's librarianship for the Gershwin and Stettheimer Collections.[79]

Gallup got to know the professional side of Bontemps's personality fairly well during the latter's stay at Yale, but the subject never came up in their conversations. Not only did this whole misunderstanding with Van Vechten result in Fisk's eventual loss of the Jean Toomer papers, but it remained a painful subject with Arna, who had throughout his life tried to avoid conflict with his friends and who had always exhibited remarkable tolerance for the quirks and idiosyncrasies of others. He never failed to regret the loss of a relationship, but was also supersensitive about some subjects and possessed a strong sense of correctness and personal dignity.

But this estrangement was not Arna's biggest problem during the Fisk years. His inadequate salary and poorly maintained campus residence continued to tax the writer throughout this period. Isaiah Creswell, husband of his old friend Pearl Creswell of the Fisk Museum, still had charge of buildings and grounds as he had when Bontemps first joined the faculty. With his limited budget, Creswell did his best to keep the faculty residences—all old houses—repaired, but Bontemps's correspondence reveals that repairs and maintenance were rarely completed and were often patchy and accompanied by delay.[80] But Arna had learned it was far easier to get one's house repaired than to get a raise in salary at Fisk. Despite the low rents, the salary Bontemps received during his entire tenure was never enough to supply all the needs and wants of eight persons. It is no wonder the poet's widow still remembers that the only trouble she and her husband had during forty-seven years together stemmed from a lack of funds.[81]

At the beginning of spring quarter 1950 Bontemps, recalling the wisdom of the old proverb—"he that asketh faintly beggeth denial"—sent a memo to Charles S. Johnson concerning his 1950–51 salary. By this phase of his career, his list of publications was impressive and most of his writings had been well-received; yet his salary had never reflected his hard work, nor his contributions to Fisk and to humane letters. A portion of the memo reads: "This is to ask if you will consider . . . the possibility of increasing mine [salary]. It occurs to me that there might be grounds for . . . increase. . . . My salary has not yet reached . . . the expected maximum. . . . There have been new achievements and recognitions since my salary was last increased."[82] Correspondence from the same period indicates he was having trouble retaining a competent library staff for the same reasons he himself was complaining—long hours, a heavy workload, and low pay. He lost, that year, three of his best cataloguers: one to Houston College for Negroes (now Texas Southern University) and another to Wilberforce, at much higher salaries; and another who quit.

Furthermore, his efforts to attract personnel from such places as the Schomburg Collection or the Chicago Public Library nearly always fell through because of Fisk's low salary offers. After recommending that Johnson add a minimum of two hundred dollars per year plus a word of encouragement to the salaries of two of his top cataloguers, Bontemps attached a reminder that cataloguers came at a premium.[83] He himself did receive a slight raise in salary during the 1951–52 term, bringing his yearly pay to a miserly $4,750 to be issued in twelve equal monthly installments. With the amount of responsibility heaped onto his shoulders, this was low pay indeed.

Spring 1950 was a busier time than usual for the scholar-poet, for his list of commissions and appointments appears staggering. Public schools all over the South wanted him as their commencement speaker, and *Phylon* again commissioned him to write an article, this time on literary landmarks and contours of "the Negro" in American literature immediately after the Harlem Renaissance, during the late 1930s and all of the 1940s. The symposium was to be published in the September issue, a special number on the theme "The Negro in Our Literature: The Current Scene." The assignment provided Bontemps all the leeway he needed, for he was given the impossibly broad subject: "the poetry of the last three decades," or "poetry of the 'Old Guard,' " as *Phylon*'s editor, Mozell Hill, described the topic.[84] Bontemps was one of an impressive array of scholars who wrote articles for this issue, such outstanding personalities as Richard Wright, Frank Yerby, Willard Motley, Sterling Brown, J. Saunders Redding, Horace Cayton, and Alain Locke. The article did come out but not as early as originally planned.[85]

Also during the spring of 1950 Bontemps submitted a brief but important article to *Negro Digest* for its June issue under the title "Famous W.P.A. Authors."[86] But the most exciting development of this first phase of the fifties was a promise from Helen M. Chesnutt, daughter of African-American novelist Charles Waddell Chesnutt, that she would donate to Fisk her father's papers, a large collection of letters, publications, scrapbooks, original manuscripts, and other artifacts, in exchange for Bontemps's assistance in placing one of her father's unpublished books with a publishing house. She had already sent a few items to the James Weldon Johnson Collection at Yale but still had the bulk of the materials in her possession.[87] Ostensibly, negotiations worked out to her satisfaction, for Fisk currently owns the Chesnutt Collection. It was primarily through Bontemps's diplomacy and tact, as his correspondence at Fisk and Syracuse reveal, that Miss Chesnutt decided to follow through on her commitment.

Arna spent most of the summer working on two major projects and a minor one. Omega Psi Phi had asked him to write a brief review of Langston Hughes's newest book, *Simple Speaks His Mind*, for the September issue of *The Oracle*. This was no large project but seemed an added burden to that of the two books he had promised to deliver for two separate publishing houses. The first was a book for children and juveniles, *Sam Patch, the High Wide and Handsome Jumper*, written jointly with Conroy, which had been promised to Houghton Mifflin; and the other was a longer work he was writing for adolescents and adults titled *Chariot in the Sky: A Story of the Fisk Jubilee Singers*, a manuscript that had been promised to Winston of Philadelphia. Both manuscripts were published early in 1951. In the midst of this schedule, Lillian Bragdon of Alladin

Books sent him a wire inviting him to be her guest at the annual Newbery Awards Dinner at Cleveland, an invitation he accepted graciously.[88]

The 1951–52 school year brought an invitation from an unexpected source— Oakwood College. Eva B. Dykes of the Department of English asked him to present a twenty-minute speech during the vesper service in October. The department was celebrating ''Good Communication Week'' and could pay his travel expenses but could offer no honorarium. Eager to see his old friends, he agreed to go and Dykes was delighted. They reminded him that he and his entire family would be expected to ''spend the Sabbath'' with them.[89] Meanwhile, Arna kept busier than usual presenting *Sad-Faced Boy* and *Slappy Hooper* to schoolchildren. This busy period was punctuated by a letter from Herb Nipson of *Ebony* saying he was outlining a story on the Seventh-day Adventists and needed help. With his memory refreshed by the trip to Oakwood, Arna wrote the following lucid explanation of the religious beliefs of the sect, their feelings toward the Old and New Testaments, and why they, like the Orthodox Jews, observe Saturday as the Sabbath.

SDA's are frankly fundamentalists. . . . They take the whole Bible as their creed, including the Old Testament. Miracles, creation, verbal inspiration, virgin birth—everything. If you ask about the ceremonies of the tabernacle . . . sacrifices of sheep and goats . . . they explain that all these pointed to Christ, the Lamb of God, and his life on earth. . . . The rest of the Old Testament holds, including the laws relating to clean and unclean meats. Naturally Saturday, the 7th day of the week, as identified by the 4th commandment, is their day of rest and worship. . . . This is the cornerstone of their doctrine.

The other relates to prophecy. They believe in prophecy in the New-Testament sense. They show how prophecies of the Old Testament were fulfilled in the New, and they believe that those of the New have been or will yet be fulfilled in the earth, including the Second Coming of Christ through the sky on a cloud of angels. This phase of their teaching goes back to William Miller who preached that Christ would return in 1844. (William Still of Underground Railroad fame became interested at one time. Fred Douglass, who lectured in towns where the movement was strongest, evidently didn't.) SDA's refer to that movement and the mistake about the date as ''the Great Disappointment.''

Boiled down then, the SDA hope is that Christ will literally return to the earth in ''this generation'' to redeem the godly. The rest is preparation for that event. . . . Hence their extensive health program, their system of schools, their many publishing houses and books defining the good life.[90]

Bontemps's explanation also includes commentary on the SDA system of education, the tone of which is complimentary to Adventists and a tribute as well to his own capacity for objectivity. The letter reveals, through the repeated use of ''they'' and ''them,'' that Arna no longer considered himself a member of this sect. He went on to explain:

That is one side of the coin. If you earmark Adventists as just another small fundamentalist sect . . . you fail to account for the type of people they have been able to attract and to hold . . . Richard Wright and Willard Townsend were both touched by their influence at impressionable moments in their lives . . . many lawyers, doctors, teachers . . . even some jazzmen: Tiny Parham and Arthur Whetsol (Duke's first trumpet player). Not to mention Hank Johnson . . . and William Patterson. . . . None of these remained in the Adventist fold, but all were sheltered in it at one time.[91]

In December 1950 Arna joined the lecturing staff on race relations of the American Friends Service, but managed as usual to spend Christmas with Alberta and his children. He wrote as usual and the others entertained themselves as best they could. Joan, his eldest, recalls that he was a "very good father," managing to spend a great deal of time with his children, especially in activities related to their education, teaching them to read and taking them to libraries and on vacations. She said in an interview: "We had to keep very quiet so that he could write. Since he was working full time, and his weekends and holidays were spent writing, we didn't have a lot of those kinds of times together."[92] And Christmas 1950 was not much different from all the other Christmases for the writer who, in addition to working on some of his newest writing projects of which he always had an abundance, spent the vacation proofing galley sheets for *Chariot in the Sky* and *Sam Patch*.

The lecture season of 1951 was heavier than usual. Occurring as customary during "spring break," it had begun with several stops in Texas, one of his few visits to the "Lone Star State." First on his Texas itinerary was a two-day program at Houston's Texas Southern University, sponsored by the Department of English during Ollington Smith's tenure as Chair. Smith recalls that he had met Arna Bontemps through their mutual friend Langston Hughes during the waning years of the Harlem Renaissance, when Smith, a recent Fisk graduate, was pursuing graduate studies at Columbia. He recalls that Bontemps's visit marked the first of Texas Southern's lyceum series. While in Houston, he stayed at the Smith home on O'Neill Street, for in those days the better hotels did not accept persons of color. Smith also recalls that Arna wanted to "see" the campus of Rice University and that he drove the poet-novelist through at night, for that campus was also off-limits to "coloreds."[93] Leaving the Houston school, Bontemps went on to Wiley College at Marshall at the request of the poet and English teacher M. B. Tolson, and then to Dallas where he was a lecturer and banquet speaker for a convention hosted by a federated women's group.[94] The tour culminated with a trip to Milwaukee, Wisconsin.

Arna's restless energy kept him going, kept him writing. He was never happy unless he had a book in progress. The late winter of 1951 found him working on three books: two juvenile novels and a biography. The biography was an ambitious work he had conceived as an interrelated interpretation of Frederick Douglass, Booker T. Washington, and W.E.B. Du Bois, a plan he later abandoned in favor of separate volumes on the three personalities.[95] Simultaneously, a new biographical dictionary titled *American Novelists of Today* included among its roster of leading writers two Nashvillians, Arna Bontemps and Alfred Leland

Crabb. This was a singular honor because the book was edited by Harry R. Warfel, an important name in American literary criticism.[96]

Chariot in the Sky began to attract a great deal of attention, and newspapers across the country in late April and early May gave it due recognition. Reviews in magazines and scholarly journals came later but were superficial, though not hostile. One critic dismissed it in one line as a book for boys and girls.[97] This book represented the fulfillment of one of Arna's long-held dreams. It was a story he had wanted to write since joining the Fisk faculty in 1943, for he had been fascinated with the singers who gave to the world Negro spirituals and to the South its foremost liberal arts college for African Americans. The original Jubilee Singers, even today, are a living presence on Fisk's campus. On entering the Fisk Memorial Chapel, where funeral services for John Work, Arna Bontemps, and many other faculty members have been held through the years, one beholds an impressive life-sized portrait of the Singers painted by Edmund Havell, Jr. (Queen Victoria's favorite court painter) when the group was touring the British Isles in 1871.

The painting recreates those tumultuous days just after the Civil War when Fisk held classes in abandoned Army barracks and the idea of a fundraising tour by the Singers was still a dream. *Chariot's* most appealing character is Caleb Williams, the protagonist through whom Bontemps tells the Singers' story. It offers excellent insight into African Americans' struggle during and immediately after slavery. Though its style appeals to young readers, it is also useful for adults, especially in courses on slavery, the Civil War, and Reconstruction. The May–June issue of the *Chicago Schools Journal* carried a brief biographical sketch of the author in a special edition titled *Chicagoland: Authors and Illustrators of Children's Literature.*[98]

May 1951 included a visit from Ida Cullen to the Bontemps home on Meharry Boulevard. By this time Mrs. Cullen, remarried, had opened a gift shop in Harlem called "Afro-Arts Bazaar." Hers was a timely visit, for Edward Gross was still trying to get *St. Louis Woman* staged again.[99] Cullen and Bontemps compared notes.

Mary L. Morse of the Association for Childhood Education International had asked Arna to write a children's story with a typical regional backdrop, a work that she would include in the association's volume of regional American stories.[100] In early July Arna was present at the Newbery–Caldecott Award Dinner in New York when Elizabeth Yates received the Newbery Medal for "Amos Fortune, Free Man," and Katherine Milhouse received the Caldecott Medal for "The Egg Tree."[101]

In the fall, Fisk published its periodic report on the creative activities, research, and publications of its faculty. The last report had come during Bontemps's first period at the Nashville College. His list of publications was as lengthy as those of any of the faculty whose names were listed, and longer than most, but the writer-critic was not content to rest upon the laurels of this difficult-to-emulate list of publications. He continued his schedule of writing, always with more projects outlined than he had time to finish. But monetary awards remained low while workloads remained high, a problem that plagued all of the African-American writers who, like Bontemps, had to hold down professorships while trying to remain active as writers—people such as Sterling Brown, Robert Hayden, John Mattheus, Margaret Walker (Alexander), Melvin B. Tolson, and Arthenia Bates Millican.

Bontemps wrote to Tolson at Wiley to keep in touch with his old friend, and had received a reply by the middle of September. This portion of Tolson's letter summarizes some of Bontemps's own problems and feelings on literature and the African-American writer:

This has been a long hard road to travel, but I'm glad that years ago I saw the necessity of traveling it. I wish some of us who see the light could get together and bring pressure to bear on the heads of our leading Race institutions to establish at least one chair in each institution for those interested in creative work—especially literature. We are away [sic] behind in this. And the race suffers. In my talk this summer with Karl Shapiro, he was shocked to learn that I was carrying the regular load of a routine professor. . . . Negro life offers the only Virgin field left for exploitation. If we fail to seize the opportunity, others will! Since the complexity and irony of modern life are the principal themes of literature today, where can one find a field greater in scope and depth than among us?[102]

Bontemps, like Tolson, continued to exploit the field that lay before him and welcomed even a limited opportunity to write.

With the opening of the 1951–52 term, the writer's third child, Poppy, had entered Bennett College and he was elated about her achievement. His book earnings were beginning to increase, making it easier for him to pay tuition. In a letter to "Lang" he wrote: "Yes, the Doubleday check arrived finally and surprised me by being twice as big as I had expected. After some delay I also received my book club money which pleased me by being enough to cover Poppy's expenses for her first year at Bennett."[103] This letter also contained an allusion to a joint lecture tour the two friends were planning, one of many they planned and executed jointly between 1931 and 1967, the year of Hughes's death.

More frequently now Bontemps was receiving requests from book companies and individual authors to include his poems and short stories in anthologies. Among the poems, "Southern Mansion" and "A Black Man Talks of Reaping" remained favorites, with "A Summer Tragedy" leading the short stories. Colleges across the country became increasingly interested in securing him as a lecturer. He received from Jackson, Mississippi, a telegram from his friend and colleague Margaret Walker Alexander with news that she and other faculty members there were planning a huge literary festival to celebrate the college's seventy-fifth anniversary in October 1952. The telegram asked Bontemps to name his fee if he could accept.[104] He said yes to his friend's request and also spoke that fall at Savannah State College during an observance of National Book Week, while turning down offers to travel larger distances from Nashville.

News also came of the publication of Van Vechten's autobiography, *Sacred and Profane Memories*. Bontemps, to his utter surprise, received a copy inscribed in Van Vechten's own hand, a book he was happy to receive and which he devoured with much relish, especially the parts pertaining to the Harlem Renaissance, a period that remained his favorite literary topic, as it did with Ida Cullen, Louise Thompson, Aaron Douglas, and others who had "been there."

The year 1952 was relatively quiet for the writer where publishing books was involved, but in another respect it was one of the most triumphant of his twenty-one years as Fisk's Head Librarian, for Helen Chesnutt sent her father's papers to the Fisk library. And his friend, Fisk's President Charles S. Johnson, would be granted the honorary degree of Doctor of Laws by the University of Glasgow, and was asked by the Fulbright Board of Foreign Scholarships to be their representative at the United Kingdom Institute on American Studies at Cambridge University, scheduled on a date that would coincide with the administrator's stay in Scotland. Bontemps could appreciate the value these contacts would have for Fisk's international outlook and relations.[105]

Where his private life was concerned, the writer was busy helping Alberta mail invitations to an observance of their twenty-fifty wedding anniversary. They held the reception prior to their August 26 wedding date, for Arna had already made plans to take Alberta to Wildwood, New Jersey, to a summer resort they had visited previously and which remained their favorite vacation spot. They stayed there for two weeks of August in the Bonnelli house on West Roberts Avenue, the perfect place for him to write. Just prior to going to Wildwood, he had served as a lecturer in contemporary literature at Nashville's Peabody College, a special feature the college had added for summer term 1952. John Mason Brown opened the forum in June with a lecture titled "The Writer and His World in 1952." Others on the lecture schedule included Edward Weeks and A. L. Crabb. Arna Bontemps and Louise Cowan closed out the series in late July— Bontemps's talk was on Ellison's *Invisible Man*—after which he and Alberta left for the New Jersey resort.[106]

Joan Bontemps, the writer's first child, had finished college and had earned a graduate degree in library science by summer 1952 and her father, soon afterward, hired her as a cataloguer for Fisk's library. She had agreed to work for her alma mater at a salary less competitive than she could have earned at one of the state colleges, whose coffers were full. Charles S. Johnson had no objection to her being taken on, and he acknowledged that she was not only a hard worker but an intelligent one as well. She was to remain in this job until a short time after her father retired from the Librarian's post in 1964. It seemed that the children of Bontemps's Fisk colleagues, those with whom he had worked since the early forties, were finishing or entering college, or were at some point between.

But grief came again to the poet's heart. Sarah Pembrooke, his maternal grandmother, whom he loved and admired as much as he had his own mother, died at her home in Los Angeles County on September 14, 1952, a little less than two months past her one hundredth birthday, and one day after Arna's fiftieth. She had resided in California for all of forty-two years and died in her own home in Willowbrook, in the southern portion of the county. With her when she died was a relative, Rosetta Pembrooke. Arna and Alberta were notified at once and were present at the funeral, held around the time Fisk's fall term commenced. Sarah Pembrooke was buried near her daughter and the writer's mother, Maria Pembrooke Bontemps, in Los Angeles' Evergreen Cemetery.[107]

Amid these developments *St. Louis Woman* was making its mark, despite the many setbacks it had endured. Leah Salisbury had entered negotiations with Metro-Goldwyn-Mayer, which eventually purchased the movie rights to the play. Prior to this, there had been many false indications of its sale to the movies, but the current negotiations seemed fairly assured to Salisbury. She had succeeded in forcing the hand of Mercer and Arlen, who had thrown a monkey wrench into earlier negotiations on the grounds that Metro planned to use a white cast and wanted the right to acquire new tunes and lyrics. Bontemps (and Cullen, too, while he was still alive) had not objected to a white cast, hence Bontemps felt it was unfair of the two musicians to attempt to halt the sale of the movie on those grounds. The movie rights were to be sold for $75,000, a healthy sum in 1952. The original plan by a Mr. Freed of Metro was to use Frank Sinatra and Ava Gardner as stars of the musical. Bontemps thought this inappropriate, but both he and Ida Cullen, along with Salisbury, took the attitude: let them have the credit as long as we get the money.[108]

But the sale of the play also brought new woes, most associated with the problem of W. C. Handy's claim to the title. Handy, when *St. Louis Woman* was running on Broadway, had muddied the waters of the play's success by making a claim on it on the basis that it was an alleged infringement on his song, "St. Louis Blues." He also notified producers at the various studios of his claim, and now in 1952, just as Bontemps and his co-author's widow were ready to sell, Metro expressed some degree of apprehension, for it did not want to purchase a suit in the bargain. But since Handy eventually dropped the suit he brought against the authors and the play's producers, Metro lost their fear and agreed on a price, and Arna was beside himself with glee. As soon as this good news came he wrote to Ida Cullen: "Isn't the news wonderful! And it comes at a moment when I'm packing my bags for New York. On Monday the 6th I'm scheduled to appear at the opening of the *New York Times* annual book exhibit, Reading for Fun. I'll visit and speak to a few schools . . . but there will be time for the new St. Louis Woman business."[109]

Bontemps and Cullen-Cooper considered one aspect of the sale demeaning, however, and with good reason. Metro demanded statements of them that the two authors of the play had not been involved with McCarthy or any other subversive element. The check from Metro would not be released until such written assurances were in hand. Both authors complied. The following is the statement Cullen's widow wrote in accordance with the request: "This is to advise that my late husband, Countée Cullen, . . . was not a member of any subversive group or organization.''[110] Bontemps's statement is not available.

The October 1952 date of the literary festival at Jackson State in which Bontemps had agreed a year earlier to participate had arrived. Others taking part in the proceedings included Langston Hughes, Owen Dodson, Sterling Brown, Gwendolyn Brooks, Moe Asch of Folkways Records, and several others, including Margaret Walker Alexander, Claude Barnett (Associated Negro Press), and Era Bell Thompson (*Ebony*).[111] The festival ended on the eve of a November exhibit at the Sorbonne commemorating the centennial of Harriet Beecher Stowe's *Uncle Tom's Cabin*. Bontemps was invited to attend but had been away from his work more than usual in recent weeks and was forced to decline this and several other invitations. He did, however, send two of his books to the Paris exhibit: *Story of the Negro* (1949) and *Chariot in the Sky* (1951). He also enclosed a souvenir program of *St. Louis Woman* from its Broadway production in 1946.[112]

When he left Fisk to attend the speaking engagement at Jackson State, the author had been hard at work on a biographical narrative, *Booker T. Washington*, that Houghton Mifflin had hired him to write. Actually this was part of the ambitious project he had begun two years earlier with the help of a Guggenheim, that of treating Washington with two other personages. He was now on the home stretch of that project. Thirty-seven years after Washington's death, Arna was convinced that the right kind of biography on him would sell, for it had been fifty-two years since Washington had published *Up from Slavery* and Doubleday was still carrying it in display ads.[113]

Bontemps was elected to a four-year term (1953–57) on the governing council of the American Library Association, after he and his library staff had finished preparing Chesnutt's papers for public use. Housed in the Negro Collection Room of the Fisk Library, Chesnutt's mementos, correspondence, and original manuscripts had at last been processed. Bontemps said to a news reporter, "Charles Waddell Chesnutt occupies a unique place in American literature, and the collection of his letters and unpublished manuscripts which his daughter has given . . . promises good hunting for literary scholars. Chesnutt was the first Negro American writer to receive serious attention for his stories and novels.''[114] Fisk had nearly lost out in its bid for the Chesnutt papers, and probably would not have obtained them had the Chief Librarian not had the good sense to dispatch Leslie Collins to the Cleveland, Ohio, home of Chesnutt where his daughter still lived. Collins wrote to Bontemps:

I was dinner guest of Miss Chesnutt, her sister and brother-in-law. I spent some five hours there, wrapping, typing, listing, and attempting to get my genteel, sentimental hostess to tear herself away from each and every book. . . . I shall truly be L. M. Collins, M.D., officiating at the Chesnutt bedside to cut the umbilical cord. Miss C. said . . . she felt that had I not appeared on the scene she would not have given up the books and materials. (Incidentally, Howard tried to get them at one time. Van Vechten is still trying to get them for Yale. Van Vechten lost out by being himself: superior. Miss C. resented his talking down to her.) . . . She has made a personal ordeal of the whole business . . . saying now that I should make the trip down to Fisk with her.[115]

Just after the unveiling of the Chesnutt Collection, Arna mailed the manuscript of another Signature book he had been commissioned to write, after Lillian Bradgon invited him to come to New York to discuss doing a similar series of readers for Alladin Books' "Heritage Series." But he found himself at the beginning of 1953 having to revise his writing schedule because publishers were asking for specific revisions on more than one of his recently submitted manuscripts. He did commit himself to write for Alladin a treatment of the Jeans Foundation and the teachers it sent out, if the publishers would agree to a 1954 deadline. This topic was of special interest because he was then working on the Washington manuscript, and Washington had a good bit to do with the Jeans Foundation.[116]

And he agreed again to work in the summer program at Peabody, whose Department of English this year was offering an unusual course in contemporary literature. Encouraged by the experiments of 1951–52, they had decided to invite a number of the nation's outstanding poets, novelists, and critics to visit William J. Griffin's "Survey of Contemporary Literature." Besides Bontemps the list of writer-participants included John Mason Brown, Marie Campbell, John Ciardi, Louise Cowan, and A. L. Crabb.

April 1953 brought contract negotiation time to Fisk; and Bontemps, who had not received a raise in at least two years, was offered a contract for the 1953–54 school year of $5,000, a mere $300 above his current salary. He refused to sign this contract offer and Charles S. Johnson agreed his salary needed some "adjustment," inviting him to return the old contract in exchange for a new one.[117] He ended up getting $200 above the original offer. Aware that Arna had been patient about a raise and that he merited an upward adjustment in salary, Johnson wrote him a memo expressing his pleasure at the recognition he had brought to Fisk through his involvement at Peabody.[118]

Returning to postponed writing projects, the writer sent in June 1953 a letter to the *New York Times Book Review* on James Baldwin, whose first novel, *Go Tell It on the Mountain*, had been released earlier in the year and who had himself published an article in the *Times* only a short while before. Bontemps wrote:

The phenomenon of James Baldwin delights and fascinates me. The implication of most of the letters in response to his recent article is that in him the Negro writer appears to have come of age. The fact that he wrote about literature and . . . in a . . . general way made an impression. A generation ago, Negro writers did not do that. I have no quarrel, but I would like to point out that this looks more like the growing up of the Negro writer's audience, his editors and his publishers. Remember when *Esquire* circularized its readers to ask if they would object to the publication of a short story in that magazine by a Negro writer? Well, even earlier than that, in the days of the "Harlem Renaissance," there was lively talk about what a Negro could properly write about for American readers. . . . There were writers then (Jean Toomer, Wallace Thurman, Jessie Fauset) and there have been others since whose insights on literature might have been worth something."[119]

In midsummer, Ida Cullen-Cooper wrote to Arna to update him on the progress of his and her late husband's "Woman." She began: "here's the most recent news regarding 'St Louis Woman.' I did not know whether you had seen it. . . . Isn't this wonderful—and with such a cast it should be a terrific hit."[120] Arna was elated but busy dealing with Moe Asch of Folkways Records, who had offered to make a recording of a selection of the poets in his and Langston's 1949 anthology of Negro poetry. Both authors signed the contract while Arna was planning as usual to make the annual meeting of the A.L.A. held in New York in mid-August. He agreed to record his own poems while there, and he stayed at the Algonquin Hotel, which had replaced the Theresa as his favorite stopping place in the city. Prior to the convention, though, he and Alberta would spend the customary two weeks at Wildwood.

Spring 1954 saw Bontemps once again concerned with Fisk's annual literary festival. Though he would not accept the chairmanship of the committee, his colleagues on the committee always left it up to him to contact the writers and other artists who visited the campus in various capacities. One of the first persons he invited for the upcoming term was Gwendolyn Brooks-Blakeley. The previous winter's lecture tour had taken him back to Chicago for a brief stay; and he had brought Alberta with him so that she could see some of their old friends, Brooks included, most of whom she had not seen since their move from Chicago to Nashville in 1943. The Chicago circle of poets had entertained the pair while they were there. But Miss Brooks could not, Arna regretted, because of her full schedule, fit Fisk into her itinerary. She did write a cordial reply that got to the heart of Bontemps's personality. She described him as a grand person, "absolutely real," and assured him that everybody in Chicago was still talking about the "quiet charm" of Mrs. Bontemps.[121]

He did not get around to writing for Aladdin Books as planned in 1954, partially because of his impossible schedule, and partially because Aladdin's offer was not persuasive, especially since Signature had recently paid him a $1,000 advance against a 7 percent royalty based on retail price. The best Aladdin could do was a $500 advance and a 6 percent royalty. At last he was becoming able to select the companies he wrote for, realizing he had been exploited long enough by booksellers, publishers, and literary agents. He had more books outlined than he would ever get around to writing, and because of the limited amount of time he could spend on literary projects, he realized he had to make what little time he did have count.

Early in that year he finished another book for children and adolescents, *The Story of George Washington Carver*, published by Grosset and Dunlap. Because he received another Guggenheim for creative writing during the fall of 1954, Arna was able to secure the respite from teaching that would regenerate his depleted creative energies. The result was two major projects published early the next year: a revised second edition of *Story of the Negro* (Knopf), and a new book for juveniles, *Lonesome Boy* (Houghton Mifflin).

In July 1954, during the summer session at Fisk and just prior to the period when the second Guggenheim Fellowship was to begin, Arna and Alberta moved back to their first Fisk residence, the stately house on the campus at 919 Eighteenth Avenue. It was closer to the library and the right size, now that at least half of the six Bontemps children had either left the nest or were on the verge of doing so.[122] Simultaneously, Arna was doing another series of lectures at George Peabody College, this time on the Negro poets. He had already turned down more than one offer of a permanent job at Peabody, situated across town from Fisk.[123]

The writer was pleased with what he had achieved in *Lonesome Boy*. His favorite subject for prose fiction had produced still another work. *Lonesome Boy* is best described as a profound juvenile novel, for its author admitted that it was a bit too deep for children.[124] This book had one of the most interesting histories of any of his works. On the first printing it sold more than twenty thousand copies, even though reviews were mixed, for the book fell into the hands of a few overly zealous children's librarians who, as the author himself said, "couldn't dig it."[125] Probably the reason for its poor reception is that when he first wrote the book it was not a children's story. The Houghton staff showed it to the children's editors who wanted to publish it, but they, too, hemmed and hawed for a long time.

Written originally as a short story for adult readers, it is based on an episode the author during his boyhood heard a preacher tell in church. It was a narrative about a young man who liked jazz. He awoke one morning to find himself up high in an apple tree and announced he had been celebrating the devil's ball. Bontemps's imagination took over from there. The lesson is that this "lonesome boy" is almost destroyed by people. He starts running after jazz and jazz people and cannot stop. Actually, the book is about Bontemps's own conception of "waltziness": a person hearing a faraway music within himself is so pleased with it, so engrossed in seeking self-satisfaction, that the end result is negative. It is in this fictional statement that we see the Bontempsian philosophy of life at its purest. Bontemps had seen this kind of hedonistic self-gratification almost destroy his friend Langston Hughes, and others of the Harlem group had succumbed to this kind of insularity: Wallace Thurman, Jean Toomer, and to some extent, Zora Neale Hurston, and some of the non-black writers who were destroyed the same way—F. Scott Fitzgerald, and Ernest Hemingway.

Bontemps had always felt strongly that it was bad for a person to be alone, isolated within his own heart; caught up entirely with his own mental and artistic pursuits, shutting out all the rest of experience. He believed, in the deepest sense, that to violate oneself is wrong. He was convinced that the literary artist, like the average person, should get out and do something else, anything else, besides write. It is this philosophy, no doubt, that made Arna Wendell Bontemps unique among the circle of Harlem writers. It also explains the high value he placed on family and on human relationships. This attitude is only one result of the deep, inner calm that characterized his spiritual condition and that always manifested itself in his dealings with others.

Arna wrote *Lonesome Boy* in just one day, on a Sunday—a day of the week he almost always devoted to writing. He commented near the end of his life that it was the kind of story that writes itself.[126] Not many of the Harlem group, possibly none of the others except Hughes, could have written this kind of story based on personal observation of a particular kind of human experience. Arna never lost the common touch and he had, more than any of the writers of his generation, an ability to appreciate the worth and beauty of all kinds of human experience. He frequently visited primitive black churches during his youth, and he possessed the ability to become thoroughly involved in the types of expression he found in their worship services. He had on more than one occasion been literally transported by the shouting, the testimonies, the "talking in tongues."[127] And he had learned, during the Harlem years, that he could be equally comfortable at church, or at Alelia Walker's Dark Tower, or at a "house-rent" party, or a game of baseball.

Another highlight of his career came with the 1955 visit to Southern University in Baton Rouge. The occasion was Negro History Week, and the poet found himself once again in his home state. News stories of the event were numerous throughout the region and one headline read, "Famous Novelist on Negro History."[128] Lionel H. Newsome, then Professor of Sociology and who would go on to become General President of Alpha Phi Alpha and President of at least three universities—Johnson C. Smith, Central State, and Barber Scotia—had been instrumental in bringing Bontemps to Southern.[129] While he was there the historian in Bontemps came forward as it often did. He said he could not see how "any black person" could face life without knowing "Negro History." He went on to say that it is a history that dates back farther than the Middle Ages, at a time when Timbuctoo, in the heart of a jungle, had universities and libraries.

He developed his speech around his perception of three excuses for suppressing "the Negro" that have been given historically in this country by those who did not wish him well: "the Negro" has no soul; "the Negro" cannot be educated; nothing can be done about "the Negro's plight."[130] At one of the sessions he gave excerpts from the book he was still preparing on the lives of three great Americans: Frederick Douglass, whom he called "Leader as Hero"; Booker T. Washington, "Leader as Negotiator"; and W.E.B. Du Bois, "Leader as Prophet and Seer."[131] This 1955 visit to Southern University came at a time when Bontemps saw himself recognized by persons all over America as an authority on race problems.

The 1955–56 school year found the writer-librarian locked in at the $5,200 salary he had received for the previous year's work. But there was a promise of a raise during the next year, which he did receive: for 1956–57 his salary was $6,000. Meanwhile he continued his speechmaking activities throughout the United States. But in April 1955 he found it necessary to confine his lecturing to places near Nashville. The Tennessee Library Association that year held its convention at Chattanooga, and Arna gave the keynote address at the banquet. His speech, an adaptation of the one he had given earlier at Southern University, was titled "Three Visitors to Tennessee."

At Fisk's December 1955 Commencement Convocation it became the writer's task to introduce the speaker, noted South African novelist Peter Abrahams, of *Tell Freedom* and *Mine Boy* fame. The text of Bontemps's introduction is an example of his clear, economic, prose style, as well as an indication of his insights into the contemporary literary scene:

We are honored today by the presence of a major literary figure. . . . But I would not want to give him any illusions about the prevailing American attitude toward creative genius. Sherwood Anderson, whose books were nearly as well known in the twenties as Ernest Hemingway's are now, cautioned us that one might become the foremost writer in this nation and still not be known by name to more than one American in a hundred. He wasn't talking about Fisk, of course. Here we honor the creative spirit. Fisk University introduced the Negro spiritual to the musical world. It produced W.E.B. Du Bois. More recently Frank Yerby, William Demby . . . nurtured their dreams in these same buildings. . . . Peter Abrahams has already lived to enjoy the distinction of a first-page spread in the *New York Times Book Review*, a recognition reserved almost exclusively for major figures. His books have been translated into all but one or two of the languages of Europe, not to mention the Chinese and other languages. . . . But he has brought a new and arresting subject matter to the British novel. Africa is his theme, as it was the place of his birth, and he is without a doubt one of the major voices now speaking to the world for that thoroughly awakened continent.[132]

Early in 1956, Bontemps spoke at a luncheon of the Kentucky–Tennessee chapter of the American Studies Association, which that year met in Nashville. His speech was titled simply "Booker T. Washington."[133] By this time, good reviews of *Story of the Negro* a work issued late in the previous year, had begun to appear, and by fall of the current year the book had won the Jane Addams Children's Award. The Book Award Committee of the Women's International League for Peace and Freedom had unanimously selected Bontemps's work to receive the honor.[134] The Committee had waived the requirement that the book be a first edition—it first came out in 1948—and Eleanor Roosevelt presented the award.

In his acceptance speech at the awards dinner held later that fall, the author made these significant remarks about *Story of the Negro*:

When the idea of this book was first proposed, I had some trouble thinking of it as a juvenile. The distinction between the juvenile and the adult book has always been some-what vague to me. And as I think of the *Story* . . . in this regard, all I can say now is that it consists mainly of things I learned after I left school that I wish I had known much earlier. Whether or not this makes it a juvenile I don't know. These things I would like to have known as a schoolboy and as a college student in the integrated schools of

California . . . when we were given the small fragments of . . . uncomplimentary information about Negro Americans. . . . My own suspicions about this material were aroused
by certain comments on the Negro qualities of most slaves. They were pictured as docile.
But the Negroes I knew personally were not all that docile by comparison with other
people. So I made inquiries and began reading. . . . One thing led to another until I found
myself immersed in the whole question and discovering so many points of interest I have
never since been able to turn away.[135]

While Bontemps was outlining this speech, he played an important part in
planning and executing a literary evening on Fisk's campus honoring Marian
Anderson. To celebrate the publication of Anderson's autobiography, *My Lord
What a Morning*, he reviewed the book and the Fisk class that would graduate
in May of 1957 presented the biographical film titled *Marian Anderson*.

Before the end of autumn quarter 1956, Charles Spurgeon Johnson was dead.
His death marked the end of the middle years of Arna Bontemps's tenure at Fisk
University, the years during which, with the support and encouragement of his
friend, mentor, and colleague, the novelist-librarian had made a significant contribution to Fisk and to American letters. In his remaining years at that institution,
Bontemps would come even further into his own as a writer, critic, and literary
historian.

Before the end of the 1950s, the writer had begun to alter and redefine his
assessments and predictions about African-American literature. He had made in
the fall of 1956, in his acceptance speech for the Addams Award, some insightful
remarks about this body of literature. He had begun to suspect there would be
sweeping changes coming about. He described the mid–1950s as a time of
"reappraisal and change" in the South and elsewhere, and he implied that the
intellectual and artistic climate in this country would require adjustments in
literature and in almost every phase of American life.[136] In an interview with
Judy Brimberg of Hampton, Virginia's *Daily Press* he said: "We are coming
to a period in which writers will not deal with white or Negro characters, but
paint them in terms of the total situation."[137]

Hence, long before the 1960s Bontemps had come to believe that the so-called
Negro novel, so popular in the late 1920s and early 30s, was passé. He attributed
some of the causes of this change to television, for it had brought about a change
in the fiction audience: The reading public no longer tolerated serious fiction.
He had observed that in the place of the typical "Negro novel" books dealing
with personalities had emerged. In 1956 alone works about Langston Hughes,
Hank Armstrong, Marian Anderson, and Eartha Kitt had appeared.

In his fellow African-American writers Bontemps had also noticed a change.
He saw a deep significance in so many of them living abroad—William Demby,
Ben Johnson, Richard Wright, Frank Yerby, and James Baldwin. They were
not necessarily writing about the problems of minorities. Demby had not written
a book about blacks since 1947, and though Baldwin's first novel, *Go Tell It
on the Mountain*, can appropriately be called a novel about African-American

life, he followed it with a book about life in Paris (*Giovanni's Room*). This kind of change in the thematic concerns of contemporary black writers led Bontemps in the late fifties to predict the decline of the Negro stereotype as an acceptable character in fiction by American writers regardless of their color. He believed that African-American dramatists, for instance, were going to write an ever-increasing number of plays for all-white casts, such as those seen in the television plays of Louis Peterson.

Considering his own works, Bontemps felt that perhaps the key to his writing was variety. He explained in an interview that he had written for all kinds and levels of people.[138] And of his works for children, his *Slappy Hooper*, *Fast Sooner Hound*, and *Sam Patch* were equally liked by white and black children. This he had been able to prove through his frequent public readings of these works. He was convinced that a book interesting to a black child will also appeal to a white one, and vice versa. "It may be," he said, "that I speak the language of children better than the language of adults."[139]

The middle and late 1950s found Arna still searching for a genre in which he could best make real for readers the truths of the human experience. He had settled on prose, but within that broad genre he was still searching, still experimenting, trying to find the perfect medium, the most efficient style. He had not abandoned, however, his dream of making a special, worthwhile contribution to American literature. Consequently, he would continue to experiment with new techniques and new genres that would improve the quality of his literary output.

Early in 1953, while thinking and experimenting, he was asked to serve on the panel of judges for the largest literary prize given to American writers, the Fellowship of the Academy of American Poets. The prize was a cash award of $5,000 that year and was given to William Carlos Williams.[140] This period saw Bontemps involved more than ever before in goodwill projects. His name had become synonymous with friendly outreach and wholesome public relations. It was his nature, though, to avoid public fanfare. He was modest and derived enough pleasure from quietly promoting a young writer here, encouraging a deserving student there, assisting them with career decisions and employment needs. And everyone who knew the writer appreciated this quality in him. Everything about him bespoke breeding and caring.

His office was still in the Cravath Library building, the structure that, since the new library was built, has housed Fisk's administrative offices. The building itself, from its vantage point in the center of the quadrangle separating Jubilee Hall on the north from Livingstone Hall on the south, still stands like a medieval citadel. Its ageless spice color and telescopic architecture create an aura of the intellectual, of the mind's aspirations. But inside this building that reaches toward the sky was an unpretentious, stuffy, little office on the second floor, where at almost any hour during the day and sometimes into the evening hours one could find the Head Librarian of Fisk University. He was sure to be busy, his desk littered with books, periodicals, and manuscripts, but he was always gracious to those who entered this sanctum, even when they interrupted his work.

Those of the library staff who worked with him and who still remember him fondly, will testify that he was never rude, never turned anyone away in haste. Sue Chandler, Leslie Collins, Beth Howse, and Ann Schockley remember that he would invite any visitor to sit down, letting him or her know by the sparkle in his eyes and the quiet sincerity of his well-modulated voice that he or she was accepted. He managed never to suggest to visitors, expected or unexpected, that they had caught him at an inopportune time. His colleagues, including Pearl Cresswell, who is one of the last remaining faculty members from the time when Fisk was in its glory, recalls that after leaving Arna's office, the visitor would experience a sense of enrichment, encouraged by the warmth and charm of his unique personality. She still recalls that Arna was sincere, "genuinely friendly, a real aristocrat."[141]

C. Eric Lincoln also understood this quality in the writer, and in a 1954 article on *God Sends Sunday* he described the novel's author as "one of our best writers, [who] shuns the bright light of publicity as Librarian of Fisk University. . . . [and who] succeeds in being intellectual without being either obtrusive or 'egg-headed.' "[142] These qualities are what kept Arna in the good graces of the two Fisk presidents with whom he had worked and with its seventh president, Stephen Junius Wright, who came to the campus in 1957, several months after Johnson's sudden death. Wright remained until 1966, by which time Arna had retired from Fisk and had gone to the University of Illinois system as a visiting professor.

Wright saw at once that in Arna Fisk had a jewel, and he enlisted his help at once in the transition from a college that historically served black students—though most of its teachers and administrators during the early years had been non-black—to one that welcomed all students, regardless of race, color, or creed. It was not difficult for Fisk to accept the white students who began to apply during these years, because its charter contained a commitment to train young men and women "irrespective of color."[143] From its earliest days, the school had clearly and proudly proclaimed that "nothing which smacked of racial discrimination was to be tolerated in the life of the school . . . [that]was to measure itself by the highest standards, not of Negro education, but of American education at its best."[144]

Arna was delighted to have non-black students at Fisk, for he believed integration would be good for the school's academic climate, and because it represented the kind of liberty he had longed for many years to see in the South. He did all he could to ensure that integration took place without incident. As he had done in his prize-winning book *The Story of the Negro*, Arna continued to build for peace by working to overcome prejudice, fear, suspicion, and by encouraging world-mindedness.

By fall 1958 the Bontemps nest was emptying, for there were only two of the six children left to educate, Constance and Arna Alexander, who had turned twelve the previous June.[145] While his children were entering and graduating from college, the proud father was involved with his own alma mater, Pacific Union College. For a special history of the college published as part of the 1957–58 *Diogenes Lantern*, Arna sent a snapshot of himself along with a completed questionnaire for a statistical study conducted in the current academic term. He carefully answered the questions and included additional comments in the margins. The questions he answered "Not at All" were the following: "Do you feel the counseling service was adequate?"; "To what degree do you think the guidance service was equipped to give you help in choosing a vocation?"; "Do you feel PUC adequately met your social needs?" He also felt that PUC was too greatly restricted in its social viewpoint but that the religious program had met his needs.

Yet he did feel, as he had during his college days, that the religious program had been forced upon him. While there, he had participated in two extracurricular groups: "Men of Grainger" and "Mountain Echo," the glee club. The part of this three-page questionnaire most interesting to a biographer is a section that includes such questions as "Would you recommend the areas of employment that you have had as areas to which our Seventh-day Adventist youth should look for employment?" His answer was "no" with this attached comment: "It would be awkward. The writer's lot is hard and likely to be misunderstood."[146]

In April 1957, at the request of the A.L.A., Bontemps presented its "Liberty and Justice Book Award" in imaginative literature to James Thurber for *Further Fables of Our Time*. Arna opened his speech with these remarks: "The literature of escape appears to be on the way out. Easier and quicker ways of getting-away-from-it-all have been discovered. But there is no reason why this circumstance should make imaginative writing obsolete. There are still people who read fiction and poetry and published drama in the hope of somehow being instructed, or at least given hints on how to order their lives or comprehend their world."[147] He revealed here a lasting commitment to fiction, an enduring faith in literature and the role it plays in society. Meanwhile he continued to do his part—writing books and teaching his students to appreciate good literature.

Arna's contributions and accomplishments did not go entirely unnoticed. S. J. Wright at the end of the 1957–58 school year raised his salary, with the Board's approval, by $500 for the year, bringing his new salary to $6,500.[148] Not only was he appreciated by the administration at Fisk, but his faculty colleagues also appreciated the contribution he had made to Fisk and to literature and librarianship. Several of them were using one or more of his books in their freshman composition classes. The titles they found most useful at that level were *Anyplace but Here* and *Story of the Negro*.[149]

This recognition by his peers inspired Bontemps to continue creating literature. He and Hughes were finishing a new anthology to offer educators, *The Book of Negro Folklore*, published by Knopf in 1958. They saw this work as a companion piece to their 1949 volume, *The Poetry of the Negro*, and it was received equally well.

Negro Folklore was a larger-than-usual anthology, 624 pages of folk songs, dialect compositions in verse and prose, "lies," tall tales, even African-American versions of the fabliau and the merry tale. It also presented examples of "rapping," though the term had not come into the language, of signifying and professing. Not only did the editors provide ample entertainment for readers of all ages, they also provided support for scholars in folklore, anthropology and related fields. *Folklore* did its part toward restoring folk materials to their rightful place in schoolrooms and on adults' bookshelves. Bontemps wrote the book's insightful introduction, revealing his appreciation of folklore as a legitimate branch of scholarship. Between this introduction and the final section devoted to modern prose pieces "in the folk manner," appear many old favorites, entertaining pieces with overtones of protest and resistance, and of mockery as well.

A few of the rhymes are nonsense songs; others are admonitory and didactic; most are comic. A great many have occasional origins, rooted in such ceremonial forms as chants and imitations for weddings, funerals, and baptisms. The book also contains an ample sampling of sermons, spirituals, and gospel songs, ghost stories, conjure stories, ballads, and the blues. Some of the pieces included in the volume had not been anthologized previously. The collaborating authors had made through this anthology a worthwhile addition to available folklore materials.

Students at Fisk also appreciated Bontemps's efforts as a classroom teacher and writer, and as Head Librarian. They did not, however, always agree with his administration of the library, especially where library hours were concerned. On the frong page of the *Forum*, Fisk's student newspaper, staff writer Julius B. Lester wrote an article titled "Help Us Get an Education, Unlock the Wisdom of the Ages: An Open Letter to Our Head Librarian." Students were demanding longer library hours.[150]

There are no available written records of Bontemps's response to this letter, but reports from faculty and staff persons who recall the late fifties at Fisk indicate that he did change library hours so that the library was open seven days a week, from twelve hours a day to eighteen. In the midst of this mild campus unrest, Knopf issued the third edition of *Story of the Negro*. Simultaneously the author published another chapter in a book, entitled "An American Original: Jelly Roll Morton." It appeared in *Jam Session: An Anthology of Jazz* (Putnam), edited by Ralph Gleason.

By 1959 Bontemps had become active in the American Society for African Culture, an organization with which he maintained affiliation until his retirement. In March of that year the Society held a conference of Negro writers in New York City. Arna attended the conference and participated as co-panelist with John O. Killens on the theme, "Negro Writers' Relationships to Their Roots." The conference was well-attended and most of the well-known African-American writers were there: Lorraine Hansberry, John Henrik Clarke, Alice Childress, Arthur P. Davis, and Robert Lucas, among others. Also present was Richard Wright, who died the following year.[151]

Just prior to this meeting Bontemps had given an address to the Frontiers Club of Nashville. The speech's title was, "Why Negro History Week?" The main point that he made, according to the outline from which he spoke, was to answer the rhetorical question he used near the opening: "How much do white people know *about* Negroes?" His conclusion was that American whites know *of* Negro leaders, but do not know Ralph Bunche from Roy Wilkins; they know *about* the Negro writers, but confuse Cullen with Hughes, Motley with Yerby, Wright with Ellison; they know *about* Negro scholars, but do not distinguish Alain Locke and Charles S. Johnson from one another. They know, he insisted, only the professional athletes and other entertainers. The speech then went into an analysis of why this state of affairs existed.[152]

Shortly after the writer returned from the New York meeting, good news came again from Knopf—they had just published his *Frederick Douglass: Slave, Fighter, Freeman*. *Top of the News* published that spring his article, "Sing a Soothing Song."[153] And Mrs. Charles S. Johnson gave the first installment of her husband's papers to the Fisk library, with its chief accepting this vast and important collection on behalf of the university. In late April the University held a special ceremony in the Fisk Chapel celebrating the presentation and acceptance of these papers. Bontemps, of course, was called upon to make remarks. He said:

The public addresses and occasional papers read by Charles S. Johnson between 1928 and his death in 1956 are represented by 369 manuscripts. They include a little over one million well-chosen words. These papers have been in the custody of Fisk . . . for a number of months and have been arranged, copied and bound. . . . This significant body of scholarship is now available to researchers who may wish to use it. . . . Not every speech or paper read by Charles S. Johnson was preserved in his files. We know about several for which copies have not been found, including more than one of those delivered before the annual Institute of Race Relations here at Fisk. No doubt these missing items will eventually be located by scholars. Perhaps there will be enough of them to fill a 14th volume. . . . Unpublished manuscripts fill at least three manuscript boxes. Notes and random jottings, sparks from the mind of the scholar . . . fill another four or five boxes. We are also preserving many manuscripts of published writings. These may be of interest to those who would like to know . . . exactly what was written, as against what was left in by editors.[154]

Johnson's personal correspondence was not included in the collection. Bontemps had hoped that this wealth of comment and observation would also become available to researchers who were seriously interested in the mind, the personality, and the public figure they represented. Johnson had been an avid and discriminating reader, and his books were a reflection of their owner. His pamphlet collection was also rich and extensive. It has already provided dozens of hard-to-find items, and these Bontemps had bound and catalogued.

In the Fisk Library the Johnson papers joined the company of the Charles W. Chesnutt Collection, the John Mercer Langston Papers, the Archives of the

American Missionary Association (1839–1879), and other manuscript collections of rare value, including the Gershwin and Holtby collections. Each year since Bontemps began collecting in 1943, the manuscript collections at Fisk contributed to research on many levels. Ph.D. dissertations by Philip Butcher and August Meier at Columbia University drew upon these resources prior to Bontemps's receipt of the Charles S. Johnson Papers. Other dissertations in progress at U.C.L.A. and at the University of North Carolina made even more sustained use of the materials.

Bontemps had succeeded in establishing an atmosphere of research at Fisk. His manuscript collections continued to grow, for only a short time after the Johnson Papers were presented, he announced the acquisition of the Angelina Grimke Papers. Still other collections had been promised. The Chief Librarian believed, whether Fisk offered graduate work or not, that scholarship would continue there, and true to his vision, the library there has never ceased to provide a fruitful ground for scholars.[155]

In 1959 the Atlantic Monthly Press contacted Bontemps about an idea associate editor Peter Davison had had. He wanted Bontemps to approach Mahalia Jackson about writing her life story. But the writer learned through Miss Jackson's agent that Evan Wylie had already obtained the option, hence the story would not appear under the Atlantic–Little, Brown imprint. This suited Arna for he had not been eager to take on the assignment.

By fall Ida Cullen-Cooper had written an ecstatic letter to Arna about *St. Louis Woman*. The play would get another chance to run through the new musical version *Free and Easy*, and it opened in Paris on January 15, 1960. During 1959 it had enjoyed a brief though successful run in Amsterdam. The following is a portion of Cullen-Cooper's letter to the co-author:

We sat in on several rehearsals and last evening saw a run-through of the first act. Arna, this production is going to be terrific. Every one who was there was so excited about what they saw and heard. You've never heard such singing in your life—the voices are so beautiful—the cutest girls you could ever see any place in the world—and Miss Della Green is just the most. She is the Della that you always wanted—this girl has everything. . . . The casting of this show has been something beyond all others—just superb. If the people in Europe loved Porgy and Bess—they will go mad over this production. . . .

Quincy Jones, the young fellow who will conduct the music, and who all of the papers and especially the *New York Times* have been raving about for the last few weeks, says that by the time they return to this country they will be able to play their parts in their sleep. They all seem so enthusiastic about playing for Europe for nine months.[156]

But Arna was too engrossed in other projects to become as excited as Ida Cullen had over the play. In early December, around the time of Fisk's Fall Convocation, he ventured to write a fond letter to Jean Toomer, his elusive and long-time friend from the Harlem years. He confided,

Dear Jean Toomer:

I have been deeply moved by your William Penn lecture *The Flavor of Men*, a copy of which was given to me by our neighbors Marian and Nelson Fuson. Among other things, it reminded me of another great reading experience I had thirty-five years ago when another friend handed me CANE. . . .

What prompts me to write you, however (and I won't pretend that I didn't hesitate), is another coincidence. When I was a small boy, my wonderful old grandmother used to tell me about one of the high moments of her early married life in Louisiana. It came, she used to say, when she and her husband had the honor of entertaining Governor Pinchback in their home on one occasion. But nearly fifty years passed before I actually set out to document her memory and to learn something more about the stormy years in which he made history. I find it tremendously exciting, and I wonder that you have never written about it. How a writer of genius could keep such a story locked in his heart is one of the things that both fascinate and mystify me.[157]

This letter reveals not only Bontemps's fondness of Toomer but also, especially in the passages not quoted here, that Bontemps was at the height of his thinking about Louisiana.

In 1960 Arna was named to the Nashville Public Library Board. Nashville had led the way in integrating the state. By this time Memphis was the only major city in the state maintaining segregated libraries. To Arna it was amazing that a city just 220 miles from Nashville could be so radically different. But even more baffling to the writer-humanitarian was how anyone could bar the door of a public facility to another person simply because of color. As a member of the Nashville board, he assisted with the administration of the main library and three branches and served as consultant to several other libraries in the county. He had been disheartened over the Memphis situation, for it had been his hope that Memphis would follow Nashville's example and integrate without the persuasion of the law (Nashville's libraries had been integrated for a number of years). It had become apparent, however, that Memphis would do no such thing. Consequently a suit had already been filed to force city officials to open the Memphis library to all citizens.[158] Bontemps's sense of decency had been offended by the situation in Memphis.

As the year progressed, Arna's commitments as civic leader and lecturer grew heavier. He visited Dallas again. This time as speaker at the A.C.E. (American Childhood Education) banquet.[159] While there he lectured to students at several elementary and secondary schools, telling stories and reading poetry to more than two thousand students. Back home, Fisk was also beginning to show some appreciation for his hard work and productive scholarship. In April 1960 he received news that his salary had been raised for the 1960–61 term: He would earn $8,100.

Summer came and for the fourth consecutive year Bontemps participated in Peabody's summer program in contemporary literature. He and Alberta had planned to return in mid-August to Wildwood and to spend another of their customary vacations there, enjoying the natural beauty of the resort in peace and solitude. But they suddenly decided to go abroad instead.[160] While they were making plans for an African journey, sad news came to Arna and Alberta.

On August 6, 1960 Paul Bismark Bontemps, the writer's father, died at Loma Linda, California. The elder Bontemps was survived by his wife Letitia, his son and daughter by his first wife, Maria, and seven grandchildren: his daughter Ruby Troy's one son, and Arna's four daughters and two sons. About a week after the funeral, Arna received a letter of condolence from Garland Millet, President of Oakwood College. After using the first paragraph of the missive to place the deceased Adventist minister in heaven, Millet made bold to suggest that Arna's soul was in jeopardy. Millet had tried to arrange an appointment with Arna at Fisk during the previous spring, but Arna had refused to be tied down to a date. The tone of Millet's letter suggests that he was attempting to use the occasion of Paul Bontemps's death to inflict guilt upon his surviving son for not having devoted his time and talents to the propagation of the Adventist message in the way Paul Bontemps had thought he should.

Arna's reply showed the writer at a time when his perceptiveness and rhetorical sensitivity were at their zenith. He wrote,

Dear President Millet:

Thank you for your note of sympathy. I'm sure that I am my father's son in many ways, including my hardheadedness. But in at least one thing I think I inherit more from my mother. My father never separated the "spiritual" from the "sectarian" in his thinking, but my mind has never worked that way. I don't think my mother's did either, but she knew better than to argue with him. I hope all will be harmony with them hereafter. I loved them both deeply.

With kindest regards,

Sincerely yours,

Arna Bontemps[161]

Arna's oldest child, Joan Bontemps Williams, described her father as a "master of understatement."[162] The truth of her remark is borne out in this letter to Millet, for it is what the letter merely implies that cuts most sharply.

In early summer 1960, President S. J. Wright had given the writer a verbal commitment concerning his trip to Africa, and wrote to him a letter confirming that commitment. Arna's scheduled departure date was in mid-September, depending on transportation, and the arrangements Wright made kept the writer-librarian from losing pay during his extended absence: the first month of leave was charged to his annual vacation; and the second month was also with pay, with the understanding that Bontemps would make a special effort to purchase, within his approved library budget, rare Africana; and that he would make a special effort to recruit "exceptional" African students. Time beyond two months would be without pay.

The majority of the three-month vacation was spent in two countries of east central Africa, Uganda and Kenya. En route he was scheduled to stop in Paris for a few days, and he would not have thought of doing so without making an effort to see his old friend and fellow novelist, Richard Wright. At the end of August he wrote to Wright: "We are now scheduled to arrive at Le Grand Hotel in Paris September 15th. We'll be flying there from London that morning and expect to remain a little more than a week. Alberta and I are both looking forward to seeing you and your family. This will be our first visit to Paris, you know, and you can imagine our feelings. Till then, all good wishes, Best ever."[163]

The Syracuse Papers contain a reply on air-mail stationery in Wright's hand. His note included instructions for Arna and Alberta to meet him at his home in Paris on the day of their arrival; the address given was 4 Rue Regis, Serpes-Babylon, Cherche-midi à Rue Berite between 5:30 and 6:00 P.M.[164] The pair had a wonderful time in Paris, and one of the highlights of the trip was the time they spent with Wright and his wife Ellen. Mrs. Bontemps still recalls with delight the many trips she and her late husband had together, but this "African journey" with attached stays in Paris and London still stands out in her mind. She said recently: "When we traveled to France, we found—Arna and I—that Bontemps is a common name. And in the hotel they really carried my husband around about not speaking French—with a name like that. 'Oh, Monsieur Bontemps, shame on you for not speaking French.' "[165]

Leaving Paris, their first stop was at Makerere College in Kampala, Uganda, where Arna lectured for two months, and on to Nairobi, where they spent the last leg of this African hiatus. Their first stop after leaving the United States had been London, where they were met and entertained by Vera Brittain, the biographer and literary executor of Winifred Holtby. This was partially a business visit, for since 1955 Arna had been the custodian of the Winifred Holtby Memorial Collection in Nashville, the year in which the collection was founded at Fisk. In London the writer and his wife attended two social functions given in their honor, a cocktail party hosted by Miss Brittain and a dinner party given by Geoffrey Handley Taylor, an old acquaintance.[166] The couple also visited with South African novelist Peter Abrahams, who was living in Kingston, Jamaica, but lecturing in London. Bontemps confided to Abrahams his plan to write about some of the interesting personalities in Uganda and Kenya, preferably the controversial ones.[167] He also saw Mercer Cook during the Paris leg of the journey; Cook had accepted a job with the Congress of Cultural Freedom.

While Arna was still in Africa, Richard Wright died. Langston Hughes, who had been in Paris with Wright when he was rushed to the hospital, had written at once to Arna at Nairobi to give him the sad news. Wright had suffered from intestinal troubles prior to his hospitalization.[168] Arna sent a note of sympathy to Ellen Wright and her daughters and wrote her a lengthy letter, on a borrowed typewriter that had a bad ribbon, as soon as he arrived at his son Paul's home in Mount Vernon, New York, where he and Alberta stopped for a few days before returning to Nashville.[169]

This letter to Ellen Wright concerned a long-distance telephone conversation Arna had just had with Gayle Gibson, his secretary in Nashville, who had told him a manuscript from Richard Wright, accompanied by a note, had been on his desk at Fisk for some time. Wright and Arna discussed the manuscript at length during the stop in Paris, and Wright had written to Bontemps about it in Uganda. The project started with discussion of the 1951 novel Bontemps had written about the Fisk Jubilee Singers and the treatment Wright had written of the singers for a movie about their experience of introducing the Negro spiritual to the musical world of 1871. Wright had suggested he and Bontemps collaborate on a scenario in hope of selling it when it was finished. Arna's position as Head Librarian gave him custodianship over all the memorabilia relating to the singers, hence Wright thought Arna would be a natural for the project. Arna wrote to Ellen Wright concerning her late husband's proposal:

I was interested but declined to risk the only copy of his treatment in Africa. He then offered to have a copy made and sent to me at Fisk. I intended to read it and give him my ideas after reaching home. His death, of course complicated things. Under the circumstances I don't think I should even read the manuscript until I know what your wishes are in the whole matter. . . . Dick and I also agreed that should we move ahead on this project, we would ask Leah Salisbury to handle it for us. He told me that he was free to do this and that he was sure Paul Reynolds [Wright's literary agent] would not object, since his specialty did not appear to be theatrical properties. We have had an inquiry about the movie rights to *Chariot in the Sky*, but will hold back on this till I hear from you.[170]

The days before Arna's departure for Africa had seen him practicing his favorite avocation, keeping in touch with other writers. Harold Jackman had written in early August to report his findings on some research Arna had asked him to do for a proposed occasional piece. He replied to Jackman: "I'm tickled pink. The names, the sidelights, are just what I need. I am most grateful, and . . . will . . . let you know how I come out." And in a postscript he wrote: "You could indeed operate a successful research service, and I don't think anyone who is working seriously would balk at a reasonable charge. I think it's a good idea."[171] Jackman, who was planning to open a new research service, had asked Bontemps to give his honest reaction to the concept.

Once back at the Fisk post, the writer was aglow with inspiration. The new discoveries and friendships he had established on the Dark Continent had agreed with him. He had spent a good bit of time with Sam J. Nitro of the Art Center at Makerere College, and Nitro in turn had introduced him to his associates at the college and to many of the scholars, writers, and artists in both Uganda and Kenya.[172] Arna was gladdened, too, when shortly after his return, the Board of the William Allen White Children's Book Award placed his 1959 biography, *Frederick Douglass: Slave, Fighter, Freeman,* on the 1961–62 Master Book List.

He had also discovered on his return from Africa that during his absence the American Society of African Culture had published his fictional piece "Ole Sis

Goose'' in their 1960 volume titled *The American Negro Writer and His Roots: Selected Papers from the First Conference of Negro Writers, March 1959.* And Abingdon Press requested that he rewrite the ''Rutland manuscript'' they had earlier asked him to evaluate. But receipt of the galley proofs from his own forthcoming book had interrupted his work on the Abingdon assignment, a book titled *The Trouble with Being a Mama.*[173] A few months later, Dodd, Mead published Bontemps's book under the title *One Hundred Years of Negro Freedom*. In this work he had presented a century of history through biographies of persons who played significant roles in making that history. It was an important book, one that presented history as it should be presented—objectively. This book was free from the taint of defensiveness and offensiveness as well. Its author had long believed that personality—the personal convictions and philosophies of human beings—is a reliable mirror of culture.

Eventually Arna did get around to appraising the Rutland manuscript as Abingdon had requested, and when he had finished the task he advised that the manuscript not be tampered with by editors. Arna used his decades of experience with commercial book companies to protect the interests of a fellow writer, yet his appraisal was not dishonest.[174]

In the summer 1961 Arna received an announcement of the funeral of Harold Jackman, his friend whom he had seen only a few days before during a brief stay in New York City. Jackman had died on July 8, and funeral services were scheduled for July 13. Langston Hughes had called already to tell Arna of Harold's death. Arna reacted to this news with profound sorrow, for since 1924 Jackman's friendship, and later his correspondence, had meant much to him. He was grieved too because he realized American letters had lost a giant and that the already thinning ranks of the Harlem writers had been invaded once more. Another trip to New York for the funeral caused Arna to fall further behind on his work schedule than he had been on his return from AMSAC and caused him to decline a number of invitations, one to a benefit in Los Angeles sponsored on behalf of a liberal newspaper, *The People's World*.

By December he was caught up and ready to accept one of two engagements before the new year. On December 16 he read ''The Bedbug'' from his anthology *Golden Slippers* in Detroit before a large group of schoolchildren, and the rendition tickled their funny bones. Then he read *Fast Sooner Hound*, a fanciful story full of chuckles and an equal amount of suspense, and the kind of absurd happy ending children love. After the story, he allowed time for questions and answers and commented on the sophistication and perceptiveness of the children of the 1960s as compared to the naiveté of his own childhood. Some of the questions the children asked during the session revealed a number of facts of importance to the biographer.

Telling the children how he created his characters he said: ''I listen to people. I watch them carefully. Then I take characteristics from several people and make one character. And always I use a little of myself.''[175] He had not altered his basic method of creating fiction since the Depression days in Alabama when he wrote *Popo and Fifina* with Langston Hughes, his initial effort at writing for children. In response to a question about his own childhood reading habits, he answered that he read so much as a boy he neglected his chores and that his father had limited him to two books a week. He also revealed that he was never good at arithmetic. He went on to tell his youthful audience, some of whom had whistled at the number of books he must have been reading before his father's restriction, that his hobbies when he was very young included most sports. The article in the *Michigan Chronicle* observed, "after the program the children hung around this pied piper [sic] of literature. He was interested in them and they reluctantly left his company."[176]

By spring 1962, Bontemps's African experiences and the string of continuing interests and activities they started, had begun to culminate in publishing opportunities. Professor Edwin S. Munger of the California Institute of Technology in Pasadena, California, an old friend who had visited with Arna and Alberta in the spring of 1960 while they were making plans for the trip to Africa, contacted the writer and expressed his eagerness to hear about the trip and to discuss a writing plan of his. Simultaneously Bontemps was returning from a conference with Hill and Wang on a projected series of books for American readers about the new African countries. The editors had high hopes for the project, but Bontemps could foresee a long-range problem, that of finding enough African writers capable of writing general books on such countries as Kenya and Ethiopia.[177]

Meanwhile Arna was too engrossed in writing something of his own to spend much time on the Hill and Wang proposal. He was hard at work gathering materials for *American Negro Poetry*, an anthology for which he was under contract with Hill and Wang, and which they first issued in May 1963. He was also working on a collection of poems he had been meaning to finish since the 1920s. He published this work in 1963 through Paul Bremen, the small British publishing house. He had agreed with his friend Bremen that the volume should be called *Personals*.

In January 1962 Arna participated in a three-day series of lectures hosted by Langston Hughes in memory of Harold Jackman. At these New York lectures Bontemps spoke on his specialty, "The Harlem Renaissance." This, too, led to publication, for *Phylon* published the taped lectures after the lecturers had approved the transcripts. These arrangements were handled for both Bontemps and Hughes by Hughes's personal secretary, George Bass, who after Hughes's death became co-executor with Bontemps of the Hughes estate.[178]

The list of guest speakers at the Jackman Memorial Lectures included Zelma Watson George, E. Franklin Frazier, William Branch, Sterling Brown, and Arna Bontemps. The guest artists were Langston Hughes, poetry and jazz; Voices Incorporated, spirituals, blues, and folk songs; Betty Allen, songs of Margaret Bonds; and Clara Ward, gospel music. Bass served as chairman; Loften Mitchell was Hughes's co-host. The festival was underwritten by the John Hay Whitney Foundation and by Harlem's Market Place Gallery. The sponsors and co-hosts divided the body of African-American literature into five periods as they saw the whole in 1962: (I) 1619–1863; (II) 1864–1919; (III) 1920–1932; (IV) 1933–1949; (V) 1950–present.[179] Bontemps's speech discussed, of course, the third period.

In April 1962 Bontemps was guest lecturer at Morgan State College, Baltimore, at the school's fifth annual faculty-student conference on the humanities.[180] About three weeks after his return from Morgan, he was to see his name in print yet again. A teacher's magazine published his most recent observations about the Harlem Renaissance with a photograph of him with Arthur B. Spingarn of NAACP fame.[180] In this article Bontemps expressed his gratitude for the privilege of having seen from a grandstand seat two great awakenings, the Negro upsurge of the 1920s and that of the 1950s. Though these movements were separated, he observed, by thirty years, they were not unrelated. He was equally gratified that the Harlem poets were still read and quoted, "some of them in many languages around the world."[181] And he said the anti-folk attitude of the "New Criticism" did more to silence the confident self-expression of the Harlem group than did any other reaction.

In early October Arna received the first of a series of letters from Marjorie Content Toomer, wife of Jean Toomer, who was himself still alive but in a state of physical and psychological deterioration. Toomer had ignored letters from Bontemps as he had done in all other attempts by former friends to correspond with him. Marjorie confided to Arna that Jean's failure to answer letters did not surprise her, as he had lost all interest in matters that had sustained him in the past, and she added that the situation regarding what to do with his papers and personal effects had been further complicated by his refusal to cooperate in any way.[182]

Arna could stifle his curiosity no longer and decided to write to Marjorie, feeling her out about Jean's papers. From the series of letters she wrote back, it is clear that Marjorie Toomer had every inclination to let Fisk have the papers—permanently—to rid herself of the burden of custodianship and also because of her respect for Arna Bontemps and his genuine fondness of Jean. She decided to leave it up to Arna and his staff to arrange the papers and select what they wanted. The papers had been stored outdoors in a former pigeon house since 1955, the year the Toomers moved to the old remodeled barn in Doylestown, Pennsylvania, that they called home. Toomer had simply stuffed his papers into cartons, unsorted.[183]

Bontemps wrote to Marjorie Toomer the following reply:

Your letter helps to unfold the mystery which Jean Toomer had become for me. As I tried to indicate before, I am intensely interested in just about everything else that pertains to him, and I hope very much that there is some way in which I can be of assistance. If it can be done without upsetting Jean too much, I will gladly volunteer cooperation on behalf of this library. If you think it might help, I or someone else from our staff, might arrange to visit Doylestown and examine the material. If, on the other hand, the material could be sent here in boxes at our expense, I think our Cataloguing Department might be able to arrange it. We have had considerable experience at this sort of thing, and I can assure you that the papers would be handled with feeling.

Meanwhile I wonder if we have here copies of everything Jean ever published. Would you be willing to check a list of our holdings to indicate whether . . . it is complete?[184]

Amid these negotiations Bontemps adhered to his writing schedule, so that by year's end he had begun editing the series of short books about African countries that Hill and Wang had asked him to do. December found him on Ethiopia and already finished with several in the series.[185] At the same time the writer's youngest child and second son, Alex, was about to finish his first quarter as a freshman at Fisk. Nearly twenty years had passed since the writer joined the Fisk faculty in 1943, and more than eighteen years since the June 1945 birth of Arna Alexander Bontemps. When the new year began (1963) the author was still working on the two Hill and Wang projects, but the editing of the poetry anthology was taking up the bulk of his writing time.

In April of that year, shortly after meeting his press deadline for the new anthology that would come out a month later, Arna paused to answer once more a few misguided souls among the "New Critics" who had erroneously objected to Negro spirituals and minstrel shows as damaging to their public image. The *Milwaukee Journal* of April 22 carried an article titled, "Race's Critics of Spirituals Scolded by Negro Author."[186] Arna called these critics "falsely educated" and observed that they were doing the race more harm than good. "The minstrel show is a form. I have no more against it than I do against the sonnet form," the *Journal* quoted him as saying. He felt that African Americans who refused to sing spirituals were only "partially educated" and suffered from an inadequate sense of appreciation for the contribution of their ancestors. For similar reasons, in a speech given at Milwaukee's Central Library, the writer objected to recent changes in the Philadelphia schools by officials who wanted to "improve" the image of Huck Finn.[187]

The beginning of 1963 had found the writer needing a more organized kind of writer's retreat than those he had experienced over the past several years. The summers at Wildwood had been fine, but that place, too, was beginning to become overpopulated. He had experienced the solitude of Yaddo, the writer's colony, and knew the benefits to be derived from writing in an atmosphere where nobody was present but a small group of writers. He decided to apply to the MacDowell Colony of Peterborough, New Hampshire, for summer admission. This colony, operated by the Edward MacDowell Association, had a good reputation among creative artists in this country and abroad.

The admissions committee of the colony accepted him for the entire month of June, 1963. His daily schedule would begin with breakfast at 7:30 A.M., with lunch delivered to his studio. A 6:15 P.M. warning bell would ring for a 6:30 dinner. He would live on the campus for a month and receive meals and the use of a studio for a reasonable $100. At his disposal would be the Savidge Library, complete with books, piano, phonograph, and tape recorders, and the place would be full of graphic artists, creative writers, and composers. In fact, Aaron Copeland was a member of the Board of Directors. Between 11:00 P.M. and 7:00 A.M. the residences were kept quiet. This was exactly the kind of environment Arna needed at this juncture in his career, for he was still accustomed to rising early and writing for a few hours before breakfast.

But despite the elaborate plans he had made to attend the retreat and the intense need he felt to get away from everything, he did not attend the MacDowell Colony during the summer of 1963. He and Alberta were building their new house on Geneva Circle, at the crest of a hill overlooking the city of Nashville, situated in a residential area only a short drive from Fisk. Arna had tried to adjust his various schedules to allow him to make the trip, but the builders did not finish the house on schedule, causing him to spend the time he had hoped to have for the Colony on moving into the new house and helping Alberta unpack and arrange their belongings.[188] This was not the only plan he had to alter or abandon, for delays on the new residence also prevented him from attending the A.L.A. convention that year, the first time in many years he had missed his favorite conference of librarians.[189]

Reviews of *American Negro Poetry*, which included works by fifty-six poets, had begun to appear. These were generally good, though often not specific enough, as seems to be the rule with reviews of poetry anthologies. But Arna had never paid much attention to critics and he was not about to start trying to curry favor with them at this stage of his career. Already he was deeply involved in the writing of his next book, *Famous Negro Athletes*, which he had planned to finish at the MacDowell Colony. The book had been scheduled for publication by Dodd, Mead before the end of the year, but because of interruptions in the author's schedule it did not come out until the first part of 1964. This book answered a definite need, for before it came out it was not possible to read about the greatest black American athletes under a single cover. It traces the rise of such historic figures as Joe Louis, Jackie Robinson, Sugar Ray Robinson, Satchel Paige, Jesse Owens, Wilt Chamberlain, Willie Mays, and others. Except for one brief review published anonymously, this book was virtually ignored by scholars and critics.[190]

But while Bontemps was being overlooked by critics, his friend Langston Hughes was receiving more attention than he wanted from a particular element of society. By early fall, Hughes had been canceled as one of the participants in the American Writers' Series, a television program scheduled to air in Nashville later that year. Mrs. John B. Napier of Nashville had appeared before the Nashville board of education to protest Hughes's scheduled appearance on the program because he had been questioned by the McCarthy Committee twenty years earlier. Arna was dismayed at the injustice of the cancellation, for he too had been questioned by the Committee, and he, like Hughes, had been exonerated.

Arna believed this action against Hughes was racially motivated, for he could remember well that Arthur Miller had also been summoned by the committee and had refused to answer, claiming immunity under the Fifth Amendment. Yet Miller's appearance on this series had not been questioned. This cancellation provoked a string of protest letters to area newspapers, with at least one writer suggesting that Bontemps be placed in Hughes's spot on the program, a statement that must have embarrassed the writer, for Langston was still his best friend.[191]

The end of 1964 saw the author-librarian-teacher-humanitarian planned to sing a swan song. Arna had held the position as Head Librarian at Fisk for twenty years, and the strain of keeping up a heavy writing schedule and an ever-increasing number of public appearances, all while doing his regular job, had taken its toll. Others could perceive no change in him, but the writer himself knew he was slowing down. These years at the library post had been his best, but they also had been demanding years. He had quietly decided to investigate retirement options. Many of his Fisk colleagues had retired already; others, like Charles S. Johnson and Fred Brownlee, Executive Director of the A.M.A., had died.

Many changes had occurred in the Fisk working climate, and as a natural result, Arna's professional situation had also changed. He could anticipate the difficult times that lay ahead for Fisk and knew he did not, in 1963–64, have the energy reserves he had possessed on accepting the appointment in 1943. He had joined the Fisk faculty as Head Librarian with the academic rank of full professor, and in these twenty years had built the Fisk library into one of the best in the South.

Arna's list of writings had expanded to about five dozen books, plays, and articles, plus an astounding number of speeches and reviews. At the end of the 1964–65 school term the writer resigned his position as Head Librarian at Fisk University, bringing his total years of service in that position to twenty-one. But at the request of the administration, he stayed on another year as Acting Librarian, or until a new Chief Librarian could be found. At the same time he was named Director of University Relations, a position he held until fall 1966. In effect Fisk had refused to let him retire, but Arna Wendell Bontemps was ready to step aside, and indeed could look with pride on his accomplishments.

Chapter 9

The Mature Years

Nearing the end of a fruitful career at Fisk, Arna Bontemps had little to regret. He could look back on his decision of more than twenty years earlier to accept the job as a happy one. In an interview with his former student and fellow librarian Ann Shockley a few weeks before his death, the writer spoke of the most outstanding achievements of his tenure at Fisk. He concluded that his greatest accomplishment had been "keeping active the interest in the black experience and background." "We [the Fisk Library staff]," he continued, "sort of served as a clearing house for information on the subject."[1] While serving as librarian and teaching classes in literature and creative writing, he made an impact on American literature, both as an author-scholar and as a college professor. His personal influence as teacher and mentor to other writers was acknowledged by all who knew him.[2] He never lost interest in the preservation of African-American culture, and he did his part to aid his race in the struggle for equality.

During Arna Bontemps's mature years, he began to receive recognition from many quarters of the academic and artistic world. He lived long enough to receive more requests to write for publishing houses and journals than he had time or energy to accommodate. But he also could remember when his name had been unknown by publishers and patrons of literature. He saw himself become recognized as the person who could analyze the Harlem Renaissance with more clarity and sensitivity than anyone else. He had lived through the period, had been one of its contributors as had Hughes, but no one else had written as often or as well on this period as Arna Bontemps.

When Bontemps decided to step down from the librarian's post, he had long looked forward to a lighter workload, to an even greater amount of freedom than he had enjoyed all along, freedom to pursue his writing full time, or at least three-quarters time. But preparing to make the transition required an even greater amount of work than normal, for he had not anticipated being asked to stay on as Acting Head Librarian, nor had he supposed that the Fisk Administration would ask him to become Director of University Relations. He agreed to do both. The news of his pending retirement leaked out, and it seems that every learned society, every writer, every publisher who had ever known the name Arna Bontemps began to contact him. They wanted him to write books, chapters in books, or to edit anthologies. A flood of requests came in for him to make public appearances and submit articles to special editions of scholarly journals.

The people of Nashville had always called upon his talent, and they were doing so more than ever before. Writers and aspiring writers sought his advice as they always had, and as usual, he took time out of his overwhelming schedule to evaluate their works and to encourage them when he believed encouragement was merited. For these reasons the one and one-half years between January 1964 and June 1965 became the busiest period of the writer's life, and in some ways it was the most productive.

Fellow writers whom he encouraged and complimented during this period included Robert Breen; Wayne Cooper, a graduate student who was finishing a thesis on Claude McKay; Michel Fabre; John O. Killens; Ann Allen Shockley; Russell Atkins; Ossie Davis; Gwendolyn Brooks; Robert Farnsworth of the University of Missouri at Kansas City, biographer of his old friend and fellow poet Melvin Tolson; Carrole Fair; Thomas A. Dorsey, author of "Precious Lord, Take My Hand"; Horace Cayton; C. Eric Lincoln; and several others.[3] He also wrote to poet Frank Horne during this period offering compliments on Horne's newest poem, "Balm in Gilead."[4]

Typical of the kind of verbal support Arna Bontemps through the years had given to other writers are the following quotations from letters written in 1964 and 1965. To Russell Atkins he wrote: "I have every reason to be especially grateful to you for volume 8, No. 1 of the *Free Lance*, and I assure you I am. You are keeping a light burning and it seems to me to be getting brighter and brighter."[5] To Carrole Fair he sent his views and advice about publishing: "I am pleased to hear about your career and I would encourage you to carry out the anthology project. There is no mystery about publication. First you assemble the poems. Then you start showing the collection around to prospective publishers. If you are lucky, you make a strike. It's sort of like going fishing. In any case, do keep in touch and let me know how you come out."[6] And in his letter to Horace Cayton he allowed his sense of humor a free hand. He wrote, "*Long Old Road* was certainly worth waiting for. It packs a mighty wallop, and I predict that teeth will rattle when it lands. You have done yourself proud, old man! Your special gift, I have always felt, was a capacity to live your life up to the hilt, as they say. Obviously this has not always been without cost, but we can all rejoice that you have reached the age of reflection with literary powers still capable of transmitting the whole experience."[7] An advance copy of Cayton's work had come to Bontemps's desk while he was in Boston and New York on errands for Fisk. This was not long after *Life* had published a piece on Robert Lowell, which Bontemps had read. He and Lowell had occupied a little two-bedroom wing with a common bath one summer at Yaddo.

Arna continued during this period his correspondence with Ida Cullen and other widows of his writer friends, including Marjorie Toomer, Maureen Dover (Cedric Dover), and with his long-time friend and collaborator, Jack Conroy. He also paid a special visit, on behalf of U.C.L.A., to the ailing Arthur Spingarn in New York, whom he afterwards described as "pushing ninety" and still brisk-minded.[8]

Meanwhile, he kept in touch with librarians and archivists all over the country. With Robert Vosper, Head Librarian at U.C.L.A., he maintained a stimulating exchange of letters concerning that University's efforts to acquire the Cedric Dover papers and about several other special collections Vosper wanted to acquire. Arna's family and friends had often wondered how he managed to complete successfully so many duties at once. But he kept up his pace without slowing down. In February 1964 he was one of nine members named to Nashville's new Metro Board of Education, an office into which he was installed the following July. But between spring and fall of that year, the strain of his impossible schedule bore down upon him more heavily than usual. As early as March he wrote to Paul Bremen, publisher of his collected poems, *Personals*, "I understand what you mean by *hectic*. That describes what we have here also."[9]

But Arna did not neglect his writing schedule during this demanding period. Now that *Famous Negro Athletes* was off the press, he was able to begin preparing, with Jack Conroy, their new, revised edition of *They Seek a City* (1945), which Hill and Wang reissued in 1966 as *Anyplace but Here*. Macmillan also published a new edition in 1964 of *Black Thunder* with a new introduction by the author containing much that is nostalgic, a Bontempsian ingredient. Before the end of 1964 he had finished one of his most important critical articles, "Harlem the Beautiful Years," published in January 1965,[10] and had put finishing touches on another he had been asked to write for *Harper's*, a nostalgic memoir that is perhaps his most autobiographical piece.[11]

He also completed a newsletter piece on Du Bois for AMSAC, and in February 1964, at the request of the Du Bois Memorial Committee, he attended the New York tribute to the late scholar. The highlight of this affair was a skit based on the Du Bois career featuring such notables as Ossie Davis, Ruby Dee, Beah Richards, Godfrey Cambridge, Clebert Ford, and Eva Jessye Choir. Bontemps presented a special tribute, followed by personal statements from John Hope Franklin, Arthur Spingarn, and Nadine Brewer of the Metropolitan Opera, among others.

By the end of spring quarter 1964, most of the job of cataloguing the special collections of the Fisk Library was complete. Bontemps had secured a special grant enabling him to hire enough staff to fully catalogue the American Missionary Association Archives.[12] At the end of the quarter he traveled to Worcester, Massachusetts, to speak at the opening of the new public library building.

In his remarks he said this country's literary history revealed a tendency to neglect books that challenge prevailing notions "about Negroes, no matter how truthful or well-written."[13]

Describing this cultural blackout, he implied that "Negroes" need to read about themselves and their situations, and that it is equally important for white readers to become acquainted with some of the same books if both are to live, work, and worship together. He depicted this tendency to ignore the literary and artistic contributions of minorities as an ostensible "self delusion," using as an example Ira Aldridge, the nineteenth-century figure whom critics called the greatest Shakespearean actor America has produced. Aldridge's name did not appear in the *Encyclopedia Britannica*, *Who's Who in Theater*, or the *Dictionary of American Biography*.[14]

As soon as Bontemps returned from this Massachusetts jaunt, President S. J. Wright formally appointed him Fisk's Director of University Relations at an annual salary of $14,000. In this position his duties would encompass assigned responsibilities for fund-raising and coordinating the public relations program.[15] He was also appointed to the editorial board of the *Negro History Bulletin*, one of two journals published by the Association for the Study of Negro Life and History, an organization in which he had held membership for a number of years.[16] And he attended a four-day conference for writers at the Asilomar Conference Center, an extension of the University of California.

Its theme was "The Negro Writer in the United States." Bontemps was one of the panelists at the conference, appearing along with several other African-American writers and scholars: James Baldwin, Robert Bone, Gwendolyn Brooks, Horace Cayton, Ossie Davis, Ralph Ellison, Nat Hentoff, Herbert Hill, LeRoi Jones, Saunders Redding, and Harvey Swados. Throughout, the meeting was tense. Goldwater had received the Republican nomination for president. The Harlem riots were in full swing. Everybody, it seemed to Arna, was a little too emotional. Most of the speakers became overly charismatic under the pressures of audience response and performer projection. Not that Arna was incapable of emotion—on the contrary, he was both intense and emotional, but it was his nature to display his feelings quietly. So Arna kept his characteristic "cool" and was the only one of the conference participants who favorably impressed columnist Kenneth Rexroth, who attended the entire meeting. Rexroth described the proceedings as a discussion turned into a "civil rights rally," but he complimented the reserve of Arna Bontemps, whom he regarded as a much-needed stabilizer during the conference. He described Arna as "a Creole of color and a gentleman of letters of the type who once made French literature so humane."[17]

Rexroth asked Arna a question during the meeting that the poet-novelist had himself pondered for many years: What happened to the children of "the Negro elite" of the years before the First World War? He replied: "As a teacher, I have met descendants of John Mercer Langston who did not know who their great ancestor was and who were embarrassed when I told them about him. They, like most other middle class Americans, have been snowed under by the standards of the television culture.''[18] How the other conference participants regarded Bontemps's stance has not surfaced.

In early February 1965 Fania Marinoff, the widow of Carl Van Vechten, sent Bontemps a copy of Edward Leuder's recent biography of her husband, titled *Carl Van Vechten*. For this gesture the writer-archivist was grateful, and he promptly read the book with sustained interest. It had arrived around the time he and his staff were boxing and mailing all of his original correspondence with his sometime friend "Carlo," which he was sending to the Manuscripts Department of the library at Syracuse University. He had effected a sale of these documents to Syracuse, although Van Vechten would have wanted them to go to Yale.[19]

On June 4, 1965, finishing the first of his four years as a member of the Metro School Board, Arna handed diplomas to 277 Pearl High graduating seniors. On this same date eight years later, at about the same time of evening, he would keep his final appointment.[20] But even if he had been aware of the exact time of this irrevocable assignation, the poet-humanitarian would not have had time to worry over the inevitable; he was too busy writing and enjoying life each moment. As soon as Jack Conroy returned from the extended stay in Europe he had taken in early summer, he and Bontemps put the finishing touches on *Anyplace but Here*, which they promptly mailed to Hill and Wang.

Arna then went to U.C.L.A. during Negro History Week to speak at a convocation. His topic was "Old Myths—New Negroes," and the occasion was the acquisition by the U.C.L.A. library of the five thousand-volume Arthur B. Spingarn Collection of books by and about African Americans. Bontemps had used his influence with Spingarn to assure the acquisition. Alberta made this trip with her husband, and they could both recall their difficult days in Watts in 1934–35 and smile about them. Arna recalled for his U.C.L.A. audience aspects of his boyhood in Watts. He recalled a happier Watts, while all around were predictions of a "long, hot summer." On his return to Fisk, he finished preparing for a writer's conference held there from April 22 to 24, 1965. Fisk was celebrating its one hundredth anniversary, and the conference featured Bontemps, Fisk Writer-in-Residence John O. Killens, and poet Robert Hayden, also a member of the Fisk faculty. Saunders Redding gave the conference's keynote address. In fact, many of the greats attended that year: Margaret Walker Alexander, Melvin B. Tolson, William Melvin Kelley, Richard Rive, Alice Childress, and Loften Mitchell, to provide only a partial list.

Anyplace but Here was issued early in 1966 and experienced good sales. Bontemps also received a letter from the University of Illinois' Chicago Circle campus offering him a tenure-track position as an Associate Professor in American Literature at a salary three times his highest pay at Fisk. This was an offer he could not refuse. Moreover, he was excited about the prospect of living in Chicago again. He and Alberta would see old friends and familiar places, and he would enjoy the stimulating company of the Chicago literati. He was more than a little proud of this appointment: at last he was being recognized, not for his color but for his competence, a rare experience for the African-American professional. Illinois was more than happy to have Bontemps, as his correspondence from this period reveals. The salary offer was "negotiable" and his course schedule flexible, giving him a free hand to design his own teaching activities.[21]

Explaining to Ann Shockley how it happened that he took the job at Chicago, Bontemps said that at age sixty-four he left Fisk on a sabbatical and went to Illinois. He had not intended to take another job, but after being granted a sabbatical by Fisk's trustees and president, he was invited to come to Illinois to replace Gil Osofsky, who had just been awarded a Guggenheim grant and wanted a year's leave. He went to teach a course in history and was also asked to teach a topic in literature, which was one of the areas he had promoted all along: Bontemps believed that the African-American experience is seen better through the literature than through history.

So he went to Illinois, and after his first year, officials there promoted him to full Professor of English. He had planned to stay at Illinois a while longer, but in the middle of his second year, not long after the promotion was announced, he had "a little unexpected occurrence" [the stroke he suffered in the winter of 1968]. His doctors advised him, he said, to "cool it," which he tried to do, returning to Nashville to spend a year at home, while remaining on salary at Illinois for an additional two years.[22]

To accept the Illinois offer without burning his bridges at Fisk, Arna had requested that his sabbatical be changed to a regular one-year leave without pay. This left him free to accept Illinois' offer. His leave of absence during the 1966–67 school year coincided with S. J. Wright's resignation as President of Fisk University. By August 1966 Arna and Alberta had moved into an apartment at 4939 South Dorchester Avenue, Chicago. They had not lived in the "Windy City" since August 1943, all of twenty-three years.

But Arna wisely did not sever his ties at Fisk. During his absence he kept in contact with his closest Fisk colleagues. He also continued to write books and articles, all of which were announced at Fisk. Only a few years before this period, an increasing number of schoolbooks had begun to include selections from Arna's writings, a trend that continued throughout his stay at the Chicago Circle campus. Furthermore, he began to receive an increasing number of requests from publishers of school books to serve as editor-consultant. Besides his relationships with Aladdin, Beacon, and several other firms, he also served as writer-consultant for the *Negro American Heritage* series (Century Schoolbook Press, San Francisco, 1965).

Before he left Nashville for Chicago, he published two additional chapters in books, "The Negro Contribution to American Letters," in *The American Negro Reference Book*, edited by Howard University's John Paul Davis and published by Prentice-Hall in 1966; and "The Negro Renaissance: Jean Toomer and the Harlem Writers of the 1920s," in *Anger and Beyond*, with Herbert Hill as editor (Harper and Row, 1966). In the fall of 1966 he gave a speech on his own use of the "lonesome boy" theme. A slightly revised version of this speech was later published in *Horn Book*.[23]

In the spring of 1967, all was going well for Arna and Alberta. They had no more "babies," for Alex, their youngest, was in his junior year at Fisk, and the others had married and were pursuing their individual careers—Joan as a college librarian, Paul as a college professor, Poppy, Camille, and Constance as teachers in public schools. But twice in one week, amid Arna's happiness, grief came again to his heart. John Wesley Work III (1901–1967), his close friend, fraternity brother, and Fisk colleague for nearly twenty-four years, died in May—Jean Toomer had died only a few weeks before—and within the same week of Work's death, Langston Hughes died in New York City. Returning from Chicago to Nashville by plane, Arna and Alberta attended Work's funeral at 4:00 P.M. on May 20 at the same chapel on Fisk's campus where the writer's own funeral would be held six years later.[24] As soon as Work's funeral was over, Arna and Alberta made a furious dash for Nashville's airport to board a plane that would get them to New York in time for Hughes's funeral.

In their work together Langston and Arna had reinforced each other. The writer's son, Arna Alexander Bontemps, in a speech made in April 1991 at the College Language Association's annual meeting in Columbia, South Carolina, said of his father's collaboration with Hughes: "In the areas where their egos were most vulnerable, they did not compete. Poetry was Hughes's thing, and my father was a writer of prose fiction." And speaking of the effect Hughes's death had on Arna, his friend and collaborator, his son and namesake said of his father that he went to New York for Langston's funeral and returned a changed man: in Langston's death Arna had confronted his own mortality. The hurt and shock of losing both Work and his beloved "Lang" simultaneously cut deeply into Arna's sensitive, caring heart.

In 1968, after he had returned to Chicago and had begun his work as co-executor with George Bass of Langston's estate, Arna suffered a stroke. For the first time in his nearly sixty-five years he was hospitalized. After one week in the hospital, he was released with a warning from his physicians to slow down. But he did not take this illness seriously, though family and friends did prevail upon him to return to Nashville and to cut down on his globe-trotting. For the remainder of his life, the writer referred to the seizure he had experienced as his "little accident" or his "unexpected occurrence."[25] Poet Gwendolyn Brooks and other friends and poets had pampered the bard in Chicago during his hospitalization. A year after his release from the hospital, in a letter that opened "Dear Gwen," he wrote to Brooks from Nashville:

I am back at the typewriter, after the imposed hiatus, and the first thing I want to say is that you are a true laureate, in kindness and thoughtfulness as well as in writing. The flowers, the poems and the presence of the others you brought all helped wonderfully. They almost overcame the embarrassment of my first hospital illness in my whole sixty-five years! Except that I have lost a few pounds and my voice is still somewhat unpredictable, I hope you would not be able to detect that I had ever been there. Actually, it now begins to seem like a dream.[26]

But contrary to what Arna implied in the Shockley interview, he did not exactly "cool it" after his stroke. His recovery seemed complete. There had been no paralysis, and his speech was not permanently affected. In the first months after the stroke, only Mrs. Bontemps could tell he was "dragging his left side a little."[27] Since childhood he had a strong physical constitution and an emotional resiliency to match. These he had called upon to help him through this illness. He overcame the effects of the stroke and by late spring of 1968 was accepting lecture engagements, but on a more limited scale than previously.

Arna found himself more sought after than ever before by the large Northern universities, coming in 1969 to the University of Wisconsin at Madison where I was a graduate student to participate in the Black Students' Association's first Black Arts Festival. It was around this time that he decided to accept Yale's offer, and began to teach there in the fall of the 1969–70 term, when he was named Curator of the James Weldon Johnson Collection, an honorary title he had not expected to receive. The writer has left an explanation of how he wound up at Yale: "and Yale visited me. I was speaking at the University of Connecticut, and they sent somebody up there to ask me . . . gave me the treatment and offered me whatever I would ask to come. And I asked for what seemed a large salary at the time . . . so large, I didn't expect them to give it to me, but they gave it. So I went there and stayed until I reached their mandatory retirement age [seventy]."[28]

While at Yale he taught an advanced undergraduate course in the Afro-American Studies Department titled "The Afro-American Literary Tradition," and a graduate course in the same department titled "The Harlem Renaissance." As a teacher at Yale Bontemps was popular with his students, for as recently as the fall of 1986 I met persons still at Yale who recalled his courses. Many of the graduate students whom he taught there went on to become professors in major universities. All in all, it was a rewarding experience for both Arna and Alberta. Mrs. Bontemps still remembers the events leading to their hiatus in New Haven. Speaking of the period between Arna's work at the Chicago Circle Campus and his decision to go to Yale, his widow said: "And then after a year, Yale asked him. First some other college; I think Brandeis. I remember our going up to visit Brandeis because they had invited him. And some other college invited him around the same time. . . . And when we came back home, he had a letter from Yale."[29]

Arna adjusted well to Yale and the New Haven community, and he would have stayed longer if Alberta had been content to stay. But she was not prepared to leave her Nashville home indefinitely. She explained: "I said, 'you've been on the retirement circuit, and I think you've done enough.' So I began packing the things up to come to Nashville. But they wanted him to stay. And they moved him into an apartment over at Brandeis. And so he stayed on another year. . . . And I'd go back and forth and be with him there.''[30] During this period at Yale and afterward, Arna's health remained good. He had no reoccurrence of the symptoms related to his stroke. On October 13, 1971 he turned sixty-nine, and though he could have worked until the end of the semester in which his seventieth birthday occurred, he chose to return to Nashville at the end of the 1970–71 term.[31]

The years between his Fisk retirement and the professorship at New Haven were filled with literary activity. In Chicago there were radio and television appearances and a lecture trip to the Azalia Hackley Memorial Collection at the Detroit Public Library. Late in 1966 he published an article in *Crisis* that appeared, to use his own language, ''cheek by jowl'' with one by Loften Mitchell.[32] In May 1967 he and Conroy received the James L. Dow Award for *Anyplace but Here*; the prize was $500. And after he had recovered from the stroke, he continued to lecture on African-American writers and their works.

In 1969 he published two books and a chapter in another. Both books were anthologies; one titled *Great Slave Narratives* published by Beacon, and another collection for juvenile readers titled *Hold Fast to Dreams: Poems Old and New* (Follet). The chapter appeared in *Black Expression*, edited by Addison Gayle, Jr., and was titled ''Negro Poets Then and Now.'' In February of that year President Lyndon B. Johnson chose his *One Hundred Years of Negro Freedom* as one of the 250 books he purchased for the White House Library. The White House Librarian listed the book under ''History.''[33]

At the end of the school term, Arna traveled again to Morgan State University at Baltimore; this time to receive the Doctor of Humane Letters degree, an honorary title the school conferred upon him. Nineteen sixty-nine was a time of unrest on college and university campuses throughout the nation, and Arna tried to offer some explanation of the causes, admitting while doing so that he had no solutions.[34] He saw the young militants of the 1960s and 1970s as sensitive youths whose hearts were quick to bleed, still caring enough to feel the world's injustices more keenly than did their predecessors. Bontemps said that as a young man he had been just as militant, but it never occurred to him to protest in the manner in which his son Alex's generation protested.[35]

As soon as he moved back to Nashville from New Haven, Bontemps was asked again to serve Fisk University. This time he would teach creative writing and his title would be ''Writer in Residence.'' He accepted the offer and began functioning in his new role at the beginning of the fall quarter 1971. Members of the Fisk family were elated to have him back, and they showed it by rolling out the red carpet, honoring him and Mrs. Bontemps at a reception. The reception, one of the high points of his Fisk experience, was held on Sunday, October 21, 1969 at eight o'clock in the evening in Jubilee Hall's Appleton Room.[36]

A few Fisk faculty members still recall this social event with pleasure. Their eighth president, James Raymond Lawson (1967–75), had been appointed about a year after S. J. Wright resigned and Bontemps left on sabbatical in 1966.[37]

Lawson, too, understood the value of having Arna Bontemps back on campus. Arna was now working with the fourth Fisk president since hiring on in 1943, and he would continue to work for the good of Fisk University.

As soon as the elaborate welcome home had been given and he had greeted his old friends and had become acquainted with some of the new faces on campus, Arna lent the benefit of his experience and his literary contacts to a committee planning the annual spring literary festival. And he continued to write. While at Yale he had published two new books and at least one scholarly article and had delivered several formal speeches, some of which have been preserved in manuscript form. The published article was a revision of the speech "Old Myths—New Negroes" that he had given a few years earlier at Chicago. He kept the title intact and sent it to the editors of *Top of the News* in the fall of 1969. They published it in their first issue of 1970.[38]

Lippincott published his children's book, *Mr. Kelso's Lion*, and Bontemps also published that year an updated version of his and Hughes's 1949 anthology. This volume was the best of the Bontemps—Hughes collections of African-American verse, mainly because it was more complete, presenting more new poets than had their previous versions. Bontemps titled it *The Poetry of the Negro, 1746–1970* which, like the 1949 volume, was issued by Doubleday.

In 1971, just after his formal retirement from Yale, Dodd, Mead published another of his biographies, *Free at Last: The Life of Frederick Douglass*. Once back at Fisk, Arna began to think more seriously about writing his autobiography, a plan he had decided upon not long after the death of Hughes. He had planned to write a biography of Hughes and then his own life's story, but meeting publishers' deadlines had not left him much time to work toward either of these goals. In early 1972 he was named Honorary Consultant to the Library of Congress in American Cultural History. This appointment came not long after Dodd, Mead had published another of his historical books, this one titled *The Harlem Renaissance Remembered*, and by fall of that year they had published his last biography, *Young Booker: The Early Days of Booker T. Washington*.

Just prior to this book's release, he granted Ann Allen Shockley on July 14, 1972, a lengthy, recorded "Oral History Interview," which is preserved in Fisk's Black Oral History Program and which remains the most reliable unpublished source on the life of Arna Wendell Bontemps. One of the questions Shockley asked him during this interview evoked a response about the writer and his craft that is still good advice to writers and that also illustrates how Arna himself approached the writing task during his nearly fifty years as a writer. He agreed that a writer needs "basic talent" but also stressed that technique is important, for technique, as he saw it, made the writer's task less burdensome.[39]

As the fall 1972 term at Fisk opened, a letter came to Bontemps from Audrey N. Jackson of Zachary, Louisiana. She had been asked by the library section of the Louisiana Education Association (L.E.A.) to contact him and secure his services as a speaker during their annual November conference. Though his schedule was busy, and though he had made prior commitments, he was irresistibly drawn by one feature of this invitation—the meeting would be held in Alexandria. He had been longing for a chance to visit his birthplace and the surrounding towns to complete research for the autobiography he had already outlined. He had decided to title the work "A Man's Name."

He gave Jackson an affirmative reply with one condition attached, that she promise to take him to his birthplace at Ninth and Winn in Alexandria and to the St. Francis Xavier Church there; and to the various other churches and courthouses in the Rapides-Avoyelles area, including the Rapides Parish Courthouse at Alexandria and Marksville's Avoyelles Parish Courthouse. He also wanted to examine records at churches in Mansura and Pineville and to visit some elderly individuals who had been friends of his Bontemps and Pembrooke grandparents.[40] All of this Audrey Jackson agreed to do, and she kept her promise. On November 20, 21, and 22, during Thanksgiving week 1972, Arna Bontemps was a guest of the Louisiana librarians, and he remained in Alexandria a few days after the conference had ended to complete research for the projected autobiography.

Audrey N. Jackson had first encountered Bontemps through his books. But she had also met him in person when he went to Baton Rouge to address the librarians there in 1955. During the conference she had spoken to him about coming to Alexandria, and this is the account she gave: "he promised he would come back to Alexandria, because Alexandria was his home."[41] Following is a segment of the interview of Audrey Jackson I conducted and recorded on January 29, 1986:

Jones: Was Bontemps excited about finding roots?

Jackson: Very excited . . . and when he found that his grandfather was listed as a free man of color on there [the courthouse records at Marksville], it was just amazing . . . he showed me something about his grandfather and his grandmother at that time. And they didn't want to make copies. But by it being court records they couldn't deny him.[42]

On the day of his arrival at Alexandria, the city declared Arna Wendell Bontemps Day and the *Alexandria Town Talk* and other newspapers, those in Pineville and the surrounding towns, carried stories about his arrival and itinerary. When I interviewed Audrey Jackson, she gave the following account of Bontemps's time in Alexandria:

When he arrived, he had a press conference, and I have the article that you can see. . . . And then we had a radio interview [the Irving Ward-Steinman show]. And on this . . . interview he talked about the town, and how it had changed. . . . And then . . . he spoke to us at the luncheon. And after the luncheon, we decided to get together the next day, my daughter, and Rose Metoyer, and I, . . . to go with him on this tour around Alexandria . . . to locate information about his family. And when the conference was over, he stayed there [Alexandria] a couple of more days, and he returned [to Nashville]. . . . We went to the courthouse in Marksville, and on to Mansura. He wanted to get records. Of his mother's marriage license, of his father's baptism. And there was some land he knew about that he wanted records of.[43]

The same interview reveals that Audrey Jackson had in her possession a number of documents and artifacts she has graciously shared with me:

Jones: Do you know of any papers or artifacts . . . that would help my research?

Jackson: I have several things, like the last speech he made at our luncheon meeting.

Jones: Do you have the original manuscript?

Jackson: Right. I have the original manuscript. I also have the remarks he made before the speech. And I also have the autograph . . . two autographed copies of his book. And he also just put his name in about four other copies of *Young Booker* for me.

Jones: Did you perceive that he had a sense of leaving a record behind?

Jackson: A very strong sense, in fact. And he talked about the fact that he was going to write the life of Langston Hughes, and that he wished to do his [Hughes's] book first.

Jones: And, the book he was doing on his own life?

Jackson: Yes, story of his life. And he talked about the fact that he had another book coming out and that the publishers were going to—probably—change the name of it. He said he wanted it to be *The Old South*, or something in that vein. . . . On the tape . . . he was supposed to give his speech first, but he asked us to let him talk about Alexandria . . . as he remembered it through his two uncles' eyes [Joseph Ward ("Uncle Buddy") and Ward Pembrooke]. . . .

Jones: In what physical and mental condition did you perceive him to be?

Jackson: He seemed very alert to me. And he seemed to be such a happy person . . . that when I heard of his death it shocked me. . . . There was nothing about him to suggest sickness . . . I thought he was a very happy person, a very warm person. He treated me like a father would treat a daughter. He was just delightful, the things he would say when we were riding along, and he would look at the fields, and you could see the churches, and he would make comments that made you feel beauty. He'd talk about the soil, and the trees, and how the sky was. . . .

Jones: He loved nature and he loved beauty.

Jackson: Yes, and he loved people. . . . It was just a beautiful thing to listen to him, and his voice was so soothing . . . soft-spoken. . . . And when you're listening to this tape, when he was talking in Alexandria, you'll realize all this warmth.[44]

Bontemps, at this library conference in Alexandria in November 1972, did not get around to reading his prepared speech, which is a revision of a talk he had given a short time earlier on the Eastern Shore campus of the University of Maryland. He gave this manuscript to Audrey Jackson with a note scribbled at the top of the first page that reads: "Before printing contact my agent for directions: Harold Ober Associates, 40 East 49th Street, New York, N.Y. 10017." He titled this typewritten speech "Black Writing Today" and opened the twenty-odd pages with a statement about writers and their critics, using the analogy of a person who runs for political office and his dealings with the press as an illustration of the black writer and his critics. He wrote:

There were in days long gone by and in a far country critics who did not exactly throw their hats in the air when William Shakespeare was writing. John Keats had an abominable press at one time. Many writers who were worthy and some who seem almost sublime in retrospect have been neglected or brushed aside with contempt, while others, tawdry and vulgar, have been extolled. For reasons such as this, critical comment, even good comment, (like political rhetoric), tends to become the most ephemeral of all writings. Now I am not against literary or critical comment, . . . and certainly do not recommend that any of it be suppressed. I may have been guilty in indulging in some of it myself at times. But the new black writer, I would say, will do himself a favor if he tries to put it all in perspective. Certainly he need not be intimidated by criticism, even if the critic is someone in his own home or classroom. The critic can't hurt him if he is good, and can't help him very much in the long run if he is tawdry or unworthy. At least this is my considered opinion, as the expression goes.[45]

The original manuscript was typewritten by Bontemps himself and is laden with handwritten emendations; it is still in the possession of Audrey Jackson and has not yet been published. It is a good example of Bontemps's writing method, his habit of sitting down at the typewriter and pounding out an entire composition before stopping to appraise what he had written. This manuscript was not typed by a secretary or stenographer, for it matches many of his type-written documents in the Fisk Archives and at Syracuse. At some time between his reading of the paper at the Maryland campus and the conference in Alexandria, he had written in ink a number of insertions and emendations. At Alexandria, the Louisiana librarians became so enthusiastic over his reminiscences of Louisiana, and of the town of Alexandria, that there was no time left for him to deliver this speech.

While in Alexandria, he enjoyed visiting with his friend Irving Ward-Steinman, the journalist on whose radio program the writer appeared during the visit. He also saw his godmother Ida Hines, and others who knew his parents and grandparents. In early January 1971, Alexandria's *Town Talk* had published an article written by Ward-Steinman complimenting Bontemps and his works. Ida Hines had sent the clipping with an attached note to Leslie Collins, which he handed over to the novelist. Bontemps wrote the following reply to his godmother:

The clipping . . . is both interesting and moving. I am grateful to you for sending it to Leslie, who promptly relayed it to me. I believe this is the first thing I have seen about myself published in my birthplace, and it therefore has double meaning from my point of view. . . .

The *Town Talk* is obviously a venerable Louisiana institution. I remember my parents occasionally receiving copies in California during my childhood. I liked the name of the paper then, and I still do.[46]

Arna Bontemps has remained the finest African-American author-scholar Louisiana has produced.[47]

Bontemps kept up his correspondence with Ward-Steinman during the winter and spring of 1973, and in mid-March sent him a postal card with this message:

Thank you for the copies of your most gracious review of *Young Booker* in the Louisiana papers. I hope the publisher has had a chance to see it. My next book is scheduled for May publication by Dodd, Mead, *The Old South*. . . . Several of the stories have CENLA [Central Louisiana] settings, and I hope to bring my two sons with me in late May or early June to have another look at their grandparents' stomping ground. (Both are college teachers.) So thanks again and best wishes.''[48]

But *The Old South* did not come off the press in May 1973 as scheduled. It would be published posthumously during the summer of that year, only weeks after its author died and was buried.

During the last few days of May 1973, Arna Bontemps traveled to Berea, Kentucky, where Berea College on May 27 bestowed upon him his second honorary doctorate degee, naming him Doctor of Humane Letters as Morgan State University had done previously. Eight days after receiving this honor, the author-scholar died in Nashville, less than five months before his seventy-first birthday. His death was sudden and without struggle.

June 4, 1973, the last day of Arna Wendell Bontemps's earthly pilgrimage, had begun like any other day in the Bontemps household. Alberta Bontemps, recognized in Nashville for her culinary skills, prepared breakfast as usual. School had recessed for the summer, and the house on Geneva Circle was full. Arna had been out in his wife's garden cutting roses during the morning. (Alberta always raised the roses and Arna gathered the blooms.) It was a beautiful day— sunny and bright. The weather was perfect. In a recent interview his widow recounted events of her husband's last day. She mused:

Yes, I can tell you about that day. . . . There had been many days since he had his stroke that I was always watching. Because I sensed that something might happen. But this particular day . . . he was in the study writing, and I was here at the telephone, trying to contact friends. This friend of ours, Mrs. Perry [Clara Perry] had passed. . . . So . . . knowing that he never liked to go to funerals, or to anything even connected with funerals . . . I was calling around to see who was going, so that I could go with them. And he came out of the study . . . he said, "I'd like to go." And I said, "You would?" I said, "All right." . . . I had two other friends . . . trying to find a way to go. So I offered them rides, and so we, the four of us, did go. And on our way, Arna stopped at the Peoples Drugstore. He needed some of his medicine. . . . He didn't seem to be ill at all. And so, we went on to the house to the wake.

By the time this party of four got to the wake, the house was extremely crowded. They made their way through the crowd, greeted their daughter Joan and her husband, among others they knew, briefly viewed the remains and went out front to the yard, where Arna's physician, Ludlow Perry, husband of the deceased, and his brother, a Catholic bishop, were standing. Mrs. Bontemps described what happened this way: "My husband admired the Bishop very much. So he became sort of excited, glad to see him. And I was walking on. He stopped to greet them . . . and I looked back just as he was going down. Just going down. And the doctor caught him, and they laid him on down. And that was that day."[49]

Funeral services for Arna Wendell Bontemps were held at twelve noon on Thursday, June 7, 1973 at Fisk University's Memorial Chapel with interment in Nashville's Greenwood Cemetery. A Presbyterian minister, Reverend William A. Alexander, presided, assisted by Father Neil O'Connel, O.F.M., of the Fisk faculty. This was a fitting arrangement, for Bontemps had always had an ecumenical outlook and could not abide religious insularity, no matter where he found it. Bernard Hunter, Fisk's organist, played for the prelude J. S. Bach's "Before Thy Throne I Now Appear," followed by scripture and prayer by Reverend Alexander. The congregational hymn was "Onward Christian Soldiers," and a personal tribute by Hughes's personal secretary, George Bass, followed. Then came a musical tribute by Dr. Oscar Henry, Professor of Music at Fisk, with the benediction pronounced by Father O'Connel. The postlude was Cesar Franck's "Pièce Heroique."[50]

The *New York Times* obituary was headed, "Arna Bontemps, Writer, 70, Dies—Harlem Renaissance Figure Had Taught at Fisk U."[51] His immediate survivors were his wife and their six children: four daughters, Joan Williams, Poppy Thomas, Camille Bontemps (Strong), and Constance Thomas; and two sons, Paul Bismark and Arna Alexander. He was also survived by his sister, Ruby Troy, and ten grandchildren.

On June 20, 1973 a memorial service for Arna Bontemps was held in Christ Chapel of New York City's Riverside Church, the location of a similar service held for Langston Hughes six years earlier. This ceremony was sponsored by a group of Bontemps's literary friends. Opposite the order of service for the memorial was printed the writer's own poem on the Resurrection theme, "Miracles" ("Doubt no longer miracles . . . "). Robert McDonald provided organ music, and the Reverend Doctor Jesse Lyons of Riverside Church presided. After he had offered scripture and a prayer, there were brief litanies of remembrance offered by Lawrence Reddick of the Black Academy of Arts and Letters; by Ruby Dee, whom the deceased had counseled when she was a fledgling actress; and by Allen T. Klotts of Dodd, Mead and Company. Organist William B. Cooper played a musical tribute that included Negro spirituals arranged by John W. Work. The benediction and postlude followed.[52]

Six weeks after the writer's death, the Summer Institute in Directed Research at Jackson State College, Jackson, Mississippi, where poet Margaret Walker Alexander taught for many years, conducted another service in memory of Arna Wendell Bontemps. The service was fitting, for Arna had planned to attend this institute. This service was held on July 18 at 10:00 A.M. in the Dansby Hall

Auditorium.[53] Walker-Alexander gave her tribute, "I Remember Arna Bontemps," and Ann Allen Shockley, Special Collections Librarian at Fisk, gave hers, which she titled simply, "Arna Bontemps."[54] She said of her former teacher and colleague:

There are some writers who drift into print, and drift out, without leaving an indelible mark upon the world of letters or the thoughts of mankind. The strength and breadth of a writer is symbolized in how long his works will have lasted after his pen is forever silent. The works of Arna Bontemps will not have to face this test of duration to prove the importance of his stature as a writer. Prior to this death, this had already been established.[55]

At the time of his death Arna was still planning to write *A Man's Name*, his projected autobiography. In fact, he had outlined it. He had abandoned, it seems, the plan to finish Langston Hughes's biography before beginning his own life's story, probably as a result of complications regarding Langston's estate. When death came to steal him he was happy, doing what he had done for almost fifty years—working on several literary projects simultaneously. There was a book on Thurgood Marshall only partially finished, and he was preparing to write the definitive biography of Langston Hughes. He had gathered much of the material and outlined the work. And he had collected all the materials on his own roots that he needed to finish *A Man's Name*, but he had not actually started the writing.

He also left a partially finished juvenile story, "Wining Boy," which is in the possession of his heirs. The title shows the writer still experimenting with folk themes and folk types, a method that has paid off for present-day African-American novelists and playwrights, including August Wilson, who won a Pulitzer Prize in drama in 1990 for *The Piano Lesson*, in which a folk character, Wining Boy, appears. Over the years Bontemps had kept a scrapbook on himself that would have aided him in writing the autobiography; and Hughes had asked him to act as co-executor of his will and had given him permission to use designated materials for the Hughes biography. When death came, Bontemps had not finished administering the Hughes estate; in fact, the estate is still in escrow, for some individuals are still protesting particular provisions of the will.[56]

Bontemps had been Head Librarian when Ann Shockley, herself a novelist-critic, was still an undergraduate at Fisk. When she came back to Fisk years later as a librarian, she got to know him personally. She remembered the writer as "a handsome man with flowing white hair and . . . a natty dresser." There was an aura of youthfulness about him, she said, in mind and in spirit. "I recall," she mused, "how he stopped me in the library one day to say that he had heard one of my short stories had been made into a short film. He was delighted; I was pleased to know that he knew. He promoted and encouraged young student writers on the campus—his life was writing and writers."[57]

Memorial services and special tributes to the fallen writer, along with published memoirs, continued to issue forth. "A Tribute to the Memory of Arna Bontemps" was presented by the faculty and administration of Fisk University on January 27, 1974, at 4:00 P.M. In the Special Collections Room of the Library a brief program was held with Gladys Inez Forde presiding. The University Woodwind Quintet provided music and Sandra E. Butler, of Guidance Associates of Pleasantville, New York, presented interview tapes of Arna Bontemps, which were accepted for the University by President James R. Lawson. To end the observance, two filmstrips from the Fisk Collection were shown, "Arna Bontemps" and "Aaron Douglas." The culminating event was held that night in the Fisk Chapel. Members of the Fisk Theater Department and members of the faculty at large read selections from Bontemps's poetry and from the poetry of Sterling Brown and Margaret Walker. Eubie Blake, Arna Bontemps's personal friend, was a guest performer along with the "Orchestrated Crowd," a Fisk ensemble.

At the Riverside Church memorial service, Lawrence Reddick's speech, "Talent and Goodness," recalled the time when Reddick first met Arna. It was in Chicago, when both were graduate students and while Arna was also working for the Federal Writer's Project. The two lived around the corner from each other and talked frequently about writers and writing. Reddick had been amazed at how widely read Bontemps was and at how many well-known writers he knew personally. Reddick credited Bontemps with being the person who discovered the genius in Richard Wright, recalling how one evening Arna had brought the thin, shy Wright around to his room. It so happened that Reddick's roommate, Ulysses S. Keyes, the defense attorney in the locally famous Nixon murder case, was in. He and Wright became friends, and Wright's novel *Native Son* was at least partially the result of that friendship. Reddick spoke of the "positive spirit" that pervaded Bontemps's conversation and about the absence of envy and professional jealousy in his soul.[58]

On the same program Allen T. Klotts, Secretary and Executive Editor of Dodd, Mead gave a speech entitled "Arna Bontemps." Klotts had first met the writer in the late 1950s when Arna and Langston were preparing one of the later editions of the *Book of Negro Folklore*, a work that went through six editions during Bontemps's lifetime. In the memorial speech Klotts proudly claimed Arna as a personal friend, describing him as "eternally youthful."[59] One week before he died, Arna had returned to Klotts the galleys for the publication of *The Old South*, fourteen short stories evoking African-American life in the rural South of the 1930s.

These stories reflect the author's experience and the experience of his ancestors, revealing a nostalgia for the South that has shaped their lives. They are tales told simply, and because of their simplicity they are also moving, full of a growing boy's awakening to the environment that shaped him and his family. These stories are full of the family affection that sustained their author all of his days. This prose fiction anthology also contains an absorbing essay about his 1972 return to his childhood home in Louisiana.

Arna Bontemps was a victim of overwork. With longevity on both sides of his family, it is probable that he could have "by reason of strength" exceeded the "three score and ten" he did reach. But the labor of producing an average of two books and several shorter works each year, for nearly fifty years, not to mention his other duties and responsibilities, took its toll. It is indeed a pity he did not set aside one of his other projects long enough to write his own story. The writer's physical stamina had waned, but he suffered no lack of inner strength. Mrs. Bontemps had sensed, prior to her husband's death, that he himself had perceived the imminence of his own death. She said:

He never discussed death at all. He was a very private person, as far as that was concerned. But I could tell that he was aware of it. And he was affected by so many nostalgic things during those last months that previously had not fazed him. It could be a movie, or something on television that he'd be looking at, and you'd see the water streaming down his eyes. He'd never been like that before.[60]

Speaking of her husband's inner resources, Mrs. Bontemps said: "He was a quiet person, and . . . very spiritual. He never displayed his religion on the outside much, but deep down, he was really religious."[61] Recalling the closing tercet of his long poem, "Golgotha Is a Mountain," Arna knew that one day—soon— he would crumble and the mound of his grave, representing heaviness, grief, and sacrifice would "make a mountain," Golgotha's hill.

A portion of Arna's inner strength came from his own childhood experiences. The tribute he read in 1952 at the funeral of his one-hundred-year-old maternal grandmother, Sarah Ward Pembrooke, is symbolic of his deep sensitivity, of his faith, and of the values instilled in him during his childhood; and it reveals one of his favorite literary themes, the strength of the black woman. He wrote:

Whenever anyone asks me about my family, I start talking about Grandma. I have been singing her praises for nearly half a century, but still there is much more that might be said. This is not the time for many words, however. This is rather a moment for thought and remembrance. . . .

As a child I was impressed by Grandma's attitude when the time came to bury our dead. I was present and saw her weep for her husband, her sister, Jane, her daughter, Teal, and my own mother, Maria, and I felt that at these times, when grief was heaviest, the greatness of her character was most clearly revealed. I passed by the door and saw her putting drops of water on my mother's parched tongue when the latter was too weak to sip from a cup. It was early morning and Grandma had been up all night. She never tired or lost hope. Though she knew the power of death, having lost so many loved ones, she refused to surrender a single one without a struggle. I shall always remember Grandma's stout heart. I shall always remember her way of life, her gardening, her needlework, her love of every living thing. Once in my kindergarten days . . . I dug up a tree I found in the woods and brought it to her in a can. She planted and nurtured it for years and reminded me of the incident after I was full grown.[62]

Arna's experience had been enlarged during his boyhood by the stories his grandmother told, for she had enjoyed a panoramic view of history. She had lived through the whole of the Civil War and remembered vividly her community's involvement in the struggle. She told her grandson about Reconstruction and about the Spanish-American War. She told him of how she had seen her sons and grandsons march off to fight in both world wars. Arna had vicariously enjoyed her triumph over time and toil. Through his own diligence and talent he has left to America a great heritage. In a letter to United States Senator Ross Bass, he described himself as "a writer, librarian, and sometimes teacher."[63] But his true vocation was writing.

His was a full and creative life. He distinguished himself as an authority on the Harlem Renaissance, for he had been one of the movement's participants, and had guarded the period's reputation with his life and his pen. In his brilliant literary career he ran the gamut from poetry to short stories and novels, to stories for children and collaboration on a Broadway musical. He wrote countless reviews, edited several anthologies, and published dozens of scholarly articles. He established himself as a sound literary critic and was an accomplished public speaker. For many years he served as a consultant to publishers and as a mentor to young writers. He was also a Fellow of the International Institute of Arts and Letters. Exclusive of his reviews, his published works total more than seventy items. In addition, he left several unpublished manuscripts, including a novel, a couple of plays, and several juvenile novels. He appeared on lecture platforms throughout America and abroad, starting in the early 1930s and continuing until his death in 1973. His literary reputation was and is international.

During his lengthy tenure as Head Librarian at Fisk and from time to time as a classroom teacher there, he had the good sense to create his literary works for literature's sake, not to curry favor with critics. Arna Wendell Bontemps spent his seventy years and eight months being himself. He was personable, warm, generous, considerate; and above everything else, he was a gentleman and a scholar. He possessed a unique capacity for nostalgia, and his works reflect that gift. Much of what he wrote was autobiographical, for he never stopped longing for the vigor and beauty of his childhood days in Louisiana, or for the charm of his boyhood surroundings in California. His search for his roots, for his own "blackness," became a lifelong endeavor, for he understood that the most far-reaching and pervasive contributions of African Americans to Western culture have come from folk sources, those taproots of vitality that are not hard to find and that should not be underestimated. Most of his works have dealt with African Americans and their struggle for recognition and freedom in a hostile world.

In telling the story of his race, Arna Bontemps captured a great deal of realism, the emotions of individuals; the themes of life itself. This is not to imply that he was not an idealist, for this he was. He was also a perfectionist in the standards that he set for himself as a writer. And he is still remembered for his many talents, and for his versatility. All who knew him, and many who only read his books, have benefited from his unobtrusive wisdom, his gentle demeanor, his subtle humor, and his perceptive observations about the American scene, past and contemporary.

Arna Wendell Bontemps was modest about his accomplishments, and was always his own severest critic. In his work and dealings with others, he was the gentleman, the scholar, the teacher, the artist. His very movements reflected the poet. His controlled but resonant voice reflected the depth of his spirit. This pioneer African-American literary personality remained faithful also in his friendships and was a devoted family man. Above all, he was a champion of freedom and dignity for everyone. As with Langston Hughes's works, not everything Bontemps published was of uniform quality. This is sometimes true of the children's works on which they collaborated, for publishers often insisted they add materials that actually distracted. But because they always felt the money pinch, they sometimes yielded to editors' demands. When no agreement could be reached, these stories went unpublished or were left unfinished.

Arna Bontemps, perhaps as overshadowed by Langston Hughes as Zora Neale Hurston was by Richard Wright, contributed to the perpetuation of what, in his early years, was a small interest in African-American life and culture. He was never, at heart, a librarian, but his knowledge of the field and his administrative ability stood him in good stead. His pioneering collecting accomplishments have provided later scholars and writers easier access to research materials, and his early interest in children's literature has inspired contemporary writers, one of whom is Virginia Hamilton. Arna Bontemps was writing and publishing when interest in African-American life and letters was only slight, but he lived to see interest in that body of literature surge into a steady stream, a flowing fountain. And his own contribution has helped them peak into a flood.

A NOTE ON THE ARNA BONTEMPS FOUNDATION

The Arna Bontemps Foundation was organized on May 11, 1988, some two years after I completed research in the Alexandria–Marksville area. The organization's members represent a broad spectrum of the Rapides Parish community. Endorsed by the Louisiana Endowment for the Humanities, the purposes of the Foundation are to honor Arna Wendell Bontemps, a native son; to secure a historical marker for the birthplace; and to preserve his old home for posterity. In the fall of 1990 the house, formerly boarded shut at its original location, was moved from the site at Ninth and Winn Streets in Alexandria to city-owned property at the corner of Third and St. James Streets, directly behind the Bolton Home in River Oaks Square.

Notes

CHAPTER 1

1. Hughes to Simon Guggenheim Memorial Foundation, January 5, 1949, James Weldon Johnson Papers, American Literature Collection, Rare Book and Manuscript Library, Yale University. (Referred to hereafter as "The Yale Papers.")

2. Jack Conroy, "An Oral History Interview," conducted and transcribed by Kirkland C. Jones, May 23, 1986. (Referred to hereafter as "Conroy Tape.")

3. "Conroy Tape."

4. "Conroy Tape."

5. Arna Bontemps, "Bontemps Reminisces about Louisiana: An Address to the Library Section of the Louisiana Education Association," [title mine], an unpublished, recorded speech at Alexandria, La., November 20, 1972. Recorded by Audrey Nabors Jackson; transcribed by Kirkland C. Jones. (Hereafter referred to as "Bontemps's Alexandria Tape.") See also "Conroy Tape"; see also "Autobiography of Anna J. Stokes," hereafter referred to as "Anna Stokes: Syracuse Papers."

6. H. E. Sterkx, *The Free Negro in Ante-Bellum Louisiana* (Teaneck, N.J.: Farleigh Dickinson University Press, 1972), 159.

7. Sterkx, 158.

8. A mulatto is the offspring of a white and a Negro; a quadroon is the product of a white and a mulatto; an octoroon of a white and a quadroon. A griffe is the offspring of a mulatto and a Negro.

9. Sterkx, 7.

10. Record filed May 25, 1862 at the Marksville, La., courthouse. This is one of the few such records from this period that I found written in English. Most are in French.

11. See court and land records at courthouse in Marksville. Abstract recorded on May 23, 1862, by L. H. Couvillion, Clerk. Land in Louisiana is often sold in arpents instead of acres, even today. An arpent is not exactly the same as but is roughly equivalent to an acre.

12. Recorded in Avoyelles Parish Courthouse in Marksville, Book B–3, 155. Also recorded as occurring in 1861 by St. Paul the Apostle Church, Mansura.

13. Marriage license recorded on April 23, 1861, a short time after the actual ceremony.

14. See records that are housed at St. Paul the Apostle Catholic Church of Mansura. See also George C. Poret, *Vignettes of Louisiana Church History*, published by the author in 1895, and his *History of St. Paul the Apostle Church*, 1895.

15. See Tenth Census, 1880, of Louisiana, Avoyelles Parish. The same Hyppolite Bontemps was married in 1890 to Sidonia Randall in Avoyelles Parish on February 6. See records of Avoyelles Parish in courthouse in Marksville.

16. See records of St. Paul the Apostle Church, Mansura.

17. See Vol. ED–3, Sheet 38, Line 19 of 1880 Louisiana Census, Avoyelles Parish.

18. P. M. Hamer and Stanley G. Arthur, *Survey of Federal Archives in Louisiana: A Project Sponsored by the Louisiana State University*, 1941. (Referred to hereafter as "Ship Manifests.")

19. "An Oral History Interview of Alberta Johnson Bontemps," Nashville, Tenn., March 27, 1986. Conducted, recorded, and transcribed by Kirkland C. Jones. (Hereafter referred to as the "Alberta Bontemps Tape.")

20. See "Ship Manifests."

21. In her letter to me of April 17, 1986. (Referred to hereafter as "Ruby Troy Correspondence.")

22. Donald J. Hebert, *Southwest Louisiana Records: Civil Records of Settlers* (Eunice, La., Donald J. Hebert, 1974), in 33 vols.

23. Sterkx, 9.

24. Written in French, it is titled *La Code Noir, on Recuil des Reglemens rendus jusqu'à present. Concernant le Gouvernement, l'Administration de la Justice, la Police, la Discipline de le Conseils Compagnies etablie à ce Subject*.

25. Variant spelling of the last name was probably a phonetic rendition substituted by the census taker.

26. See also in 1880 census record of Avoyelles Parish a Joe Bontemps, age 50; a Noel Bontemps, age 76; and an Elizabeth Bontemps, age 44.

27. These and other facts about the Pembrooke family tree are listed in obituaries of family members that are in the possession of the poet's sister, Ruby Bontemps Troy, Huntsville, Ala. See especially the Obituary of Sarah Ward Pembrooke. See also "Anna Stokes: Syracuse Papers" for an account of how this youngest of the Pembrooke daughters came close to dying of nervous prostration while a young bride.

28. "Bontemps's Alexandria Tape."

29. 1900 Census of Louisiana, Rapides Parish.

30. "Bontemps's Alexandria Tape."

31. See Louisiana Census, Rapides Parish, 1900, Sheet 10, Line 1.

32. "Anna Stokes: Syracuse Papers."

33. The census gives his first name as "Joe." He purchased a license to marry Sarah Ward May 15, 1871, one day prior to the wedding.

34. The census gives his name as Nathan W.

35. Obituary of Sarah Ward Pembrooke. See also Anna Stokes.

36. This date is corroborated by the 1900 census.

37. "Bontemps's Alexandria Tape."

38. See Arna Stokes. She lists a grown daughter of Charlotte and Joe Ward, named

Harriet. Confusion could be result of nicknames, or middle names used in place of first names, a common practice.

39. There is no longer a Louisiana town known as "White Sulphur Springs." This resort town probably died during the Civil War.

40. Obituary of Sarah Ward Pembrooke. See also Anna Stokes.

41. Obituary.

42. See local and national newspaper accounts of the period.

43. From a May 30, 1986 telephone interview with Ruby Bontemps Troy, sister of Arna Wendell Bontemps.

44. Sterkx, 13.

45. "Anna Stokes: Syracuse Papers."

46. Anna Stokes.

47–56 also refer to Anna Stokes.

57. In a May 30, 1986 telephone interview, Ruby Bontemps Troy explained to me the correct pronunciation of her mother's name.

58. Paul Bontemps's portrait may be seen on a filmstrip with sound accompaniment, "Profiles of Black Achievement: Arna Bontemps and Aaron Douglas." (Part of Harcourt Brace Jovanovich "Guidance Series.") While at the home of Alberta Bontemps in Nashville, I examined a youthful portrait of Arna Bontemps's mother. See also Bontemps's description of his father in "Why I Returned."

59. See records of Rapides Parish Courthouse at Alexandria.

60. Marriage license of Paul B. and Maria C. Bontemps. The purpose of bond as explained by a clerk of records at the Rapides Parish Courthouse (February 1986) was to serve as alimony for the bride in case some impediment such as breach of contract should occur, or should the marriage end in divorce or annulment, or in the death of the husband before a set number of years had expired. This custom remained in force in Louisiana until about thirty years ago. See baptismal records at Alexandria's St. Francis Xavier Cathedral.

61. Records of Rapides Parish Courthouse.

62. Verna Arvey, "Arna Bontemps, Who Recreates Significant Moments in History," *Opportunity*, Summer 1944, 126. See also Bontemps's "Why I Returned," an autobiographical essay that first appeared in "The South Today . . . 100 Years after Appomattox," a special supplement to *Harper's Magazine*, April 1965.

63. "Bontemps's Alexandria Tape."

64. "Alexandria Tape."

65. From "An Oral History Interview of Hattie Roy Bontemps," New Orleans, La., January 7, 1985. Conducted by Kirkland C. Jones.

66. Ann Allen Shockley, transcript of her interview of Arna Bontemps, July 1972; "Black Oral History Collection," Fisk University. (Hereafter referred to as "Shockley Interview.")

67. "Shockley Interview."

68. "Shockley Interview."

69. See history of Straight and New Orleans Universities, the merger of which formed Dillard University, in *The College Book*, 20th Edition (New York: Macmillan, 1985).

70. "Shockley Interview."

71. "Shockley Interview."

72. "Shockley Interview."

73. The license was purchased one day before the ceremony, January 14, 1895, and

may be found among the records of Rapides Parish Courthouse, Alexandria. The parish secretary, officed in the rectory of St. Francis Xavier Cathedral, testified in February 1986 that Father L. Minard was the only priest at St. Francis Xavier for many years, and even a cursory perusal of the parish's records corroborates her testimony.

74. See the famous Thomas Gandy Collection of photographic prints and negatives at Louisiana State University Library, Baton Rouge. See also their collection of free blacks' papers, an impressive one indeed. See also Joan Gandy, "Portraits Show Natchez Had Black Middle Class Following the Civil War," *Sunday Advocate*, Baton Rouge, La., February 16, 1986, 3K.

75. Charles Vincent, *Black Legislators in Louisiana During Reconstruction* (Baton Rouge: Louisiana State University Press, 1976), 11, passim. See especially his "Population Map" of 1870.

76. "Bontemps's Alexandria Tape." See also "Why I Returned," 180.

77. See *New York Times*, September–October, 1902.

78. Vincent, 183.

79. *New York Times*, October 1, 1902.

80. *New York Times*, September 30–October 7, 1902.

81. *New York Times*, October 8–13, 1902.

82. *Town Talk*, October 1, 1902.

83. *Town Talk*, October 13, 1902.

84. *Town Talk*, September 29–October 1, 1902.

85. *New York Times*, October 13, 1902.

86. *Town Talk*, September 29–October 30, 1902.

87. *Town Talk*, September 29–October 30, 1902.

CHAPTER 2

1. Notes from an interview with Leslie Morgan Collins, Nashville, Tenn., March 27, 1986. Dr. Collins would not permit me to record this interview.

2. See baptismal records for 1902 in St. Francis Xavier Cathedral, Alexandria, La. The "Syracuse Papers" contain a document, n.d., in Arna Bontemps's own hand proving that Ida Hines was the wife of his mother's first cousin.

3. "Shockley Interview," 6. Black Oral History Program, Fisk University.

4. See baptismal records, St. Francis Xavier Cathedral.

5. "Alberta Bontemps Tape."

6. "Why I Returned," 177.

7. "Why I Returned."

8. "Why I Returned."

9. "Why I Returned."

10. "Bontemps's Alexandria Tape."

11. "Why I Returned," 178.

12. "Why I Returned." See the author's reference to the "other things" that occupied his father's mind.

13. "Why I Returned," 177.

14. "Bontemps's Alexandria Tape." See also the "Audrey Nabors Jackson Interview," Alexandria and Marksville, La., January 29, 1986. Conducted, recorded, and transcribed by Kirkland C. Jones. (Referred to hereafter as the "Audrey N. Jackson Tape.")

15. "Audrey N. Jackson Tape."

16. "Shockley Interview," 2. See also "Why I Returned."

17. "Shockley Interview."

18. "Shockley Interview," 6.

19. "Why I Returned," 178.

20. "Why I Returned."

21. "Why I Returned."

22. See the *Town Talk*, September–December 1905.

23. *Town Talk*, January 30, 1906. For other stories mentioned in text, see same newspaper during entire month of January 1906.

24. *Town Talk*, February 1, 1906.

25. "Why I Returned," 178. See also "Shockley Interview," 6.

26. Obituary of Sarah Ward Pembrooke.

27. See Bontemps, *The Old South*, 6. See also Sandra Carlton Alexander's doctoral dissertation.

28. Bontemps, "Why I Stayed," Syracuse Papers. See also Chapter 1 of the Alexander dissertation.

CHAPTER 3

1. "Shockley Interview," 9.

2. *Town Talk*, February 16, 1906.

3. *Town Talk*, February 23, 1906.

4. Obituary of Sara Ward Pembrooke.

5. "Shockley Interview," 6. This age accords with the January 1905 birthdate recorded for Ruby Sarah Bontemps by St. Francis Xavier Church (now Cathedral) of Alexandria, La. Actually, if the family left Alexandria in March or early April as facts indicate, she would have been closer to fourteen months of age than to thirteen months.

6. "Why I Returned," 178.

7. "Why I Returned," 177. Bontemps hints that this young "Susy" is connected with his father's youthful activities in another parish. It is significant that his account differs slightly from that of his younger sister in that he does not mention the presence of his mother's younger brother, Ward Pembrooke, with them on this trip.

8. "Shockley Interview," 7.

9. "Why I Returned," 178.

10. "Audrey N. Jackson Tape."

11. *Town Talk*, March 14, 1906 and April 11, 1906.

12. Obituary of Sarah Ward Pembrooke.

13. *New York Times*, April 19, 1906. See also "Bontemps's Alexandria Tape" and the "Shockley Interview."

14. Obituary of Sarah Ward Pembrooke.

15. *Encyclopedia Britannica*.

16. "Bontemps's Alexandria Tape."

17. "Anna Stokes: Syracuse Papers." See also Sandra Carlton Alexander, *The Achievement of Arna Bontemps*, an unpublished doctoral dissertation, University of Pittsburgh, 1976, 8.

18. Verna Arvey, 126.

19. Verna Arvey.

20. "Why I Returned," 178.

21. Bontemps to Verna Arvey Still, December 29, 1941, Syracuse Papers. See also "Why I Returned," 179; Sandra Carlton Alexander's unpublished dissertation, 2.

22. "Why I Returned," 179.

23. "Why I Returned."

24. "Shockley Interview."

25. "Shockley Interview."

26. "Shockley Interview."

27. When the school term of 1907–8 opened in September 1907, Arna Bontemps was about one month away from his fifth birthday.

28. Boston: Houghton Mifflin and Company, 1942.

29. *Sad-Faced Boy*, 52.

30. Verna Arvey, 126.

31. Letter to Verna Arvey Still. See note 26.

32. "Shockley Interview."

33. Telephone interview with Ruby Bontemps Troy. (She read this section from her father's obituary.)

34. Obituary of Sarah Ward Pembrooke.

35. Obituary.

36. Arna Bontemps and Jack Conroy, *They Seek a City* (Garden City, N.Y.: Doubleday, Doran and Company, 1945). (This work was reissued in a revised version in 1967 by Hill and Wang under the title *Anyplace But Here*. The Prologue, title "Mudtown," is reprinted intact.)

37. Letter to Kirkland C. Jones, May 4, 1986. See note 42.

38. "Prologue," *Anyplace But Here*, 6.

39. "Prologue," 5.

40. "Prologue."

41. "Prologue," 7.

42. "Prologue."

43. "Prologue," 8.

44. "Prologue," 6.

45. "Why I Returned," 178.

46. "Why I Returned."

47. "Why I Returned."

48. "Why I Returned."

49. Jean Toomer, "Earth Being," *The Black Scholar* 2 (1971), 7.

50. "Bontemps's Alexandria Tape."

51. "Bontemps's Alexandria Tape."

52. "Bontemps's Alexandria Tape."

CHAPTER 4

1. In my telephone conversation on August 21, 1986 with Mrs. Ruby Bontemps Troy of Huntsville, Ala., she set her mother's death as August 9, 1915. But the September 30, 1914, date accords with what the writer said about his mother's death and this is also the date supplied by the Department of Vital Statistics of Los Angeles County on a certified death certificate issued on August 13, 1986. In several of Bontemps's writings he mentions the early death of his mother. In more than one place, including interviews

and published articles, he has stated that she died when he was twelve, which would also accord with the 1914 date.

2. "Bontemps's Alexandria Tape." See also The Alexander dissertation; "Lonesome Boy," in *The Book of Negro Folklore*, Arna Bontemps and Langston Hughes, eds. (New York: Knopf, 1958), 573–78. See also Bontemps, *Sad-Faced Boy* (New York: Houghton Mifflin, 1937).

3. Betty Taylor Ashe, *A Study of the Fiction of Arna Wendell Bontemps*, a doctoral dissertation, Howard University, 1978, v.

4. Personal notes by Bontemps in the Fisk University Archives.

5. Consult Charles L. James's recorded interview of Bontemps, Fisk University, Nashville, December 7, 1971, 40–41. (Hereafter referred to as "Charles L. James Interview"; tapes are housed at the Afro-American Studies Department, Yale University; partial transcripts are in the Archives in Yale's Sterling Library.)

6. Bontemps, "Old Myths, New Negroes," *Top of the News*, January 1970, 117.

7. Bontemps, "Librarians—Words Like Freedom," *The Louisiana Education Association Journal*, 44 (January 1966), 8. An extract from the address by the author, which he read in November 1965 at the L.E.A's annual meeting. (Referred to hereafter as "Words Like Freedom.")

8. Verna Arvey, "Arna Bontemps, Who Recreates . . . ," Syracuse Papers. See also Lucinda Dorothy Jordan, "Arna Bontemps, A Study in Reserved Eloquence and Versatility," 126, also in Syracuse Papers.

9. Bontemps, "Old Myths and New Negroes," 111.

10. Arna Bontemps, "Introduction," *Great Slave Narratives* (Boston: Beacon Press, 1969), vii.

11. "Lonesome Boy Theme: An Address," 672–80.

12. "Charles James Interview."

13. "Words Like Freedom," 9–23.

14. "Bontemps Obituary," *The Tennessean*, 5 June 1973.

15. "Why I Returned," 178–79. See also "Shockley Interview."

16. "Prologue," *Anyplace But Here*, 9.

17. "Prologue."

18. "Why I Returned," 179.

19. "Why I Returned."

20. Rider, 16. See also Alexander's doctoral dissertation, 12.

21. Jordan, "Arna Bontemps . . . ," Syracuse Papers.

22. Jordan.

23. "Shockley Interview," 11.

24. See her 1976 doctoral dissertation, 8.

25. Letter to Garland Millett, 21 August 1960, Syracuse Papers.

26. "Charles L. James Interview."

27. "Words Like Freedom," 8.

28. "Words Like Freedom."

29. "Know Your Faculty," *Fisk University News*, n.d. Fisk University Archives.

30. Rider, 16.

31. This is Lourania E. Pembrooke Albans, fourth daughter of Joseph and Sarah Ward Pembrooke.

32. "Bontemps's Alexandria Tape."

33. Bontemps, "Prologue," *Anyplace but Here*, 8.

34. "Prologue."

35. Arvey, 126.

36. "Old Myths, New Negroes," 117.

37. *The Old South*, 4.

38. Letter to Herb Nipson, 27 November 1950, Syracuse Papers. See also the 1957 questionnaire from Pacific Union College; also in Syracuse Papers, it lists Bontemps's college work experiences.

39. "Shockley Interview," 11.

40. Arna Bontemps, ed., *The Harlem Renaissance Remembered* (New York: Dodd, Mead and Co., 1972), 2. (This is a collection of essays by Danforth Scholars at Yale University.)

41. "Alberta Bontemps Tape."

42. Arna Bontemps, ed., *The Harlem Renaissance Remembered*, 7. Bontemps's first published poem was not "Spring Music" as Thadious Davis reports, for "Hope" appeared almost a year earlier than her June 1925 date for his first poem. See her "Southern Standard-Bearers in the Negro Renaissance," in *The History of Southern Literature*, ed. by Louis D. Rubin, Jr. et al. (Baton Rouge and London: Louisiana State University Press, 1985), 310.

43. *The Harlem Renaissance Remembered*, 15.

44. Bontemps to Harold Jackman, 25 March 1942, Syracuse Papers.

45. *The Harlem Renaissance Remembered*, 15.

46. Charles L. James, transcript of his "Interview with Arna Bontemps and Aaron Douglas," at the home of Aaron Douglas, Nashville, Tenn., December 6, 1971, 20. Referred to hereafter as "Arna Bontemps–Aaron Douglas Interview," this transcript is available at Yale University's Manuscripts and Archives Department, Sterling Memorial Library. Published by permission of "Miscellaneous Manuscripts Collection," Manuscripts and Archives, Yale University Library.

CHAPTER 5

1. Bontemps, "Harlem in the Twenties," *Crisis* 73 (October 1966), 431.

2. "Harlem in the Twenties."

3. "Harlem in the Twenties."

4. Verna Arvey, "Arna Bontemps, Who Recreates . . . ," 139.

5. Bontemps, "The Two Harlems," n.d., Syracuse Papers. See also his *Personals* (London: Paul Bremen, Ltd., 1963), 6.

6. *Personals*.

7. "The Two Harlems."

8. Arvey, 139. This article erroneously states that the novel is *God Sends Sunday*. For an explanation of how Bontemps never got around to finishing the proposed volume, see his letter to Verna Arvey Still, 29 December 1941, Syracuse Papers. For corroboration see "Shockley Interview."

9. "The Two Harlems."

10. "The Two Harlems."

11. "The Two Harlems."

12. "The Two Harlems." See Bontemps's other articles on the period: "Harlem in the Twenties," *Crisis*, October 1966; the "Introduction" to *Personals*, 1963; "The Negro Renaissance: Jean Toomer and the Harlem Writers of the 1920s," in *Anger and Beyond*,

ed. Herbert Hill, 1966; "Negro Poets Then and Now," in *Black Expression*, ed. Addison Gayle, Jr., 1969; "Harlem Renaissance," *Saturday Review of Literature*, March 1947; "Harlem: The Beautiful Years, A Memoir," *Negro Digest*, January 1970; "The Black Renaissance of the Twenties," *Black World*, November 1970. See also his book, *The Harlem Renaissance Remembered* (New York: Dodd, Mead and Company, 1972).

13. "Shockley Interview," 12. See also Bontemps, "Harlem: The Beautiful Years."

14. Recorded interview of Bontemps, by Larry E. Thompson, Nashville, 24 March 1972. (Referred to hereafter as "Thompson Interview." Available at Afro-American Studies Department, Yale University.

15. "Thompson Interview."

16. David L. Lewis, *When Harlem Was in Vogue* (New York: Random House, 1982), 91.

17. Lewis, 99; 282–83.

18. Lewis, 92.

Notes 19–23 are references to the "Thompson Interview."

24. Blanche E. Ferguson, *Countée Cullen and the Negro Renaissance* (New York: Dodd, Mead and Company, 1966), 82. See also Bontemps, "Langston Hughes: He Spoke of Rivers," *Freedomways*, Spring 1968, 140–43.

25. "Shockley Interview," Black Oral History Program," Fisk, 14.

26. Ferguson, 82.

27. Ferguson, 83.

28. Elisabeth P. Myers, *Langston Hughes: Poet of His People* (Champaign, Ill.: Garrard Publishing Company, 1940), 92.

29. Myers, 94.

30. Myers, 94–95.

31. "Alberta Bontemps Tape."

32. "Alberta Bontemps Tape."

33. "Alberta Bontemps Tape." See Alexander dissertation, 19–21.

34. "Alberta Bontemps Tape." See Alexander dissertation, 20.

35. "Alberta Bontemps Tape."

36. Robert E. Fleming, *James Weldon Johnson and Arna Wendell Bontemps: A Reference Guide* (Boston: G. K. Hall, 1978), 71. See also Sandra Carlton Alexander's excellent "Chronology" in her 1976 doctoral thesis. The Syracuse Papers, under various headings, also document these dates. David L. Lewis, *When Harlem Was in Vogue*, documents only two of the prizes won by Bontemps.

37. Letter to Countée Cullen, 20 October 1926, "Cullen Papers," The Amistad Research Library, New Orleans, Tulane University. (This collection is referred to hereafter as "Cullen Papers.")

38. Letter to Countée Cullen, 27 April 1926, "Cullen Papers."

39. Alexander dissertation, 21.

40. "Alberta Bontemps Tape."

41. Langston Hughes, *The Big Sea* (New York: Hill and Wang, 1963), 248. See also Alexander dissertation, 21.

42. "Arna Bontemps–Aaron Douglas Interview," 36.

43. "Arna Bontemps–Aaron Douglas Interview," 36. See also Blanche Ferguson on Cullen.

44. "Arna Bontemps–Aaron Douglas Interview," 42.

45. "Charles James Interview," 7 December 1971.

46. "Charles James Interview."
47. "Charles James Interview."
48. "Charles James Interview."
49. "Alberta Bontemps Tape." The widow described her husband as "a man who loved peace."
50. Lewis, 114.
51. "Thompson Interview."
52. See recorded interviews by both Thompson and James at Yale, and one by Margaret Perry among the Syracuse Papers.
53. "Thompson Interview.
54. "Thompson Interview."
55. Lewis, 198–99.
56. "Thompson Interview."
57. Lewis, 201–3.
58. "Shockley Interview," 15–16.
59. "Shockley Interview," 14. See also *Crisis*, 19 April 1927.
60. Bontemps to James Weldon Johnson, n.d., in Collection at Yale. (Documents from the Collection hereafter referred to as "Yale Papers"; see note 1, chapter 1).
61. Yale Papers.

CHAPTER 6

1. The original manuscript is among the Syracuse Papers.
2. "Shockley Interview," 17.
3. "Shockley Interview," 17–18.
4. "Shockley Interview," 18.
5. An oral history interview of Arthenia Bates Millican, conducted and transcribed by Kirkland C. Jones, Alexandria and Baton Rouge, La., 29 January 1986. See also "Shockley Interview."
6. "Shockley Interview," 18.
7. "Shockley Interview."
8. "Shockley Interview," 18–19. See also "Charles James Interview," of 20 June 1971 for a similar account. (James did recorded interviews of Bontemps in June and December 1971.)
9. "Charles James Interview," 7 December 1971.
10. James L. Lewis, 245.
11. Lewis.
12. "Shockley Interview."
13. "Shockley Interview."
14. Lewis, 265–6.
15. Arna Bontemps, "Famous W.P.A. Authors," *Crisis*, June 1950, 43. See also Bontemps, *Personals*, 9.
16. *New York Times*, Book Review Section, 15 March 1931.
17. Lawrence Stallings, *New York Sun*, 18 March 1931.
18. Gwendolyn R. Bennett, *New York Herald Tribune*, Books Section, 22 March 1931.
19. Robert E. Fleming, 79–92.
20. See Bontemps's own remarks on *God Sends Sunday*, Syracuse Papers. See also

interviews by Charles James and by Larry Thompson, Yale University, Afro-American Studies Department.

21. Bontemps on *Sunday*, Syracuse Papers. In a letter to Countée Cullen, n.d., Bontemps documents that *Sunday* was published in Russia in 1924. Royalties were deposited for the author in the Gos Bank of the USSR. See Cullen Papers, Amistad Research Center.

22. Part One of interview, 11 December 1970, Syracuse University, George Arendts Research Library. Arna Alexander Bontemps, son of the author, supported this view in his George Houston Bass Memorial Lecture, CLA Annual Meeting, Columbia, S.C., 1991.

23. Thadious M. Davis, "Southern Standard-Bearers in the New Negro Renaissance," in *The History of Southern Literature*, ed. Louis D. Rubin, Jr. et al. (Baton Rouge and London: Louisiana State University Press, 1985), 311.

24. Arvey, "Bontemps, Who Recreates . . . ," 139.

25. The school now offers four- and five-year baccalaureate degrees.

26. New York: Hill and Wang, 1956, 3.

27. Postal card from Bontemps to Cullen from Huntsville, Ala., 2 October 1931 (postmark), Syracuse Papers.

28. Bontemps, *Black Thunder* (Boston: Beacon Press, 1963), xiii.

29. *Black Thunder*.

30. Bontemps to Cullen, n.d., "Cullen Papers," Amistad.

31. Amistad Research Center.

32. Bontemps to Cullen, n.d., "Cullen Papers." See also *Black Thunder*, xiv.

33. Bontemps to Cullen, 23 June 1932, "Cullen Papers."

34. Bontemps to Cullen, 23 June 1932, "Cullen Papers."

35. Bontemps to Cullen, n.d., "Cullen Papers."

36. Bontemps to Cullen, 14 December n.d., "Cullen Papers."

37. *Black Thunder*, xiv.

38. A recorded oral history interview of Joan Bontemps Williams by Kirkland C. Jones, Nashville, Tenn., 26 March 1986. (Referred to hereafter as "Joan Bontemps Williams Tape.") See also Bontemps's letter to Countée Cullen of 8 January 1933, Amistad Research Center, Tulane University, New Orleans. (Referred to elsewhere as "Cullen Papers" or "Amistad Collection.")

39. "Amistad Collection."

40. Bontemps to Cullen (handwritten), 11 April 1933, "Cullen Papers," in Amistad Collection."

41. Bontemps to Cullen, n.d., "Amistad Collection."

42. *Black Thunder*, x.

43. *Black Thunder*, xiv.

44. Bontemps, "Sad-Faced Author," 8.

45. "Joan Bontemps Williams Tape." See also I. M. Rider, 14.

46. See Bontemps's handwritten letter to Cullen, 7 November, n.d., "Amistad Collection." See also Rider, 14–15. See Alexander thesis, 43.

47. Rider, 15.

48. Bontemps, "Negro, Then and Now," in *Black Expression*, ed. Addison Gayle, Jr. (New York: Weybright and Talley, 1969), 83.

49. *Black Thunder*, xi.

50. "Joan Bontemps Williams Tape."

51. *New Challenge*, March 1934, 16–24.

52. "Joan Bontemps Williams Tape."

53. "Alberta Bontemps Tape."

54. "Alberta Bontemps Tape."

55. *Black Thunder*, xi.

56. *Black Thunder*.

57. "Alberta Bontemps Tape."

58. *Black Thunder*, viii.

59. *Black Thunder*, ix.

60. "A Tale of Folk Courage," *Partisan Review and Anvil*, April 1936, 31.

61. Bontemps to Cullen, 12 November, n.d.; Bontemps to Cullen, n.d., (same period). Both letters are in the Amistad Collection of the "Cullen Papers."

62. See posthumous collection of short stories, *The Old South*.

63. *New Challenge*, May 1935, 8–15.

64. This "Lonesome Boy" title is not to be confused with the author's 1955 book, *Lonesome Boy*. The other works named here are unpublished mss. that may be found either among the Bontemps Papers at Syracuse University or at Yale's Beinecke Library.

CHAPTER 7

1. Bontemps to Cullen, 25 January 1936, "Cullen Papers."

2. Leah Salisbury to Countée Cullen, 18 September, n.d., "Cullen Papers."

3. "Joan Bontemps Williams Tape"; "Alberta Bontemps Tape."

4. Bontemps to Cullen, n.d., "Cullen Papers"; American Dramatists Guild to Bontemps, 2 January 1936, Syracuse Papers.

5. "Why I Returned," 181. See also Bontemps's letter to Cullen of 22 August 1945, "Cullen Papers."

6. Bontemps, "Famous W.P.A. Authors," 43.

7. "Famous W.P.A. Authors," 43–44.

8. "Famous W.P.A. Authors, 45.

9. Jack Conroy, "Memories of Arna Bontemps, Friend and Collaborator," *American Libraries* 5 (December 1974), 602–06.

10. "Alberta Bontemps Tape."

11. *Black Thunder*, xiv.

12. "Arthenia Bates Millican Tape." (For salary information see Bontemps's 1938 application to the Julius Rosenwald Fund, Syracuse Papers.)

13. Bontemps to Cullen, 20 April 1936, "Cullen Papers."

14. It began at 5:00 P.M. on Sunday, 13 September 1936.

15. Bontemps to James Weldon Johnson, 13 September 1936, Yale Papers.

16. Conroy, "Memories . . . ," 606.

17. Syracuse Papers.

18. Conroy, 602.

19. Conroy, 603–04.

20. Conroy, 604.

21. Conroy, 606.

22. "Writers, Singers Plan for Exposition Show," a news clipping, n.d., Syracuse Papers.

23. Syracuse Papers. One of the early typewritten versions of the play appears in the

Moorland Collection, Howard University Library. Versions of the original are at Yale among Hughes's papers and at Syracuse among the Bontemps papers. Contrary to what published works have stated, this play is not from 1940 but 1938.

24. Syracuse Papers. See all documents pertaining to the "Royal Netherlands Steamship Company."

25. Syracuse Papers.

26. Syracuse Papers.

27. Bontemps to Cullen, 27 December 1938, "Cullen Papers."

28. See correspondence to and from officials of these colleges from January through June 1939, Syracuse Papers.

29. See correspondence from late 1938 through most of 1939, Syracuse Papers.

30. See letter from Harcourt, president of publishing house, to Leah Salisbury, 4 April 1939, Syracuse Papers.

31. Syracuse Papers.

32. Rayford Logan, review of Bontemps's *Drums at Dusk*, *Opportunity*, June 1939, 218.

33. "Bontemps Discusses *Thunder*," review, 1 May 1936, Syracuse Papers.

34. Transcript of 1939 radio interview in Syracuse Papers.

35. The Syracuse Papers establish 19 January 1940 as the European publication date.

36. Alexander's 1976 doctoral dissertation, 257.

37. Syracuse Papers.

38. Cameron St. C. Guild, M.D., to Bontemps, 17 June 1940, Syracuse Papers.

39. Bontemps to Cullen, 19 November 1940, "Cullen Papers."

40. Clipping from *New York Times*, 24 November 1940, Syracuse Papers.

41. See news clipping, n.d., Syracuse Papers.

42. Syracuse Papers.

43. Bontemps to Melvin B. Tolson, 10 October 1941, Syracuse Papers. Tolson's reply of a few days later is also in this collection of archival materials.

44. *The Tennessean*, 5 June 1973, Fisk University Archives.

45. Bontemps to Marshall Field III, 16 October 1941, Syracuse Papers.

46. Harold Jackman to Bontemps, 8 November 1941, Syracuse Papers.

47. M. B. Tolson to Bontemps, n.d., Syracuse Papers.

48. Bontemps to Van Vechten, 8 December 1941, Syracuse Papers.

49. Van Vechten to Bontemps, 10 December 1941, Syracuse Papers.

50. Conroy, "Memories . . . ," 602.

51. Conroy.

52. Conroy, 604.

53. Conroy.

54. Conroy.

55. Syracuse Papers.

56. Syracuse Papers.

57. Syracuse Papers. This letter from Van Vechten was written from 101 Central Park West, N.Y.

58. Syracuse Papers.

59. Syracuse Papers.

60. Syracuse Papers.

61. Syracuse Papers.

CHAPTER 8

1. See telegram from Thomas Elsa Jones to Bontemps care of the Julius Rosenwald Fund, 4901 Ellis Avenue, Chicago, 6 March 1943, Syracuse Papers.

2. Memo to Thomas Elsa Jones, 11 March 1943, Syracuse Papers.

3. Syracuse Papers.

4. *The Yale University Library Gazette*, 18 (October 1943), 19–20.

5. *Library Quarterly* 14 (July 1944), 187–206.

6. Bontemps, "Harlem, the Beautiful Years," *Negro Digest*, January 1970, 67–68. See also Betty Taylor Ashe, 1968 doctoral dissertation, 19.

7. Bontemps, "Harlem, the Beatiful Years."

8. B. Asterlund, "Arna Bontemps," *Wilson Library Bulletin* (January 1946), 332.

9. See the "Basic Information" section of Fisk University's current academic catalogue. See also "Shockley Interview" and the Syracuse Papers.

10. "Why I Stayed," Syracuse Papers.

11. "Young Readers Lose a Friend and Mentor: Arna Bontemps; 1902–1973," *Wilson Library Bulletin* 48 (October 1973), 138.

12. See correspondence for September and October 1943, Syracuse Papers; and in the Fisk Papers.

13. C. B. Jaeckle to Arna Bontemps, 15 October 1943, Syracuse Papers.

14. Bontemps to Harold Jackman, 15 October 1943, Syracuse Papers.

15. Bontemps to Cullen, 17 October 1943, Cullen Papers, Amistad Research Center.

16. Bontemps to Cullen, 20 October 1943, Cullen Papers.

17. Leslie Collins to Bontemps, 2 December 1943, Syracuse Papers.

18. Syracuse Papers.

19. Syracuse Papers.

20. Van Vechten to Bontemps, 11 January 1944, Syracuse Papers. For an even fuller account of Van Vechten's demands, see his letter to Bontemps of 15 January 1944.

21. Van Vechten to Bontemps, 17 January 1944, Syracuse Papers. See others of the letters from January 1944 to December 1949.

22. See letters to and from Mrs. Ellis in mid- to late January 1944, Syracuse Papers.

23. Syracuse Papers.

24. Van Vechten to Bontemps, 31 March 1944, Cullen Papers.

25. Syracuse Papers.

26. Leah Salisbury to Countée Cullen, 19 June 1944, Cullen Papers.

27. Bontemps to Cullen, 17 July 1944, Cullen Papers.

28. Bontemps to Conroy, 1 August 1944, Yale Papers.

29. Yale Papers.

30. Bontemps to Conroy, 5 September 1944, Yale Papers.

31. Syracuse Papers. See also Charles L. James interview, 7 December 1971, Nashville. (This is one of two taped interviews of Bontemps conducted by James; these are housed at the Fisk Library and at Yale's Afro-American Studies Department.)

32. Bontemps to Cullen, 27 November 1944, Cullen Papers.

33. Cullen Papers, Amistad Research Center.

34. Cullen Papers.

35. Cullen Papers.

36. Bontemps to Cullen, 5 December 1944, Cullen Papers.

37. Van Vechten to Bontemps, 7 January 1945, Syracuse Papers.

38. Syracuse Papers. See also the Alexander dissertation, 56–57.

39. Bontemps to Cullen, 20 March 1945, Cullen Papers.

40. Cullen Papers, Amistad Collection.

41. Salisbury to Bontemps, 27 April 1945, Cullen Papers.

42. Cullen Papers, Amistad Collection.

43. Bontemps to Cullen, 31 May 1945, Cullen Papers.

44. Cullen Papers, Amistad Collection.

45. See original ms. of *Creole* among the Syracuse Papers.

46. See *Amsterdam News*, June 2, 1945.

47. Bontemps to Philip Butcher, 7 February 1964, Syracuse Papers.

48. Syracuse Papers.

49. "Joan Bontemps Williams Tape."

50. Syracuse Papers. "Juneteenth" refers to the 19th of June, the day on which blacks traditionally, especially in Texas, and in a few other parts of the country, celebrate emancipation.

51. Charles James interview.

52. Charles James interview. See also a letter from P. Jay Sidney to Countée Cullen, 28 September 1945, Cullen Papers.

53. Charles James interview.

54. The Syracuse Papers for August 1945 contain several letters from Freddi(e) Washington trying to undo the damage she had done to Cullen and Bontemps.

55. Bontemps to Cullen n.d., Cullen Papers.

56. Bontemps to Cullen, n.d., Cullen Papers.

57. Cullen Papers, Amistad Collection; Syracuse Papers.

58. Bontemps to Cullen, VJ-Day, Cullen Papers.

59. Syracuse Papers.

60. Cullen Papers, Amistad Collection.

61. See Bontemps's papers at Yale and at Syracuse.

62. See telegrams of March 1946, Syracuse Papers.

63. Syracuse Papers.

64. Syracuse Papers.

65. Correspondence between Bontemps and Frank Wade, May 1946, Syracuse Papers.

66. Syracuse Papers.

67. *Saturday Review of Literature*, March 1947, 12–13.

68. Syracuse Papers.

69. Syracuse Papers.

70. Syracuse Papers.

71. Syracuse Papers.

72. Syracuse Papers.

73. Memo from Bontemps to Charles S. Johnson, 23 January 1950, Syracuse Papers.

74. Memo, n.d., Syracuse Papers.

75. Charles James interview.

76. Betty Taylor Ashe in her 1978 unpublished Howard University doctoral thesis documents Bontemps's involvement with the Exchange Student Program, 21.

77. Syracuse Papers.

78. Syracuse Papers.

79. Letter from Donald Gallup to Kirkland Jones, New Haven, 11 May 1986.

80. Fisk Papers; Syracuse Papers.

81. "Alberta Bontemps Tape."

82. Memo from Bontemps to Charles S. Johnson, 23 January 1950, Syracuse Papers.

83. Memo from Bontemps to Charles S. Johnson, 25 January 1950, Syracuse Papers.

84. Letter from Charles S. Johnson to Bontemps, 1 March 1951, Syracuse Papers.

85. Elizabeth Brantley to Bontemps, 8 December 1950, Syracuse Papers.

86. Pages 43–47.

87. Helen M. Chesnutt to Charles S. Johnson, 23 May 1950, Syracuse Papers.

88. Telegram from Lillian J. Bragdon to Bontemps, 5 July 1950, Syracuse Papers.

89. Eva B. Dykes to Bontemps, 26 September 1950 and 8 October 1950, Syracuse Papers.

90. Syracuse Papers.

91. Syracuse Papers.

92. "Joan Bontemps Williams Tape."

93. An Oral History Interview of Ollington E. Smith, 21 June 1986, Houston, Texas, conducted and recorded by Kirkland C. Jones.

94. Syracuse Papers.

95. Ralph Morrissey, "Under the Green Lamp," *The Tennessean*, 18 February 1951, Nashville.

96. "Nashville Writers," *The Tennessean*, 22 April 1951, Nashville.

97. *The Book Mark*, 10 July 1951, 233.

98. Vol. 32, nos. 9–10, *A Supplement*, 8.

99. Ida Cullen-Cooper to Bontemps, 17 May 1951, Syracuse Papers.

100. Syracuse Papers.

101. Syracuse Papers.

102. M. B. Tolson to Bontemps, 16 September 1951, Syracuse Papers.

103. Bontemps to L. Hughes, 25 September 1951, Syracuse Papers.

104. Syracuse Papers.

105. Syracuse Papers.

106. *The Tennessean*, 2 June 1952.

107. Certificate of death for Sarah Ward Pembrooke.

108. L. Salisbury to Ida Cullen and Bontemps, 25 September 1952, Syracuse Papers.

109. Bontemps to Ida Cullen, 20 October 1952, Cullen Papers.

110. Memo from Ida Cullen to Metro-Goldwyn-Mayer, 7 October 1952, Cullen Papers.

111. "Festival to Honor Negro Literature," *New York Times*, October 19, 1952. See Syracuse Papers for the period September 1951–October 1952.

112. Syracuse Papers.

113. Bontemps to Edward Weeks (*Atlantic Monthly*), 26 November 1952, Syracuse Papers.

114. *The Tennessean*, Nashville, 21 December 1952.

115. Leslie M. Collins to Bontemps, n.d., [December 1952], Fisk Papers.

116. Syracuse Papers.

117. Charles S. Johnson to Bontemps, 27 April 1953, Syracuse Papers.

118. Syracuse Papers.

119. "Recent Letters to the Editor," *New York Times Book Review*, n.d., Syracuse Papers.

120. Cullen-Cooper to Bontemps, 7 July 1953, Cullen Papers. A copy of this letter is contained among the Syracuse Papers.

121. Gwendolyn Brooks to Bontemps, 16 March 1954, Syracuse Papers.

122. Bontemps to Moe Asch, 19 July 1954, Syracuse Papers.

123. Syracuse Papers.

124. Charles James interview, 7 December 1971, Nashville.

125. Charles James interview.

126. Charles James interview.

127. Charles James interview.

128. Syracuse Papers.

129. Syracuse Papers.

130. Syracuse Papers.

131. Syracuse Papers. See articles from the Baton Rouge *Morning Advocate* and *The Digest*, a publication of Southern University in Baton Rouge.

132. Syracuse Papers.

133. Syracuse Papers.

134. Syracuse Papers.

135. Syracuse Papers.

136. Syracuse Papers.

137. "Prize-Winning Author Says Negro Novel Thing of Past," *Daily Press*, Hampton-Warwick, Virginia, 1 December 1956.

138. *Daily Press*.

139. *Daily Press*.

140. Syracuse Papers.

141. An Oral History Interview of Pearl Creswell, Curator, Carl Van Vechten Art Gallery and Museum, Fisk University, Nashville, March 25, 1986, conducted by Kirkland C. Jones.

142. "God Sends Sunday," *Courier Magazine Section*, 11 September 1954.

143. "Historical Background," basic information section, current academic catalogue of Fisk University.

144. Fisk catalogue.

145. Syracuse Papers.

146. Fisk Papers.

147. Syracuse Papers.

148. Syracuse Papers.

149. Julius B. Lester, "Help Us Get an Education . . . ," *The Fisk University Forum*, Nashville, 21 November 1958.

150. *Jet*, 19 March 1959. (A clipping in Syracuse Papers.)

151. Syracuse Papers.

152. March 1959, 67–70.

153. Syracuse Papers.

154. Syracuse Papers.

155. Ida Cullen-Cooper to Bontemps, 16 November 1959, Syracuse Papers.

156. Bontemps to Jean Toomer, 8 December 1959, Syracuse Papers.

157. *Tri-State Defender*, "Nashville: Negro on Library Board; Memphis: He Couldn't Enter Door," n.d., Fisk Papers.

158. "Noted Speaker-Writer to Visit Dallas," *Dallas Star Post*, 9 April 1960, Syracuse Papers.

159. Syracuse Papers.

160. Garland Millet to Bontemps, 15 August 1960, Syracuse Papers.

161. Millet to Bontemps, 15 August 1960; Bontemps to Millet, 21 August 1960, Syracuse Papers.

162. "Joan Bontemps Williams Tape."

163. Bontemps to Richard Wright, 30 August 1960, Syracuse Papers.

164. Syracuse Papers.

165. "Alberta Bontemps Tape."

166. Syracuse Papers.

167. Bontemps to Peter Abrahams, 6 August 1960, Syracuse Papers.

168. *Herald Tribune*, Paris, November 30, 1960.

169. Bontemps to Ellen Wright, 17 December 1960, Syracuse Papers.

170. Bontemps to Harold Jackman, 11 August 1960, Syracuse Papers.

171. Cynthia A. Courtney (Program Assistant, American Society of African Culture) to Bontemps, 16 September 1960; Bontemps to Cynthia A. Courtney, 21 December 1960, Syracuse Papers.

172. Bontemps to Jean Hager, 3 March 1961, Syracuse Papers.

173. Bontemps to Emory Stevens Bucke, 13 March 1961, Syracuse Papers.

174. "Arna Bontemps Entertains," *Michigan Chronicle*, December 17, 1961, Syracuse Papers.

175. Syracuse Papers.

176. Bontemps to Edwin S. Munger, Easter Sunday 1962, Syracuse Papers.

177. George Bass (on Langston Hughes's personalized stationery) to Bontemps, 17 January 1962, Syracuse Papers.

178. Syracuse Papers.

179. Syracuse Papers.

180. "Two Great Upsurges of the Negro—the Harlem Renaissance and Today," *New York Teacher News*, 5 May 1962, 4–5.

181. *New York Teacher News*, 4.

182. Syracuse Papers.

183. Marjorie Toomer to Bontemps, 1 October 1962, Syracuse Papers.

184. Bontemps to Marjorie Toomer, 4 October 1962, Syracuse Papers.

185. Bontemps to Lucie Barber, 21 December 1962, Syracuse Papers.

186. Syracuse Papers.

187. Syracuse Papers.

188. Syracuse Papers.

189. Syracuse Papers.

190. *Bibliographical Survey: The Negro in Print*, 1 (March 1966), 14.

191. Syracuse Papers. See especially Delores M. Crump's letter to the editor, *The Tennessean*, 20 October 1963.

CHAPTER 9

1. "End of an Era . . . Arna Bontemps," *Fisk University News*, Spring/Summer 1973, 7–8.

2. "End of an Era."

3. See Bontemps's correspondence at Fisk and at Syracuse.

4. Bontemps to Frank Horne, 28 January 1968, Fisk Papers.

5. 21 July 1964, Syracuse Papers.

6. 8 January 1956, Fisk Papers.

7. 27 February 1965, Syracuse Papers.

8. Bontemps to William H. Kurth, 10 November 1965, Fisk Papers.

9. Bontemps to Paul Bremen, 30 March 1964, Fisk Papers.

10. *Negro Digest*, January 1965, 62–69.

11. "Why I Returned," *Harper*'s, April 1965, 62–69.

12. Memo to Bontemps from Sue Chandler, 10 November 1964, Fisk Papers.

13. "Poet Scores Neglect of Negro Creativity," *Worcester Daily Telegram*, 25 May 1964, 9, Syracuse Papers.

14. Syracuse Papers.

15. S. J. Wright to Bontemps, 5 June 1964, Syracuse Papers.

16. Charles Walker Thomas (editor) to Bontemps, 24 July 1964, 9, Syracuse Papers.

17. Kenneth Rexroth, "Tensions at Asilomar," *San Francisco Examiner*, 16 August 1964, Syracuse Papers.

18. "Tensions at Asilomar."

19. Bontemps to Fania Marinoff, 1 March 1965, Syracuse Papers.

20. *The Tennessean*, 4 June 1965, 9.

21. Syracuse Papers.

22. "Shockley Interview," 41, 45, "Black Oral History Program," Fisk University.

23. "Lonesome Boy Theme: Address," December 1966, 672–80.

24. Printed funeral program for John Wesley Work III, Fisk Archives.

25. "Audrey N. Jackson Tape"; "Shockley Interview." Bontemps also referred to his stroke as a "little accident" in more than one of his letters in the Syracuse Papers.

26. Bontemps to Gwendolyn Brooks (Blakely), 17 July 1968, Syracuse Papers.

27. "Alberta Bontemps Tape"; "Joan Bontemps Williams Tape."

28. "Shockley Interview," 45–46, "Black Oral History Program," Fisk University.

29. "Alberta Bontemps Tape."

30. "Alberta Bontemps Tape."

31. "Alberta Bontemps Tape."

32. Bontemps to Loften Mitchell, 1 December 1966, Fisk Papers.

33. Foregoing contributions documented by the Syracuse Papers.

34. "Johnson Gets 250 Books for White House Library," *New York Times*, 16 February 1966, Syracuse Papers (clipping).

35. Floyd Creech, "Social Revolution Has Leveled Out?" *New York Times*, 25 April 1969.

36. Copy of printed invitation, Fisk Papers.

37. Current academic bulletin of Fisk University.

38. *Top of the News*, January 1970, 138–47.

39. "Shockley Interview," 20.

40. "Audrey N. Jackson Tape."

41. "Audrey N. Jackson Tape."

42. "Audrey N. Jackson Tape."

43. "Audrey N. Jackson Tape."

44. "Audrey N. Jackson Tape."

45. From "Black Writing Today," Bontemps's last speech.

46. Bontemps to Ida Hines, 29 January 1971, Syracuse Papers.

47. The Irving Ward-Steinman personal correspondence; see also the *Town Talk* for the entire month of January 1971.

48. Bontemps to Irving Ward-Steinman, 14 March 1973, the Irving Ward-Steinman personal correspondence.

49. "Alberta Bontemps Tape."

50. Fisk University Archives.

51. June 6, 1973.

52. Fisk University Archives.

53. Fisk University Archives.

54. Fisk University Archives.

55. Fisk University Archives.

56. "Arna Bontemps," Fisk University Archives.

57. Fisk University Archives.

58. Fisk University Archives.

59. "Alberta Bontemps Tape."

60. "Alberta Bontemps Tape."

61. "Alberta Bontemps Tape."

62. Bontemps, "A Word of Remembrance," loaned to this author by Bontemps's sister, Ruby Bontemps Troy.

63. Bontemps to The Honorable Ross Bass, 8 April 1965.

Bibliographic Essay

It is not my intent to list every item that Bontemps wrote, but listings of published works will be nearly exhaustive. Where secondary materials are concerned I have been much more selective.

His published books include *God Sends Sunday* (New York: Harcourt, Brace, 1931); *Popo and Fifina, Children of Haiti*, with Langston Hughes (New York: Macmillan, 1932); *You Can't Pet a Possum* (New York: Morrow, 1934); *Black Thunder* (New York: Macmillan, 1936); *Sad-Faced Boy* (Boston: Houghton Mifflin, 1937); *Drums at Dusk* (New York: Macmillan, 1939; London: Harrap, 1940); *The Fast Sooner Hound*, with Jack Conroy (Boston: Houghton Mifflin, 1942); *They Seek a City*, with Conroy (Garden City: N.Y. Doubleday, 1945); revised and enlarged as *Anyplace but Here* (New York: Hill and Wang, 1966); *We Have Tomorrow* (Boston: Houghton Mifflin, 1945); *Slappy Hooper, the Wonderful Sign Painter*, with Conroy (Boston: Houghton Mifflin, 1946); *The Story of the Negro* (New York: Knopf, 1948; enlarged, 1955); *George Washington Carver* (Evanston, Ill.: Row, Peterson, 1950); *Chariot in the Sky: A Story of the Jubilee Singers* (Philadelphia: Winston, 1951); *Sam Patch, the High, Wide & Handsome Jumper*, with Conroy (Boston: Houghton Mifflin, 1951); *The Story of George Washington Carver* (New York: Grosset & Dunlap, 1954); *Lonesome Boy* (Boston: Houghton Mifflin, 1955); *Frederick Douglass: Slave, Fighter, Freeman* (New York: Knopf, 1959); *100 Years of Negro Freedom* (New York: Dodd, Mead, 1961); *Personals* (London, Paul Bremen, 1963); *Famous Negro Athletes* (New York: Dodd, Mead, 1964); *I too Sing America*, with Hughes (Dortsmund: Verlag Lambert Lensing, 1964); *Mr. Kelso's Lion* (Philadelphia: Lippincott, 1970); *Free at Last: The Life of Frederick Douglass* (New York: Dodd, Mead, 1971); *Young Booker: Booker T. Washington's Early Days* (New York: Dodd, Mead, 1972); *The Old South: "A Summer Tragedy" and Other Stories of the Thirties* (New York: Dodd, Mead, 1973).

Bontemps's play productions all stemmed from collaborative efforts with Countée Cullen—*St. Louis Woman*, New York, Martin Beck Theatre, 39 March 1946. This play was based on Bontemps's first novel, *God Sends Sunday*. The play went on a road tour and was rewritten by its authors and renamed *Free and Easy* (Amsterdam, Theatre Carre, 15 December 1949). Later the play did a stint in Paris.

His anthologies and other edited works include *Father of the Blues: An Autobiography* by W. C. Handy, ghostwritten by Bontemps (New York: Macmillan, 1941); *Golden Slippers: An Anthology of Negro Poetry for Young Readers* (New York and London: Harper, 1941); *The Poetry of the Negro, 1746–1949*, with Langston Hughes (Garden City, N.Y.: Doubleday, 1949; revised and enlarged as *The Poetry of the Negro, 1746–1970*); *The Book of Negro Folklore*, with Hughes (New York: Dodd, Mead, 1958); James Weldon Johnson, *The Autobiography of an Ex-Colored Man*, with an introduction by Bontemps (New York: Hill and Wang, 1960); *American Negro Poetry* (New York: Hill & Wang, 1963; revised posthumously in 1974).

Also fitting this category is his monograph, "The Negro Renaissance: Jean Toomer and the Harlem Writers of the 1920s," in *Anger and Beyond*, edited by Herbert Hill (New York: Harper & Row, 1966, 20–36). Other edited works include *Hold Fast to Dreams: Poems Old and New* (Chicago: Follett, 1969); *Great Slave Narratives*, with an introduction by Bontemps (Boston: Beacon, 1969); *St. Louis Woman*, with Countée Cullen, in *Black Theatre*, edited by Lindsay Patterson (New York: Dodd, Mead, 1971); *The Harlem Renaissance Remembered: Essays*, edited, with a memoir, by Bontemps (New York: Dodd, Mead, 1972).

Bontemps's periodical publications are numerous; those listed here do not include his many book reviews.

Poetry: "Hope," *Crisis* 28 (August 1924), 176; "Spring Music,"*Crisis* 30 (June 1925), 93; "Dirge," *Crisis* 32 (May 1926), 25; "Holiday," *Crisis* 32 (July 1926), 121; "Nocturne at Bethesda," *Crisis* 33 (December 1926), 66; "Tree," *Crisis* 34 (April 1927), 48.

Fiction: "A Summer Tragedy," *Opportunity* 11 (June 1933), 174–77, 190; "Barrell Staves," *New Challenge* 1 (March 1934), 16–24; "Saturday Night: Alabama Town," *New Challenge* 1 (September 1934), 5–9.

Nonfiction: "The James Weldon Johnson Memorial Collection of Negro Arts and Letters," *The Gazette* (published by Yale University Library); "Who Creates Significant Moments in History," *Opportunity* 22 (Summer 1944), 126–39; "Special Collections of Negroana," *The Library Quarterly* 14 (July 1944), 187–206; "Two Harlems," *American Scholar* 14 (April 1945), 167–73; "Langston Hughes," *Ebony* 2 (October 1946), 19–23; "White Southern Friends of the Negro," *Negro Digest* (August 1950), 13–16; "Buried Treasures of Negro Art," *Negro Digest* (December 1950), 17–21; "How I Told My Child About Race," *Negro Digest* (May 1951), 80–83; "Chesnutt Papers at Fisk," *Library Journal* 77 (1952), 1288; "Facing a Dilemma," *Saturday Review* 35 (16 February 1952), 23ff; "Bud Blooms" *Saturday Review*, (20 September 1952), 15ff; "Harlem Renaissance," *Saturday Review* 36 (28 March 1953), 15–16; "New Black Renaissance," *Negro Digest* (November 1961), 52–58; "Three Portraits of the Negro," *Saturday Review* 36 (28 March 1953), 16ff; "Evolution of Our Conscience," *Saturday Review* 44 (9 December 1961), 52–53; "Minority's New Militant Spirit," *Saturday Review* 45 (14 July 1962), 30; "Harlem: The Beautiful Years: A Memoir," *Negro Digest* (January 1965), 62–65; "Why I Returned," *Harper's* 230 (April 1965), 176–82; "Harlem in the Twenties," *Crisis* 73 (October 1966), 431–34ff; "Langston Hughes: He Spoke of Rivers," *Freedomways* 8 (Spring 1968), 140–43.

Published letters: *Arna Bontemps–Langston Hughes Letters*, edited by Charles Nichols (New York: Dodd, Mead, 1980); use with care, for the arrangement of the letters creates problems of chronology, and the introduction makes several factual errors about the lives and contributions of both Bontemps and Hughes.

Bibliographies: James A. Page, *Selected Black American Authors: An Illustrated Bio-Bibliography* (Boston: G. K. Hall, 1977), 19; Robert E. Fleming, *James Weldon Johnson and Arna Wendell Bontemps: A Reference Guide* (Boston: G. K. Hall, 1978); James M. McPherson, *Blacks in America: Bibliographical Essays* (Garden City, N.Y.: Doubleday, 1971).

Theses and doctoral dissertations: dissertations are available through University Microfilms International, Ann Arbor, Michigan 48106. Sandra Carlton Alexander, *The Achievement of Arna Bontemps*, 1966; Betty Taylor Ashe (Thompson), *A Study of the Fiction of Arna Bontemps*, 1978 (her M.A. thesis at Fisk University is also on Bontemps); Akiba Sullivan Harper, *The Complex Process of Crafting Langston Hughes' Simple, 1942–49*, 1988; this work has only one chapter in which the author discusses Bontemps's reaction to Simple; she also discusses the Bontemps–Hughes correspondence, correcting in the process some of Nichols's errors in chronology.

Church records, government documents, vital statistics: I consulted records from several churches in the Rapides–Avoyelles area of central Louisiana: St. Paul's Catholic Church, Mansura, La., which also houses records from the formerly all-black parish, Sacred Heart Catholic Church, to which the first Bontempses belonged. At Alexandria the records of St. Francis Xavier Catholic Church, now Cathedral, were also helpful. Rapides Parish Courthouse in Alexandria has helpful records, as does the Avoyelles Parish Courthouse at Marksville. I also consulted the Vital Statistics Bureau of Los Angeles County for records of the Bontemps-Pembrooke family after their move to California. Obituaries have been especially helpful; some I found in the Archives at Fisk University; others were made available to me by Bontemps's sister, Mrs. Ruby Bontemps Troy.

Papers: A collection of Arna Bontemps's papers is located in the George Arendts Research Library, Syracuse University. Several oral history audiotapes, interviews, correspondence, manuscripts, photographs, news clippings, and other artifacts are available. Similar materials may be found in the Archives and Special Collections at Fisk University's Library. Many, but not all of the Bontemps–Hughes letters are located in the James Weldon Johnson collection at Yale University's Beinecke Library; in Yale's Sterling Library (Archives) pertinent unpublished materials may be found, and at the Afro-American Studies Department at Yale a number of untranscribed tapes and unpublished documents are available. The Amistad Research Center, now located on the campus of New Orleans' Tulane University, is a must for the student of the Harlem Renaissance; their Cullen Papers are rich with unpublished documents. I also consulted the Negro Collection at Louisiana State University, Baton Rouge; and Texas Southern University's Heartman Collection, Houston.

I also had access to the correspondence of Dr. Irving Ward-Steinman of Alexandria, Louisiana, and to the scrapbooks of Mrs. Hattie Roy Bontemps of New Orleans. Future researchers will be happy to know that Florence Borders, retired senior archivist of the Amistad Research Center, is currently setting up an archives and rare books library for Southern University at New Orleans (SUNO); this promises excellent material for researchers in African-American studies.

I conducted a number of interviews, most of which I recorded. Some interviewees would not allow me to record their testimony. I recorded an interview with Audrey Nabors Jackson of Zachary, La., at Alexandria–Marksville on January 29, 1986; on the same date at Baton Rouge I interviewed author-professor Arthhenia Bates Millican; this is also recorded. Other recorded oral history interviews follow: Joan Bontemps Williams, Nashville, March 26, 1986; Alberta Johnson Bontemps, Nashville, March 27, 1986; Ollington E. Smith, Houston, June 21, 1986; Leslie Morgan Collins, Nashville, March 27, 1986 (unrecorded); Jack Conroy, Moberly, Mo., May 23, 1986; Pearl Cresswell, Nashville, March 25, 1986.

Recorded interviews done by other scholars have also aided me in this project. These are Ann Allen Shockley's interview of Bontemps at Nashville, July 14, 1972, Black Oral History Collection, Fisk University; Larry E. Thompson's recorded interview of Bontemps at Nashville, March 24, 1972 (African-American Studies Department at Yale); recorded interviews of Bontemps by Charles L. James on two separate days, December 7, 1971 and June 20, 1971 at Nashville, available on tape at the Afro-American Studies Department, Yale; and a partial transcript of an interview of Aaron Douglas and Bontemps, December 6, 1971, Yale's Manuscripts and Rare Books Archives, Sterling Library. I was also helped by a transcript of a radio interview of Bontemps in the Syracuse Papers. Also in the Syracuse collection is a recorded interview of Bontemps by Margaret Perry in two parts, circa 1969–70. I also interviewed Ruby Bontemps Troy, the poet's sister, on several occasions, in person and by telephone.

Early newspapers of the CENLA (central Louisiana) area: I was helped most by the Alexandria *Town Talk*, 1883–1909. I was also aided by the expertise of Professor Sue Eakin, retired from the Department of History at Louisiana State University, Alexandria. She suggested to me the following early CENLA news organs covering the years 1817–1910: *The Ibervillian, The Iberville Gazette, The Weekly Magnolia, The Alexandria Advertiser, The Constitutional, The Alexandria Gazette, The Alexandria Gazette and Planters Intelligenser, The Louisiana Rambler, The Louisiana Herald, The Louisiana Messenger, The Red River Publican, Red River Whig*, and the *Louisiana Democrat*.

Other early newspapers of the CENLA region: *Opelousas Gazette, Natchitoches Reporter, Natchitoches Courier, Natchitoches Herald, Natchitoches Chronicle, Red River Chronicle, Constitutional Advocate, Marksville Villager (New Villager), The Pelican, The Prairie Star*, and *L'Organ Central*.

References: Immediately after Bontemps's death obituaries were published by newspapers throughout Tennessee and by the *New York Times*. Except for a few brief memoirs, nothing biographical had been published on Arna Wendell Bontemps. In September 1973, three months after the writer's death, *Black World* published two memoirs, one by Houston A. Baker, ''Arna Bontemps,'' 4–9; another by Sterling A. Brown, ''Arna Bontemps— Co-Worker, Comrade,'' 11ff.; and Bontemps's successor at Fisk, Jessie Carney Smith, published a memoir, ''Bontemps, Arna Wendell, (1902–1973),'' in *Dictionary of American Library Biography*, Vol. I (1978), 44–47. See my illustrated critical biography, ''Arna Bontemps,'' *Dictionary of Literary Biography*, ed. by Thadious Davis and Trudier Harris, 51 (1987), 10–21.

References: Sandra Carlton Alexander, ''Arna Bontemps: The Novelist Revisited,'' *CLA Journal* (March 1991), 317–30 (a good source on Bontemps's fiction but published too late to impact the present study); Robert A. Bone, *The Negro Novel in America* (New Haven and London: Yale University Press, 1958, 129–23); Jack Conroy, ''Memories of Arna Bontemps: Friend and Collaborator,'' *American Libraries* 5 (December 1974), 602– 06; Blanche E. Ferguson, *Countée Cullen and the Negro Renaissance* (New York: Dodd, Mead, 1966); Hugh M. Gloster, *Negro Voices in American Fiction* (Chapel Hill: University of North Carolina Press, 1948); Ione Rider Morrison, ''Arna Bontemps,'' *Horn Book* 15 (January 1939), 13–19; H. E. Sterx, *The Free Negro in the Ante-Bellum South*,

(Madison, N.J.: Fairleigh Dickinson University Press, 1972); Darwin T. Turner, *Black American Literature: Poetry* (Columbus, Oh.: Merrill, 1969); Dorothy Weil, "Folklore Motifs in Arna Bontemps' *Black Thunder*," *Southern Folklore Quarterly* 35 (March 1971), 1–14; Roger Whitlow, *Black American Literature: A Critical History* (Chicago: Nelson-Hall, 1973); James D. Young, *Black Writers in the Thirties* (Baton Rouge: Louisiana State University Press, 1973).

Index

"Aaron Douglas," 169
Abrahams, Peter, 134
Academy of American Poets, 136
Adventism, 51
Adventists, Seventh-Day, 3, 79; family's
  conversion to, 33; sect's mistreatment
  of Bontemps, 33; schools, 47–52, 101,
  138
African-American literature, 156–58,
  160–61; Hughes's five periods of, 148–
  49
"Afro-American Literary Tradition,"
  160–62
Alameda Highway, 30
Aldridge, Ira, 156
Alexander, Rev. Neal A., 167
Alexander, Sandra Carlton, 48, 177
The Alexandria Daily Town Talk, 17–20,
  25, 27, 163, 165–66
Alexandria, Louisiana, 164–66;
  population of, 2–3; social climate of,
  9, 29–30; township of, 7. *See also*
  Bontemps, Arna Wendell
Alexandria-Marksville, 172
"Alexandria Tape," 173 n.5
Algonquin Hotel, 131

Algren, Nelson, 87
Allen, Betty, 147
Alpha Phi Alpha Fraternity, Inc., 133
American Library Association (ALA),
  102, 129, 138, 150
American Mercury, 59
American Missionary Association
  (AMA), 15; archives of, 140, 151, 155
American Negro Exposition (Chicago),
  90
American Negro Poetry, 147; reviews of,
  150
The American Scholar, 110
American Society of African Culture
  (AMSAC), 145–46, 155
American Studies Association, 134
Anderson, Marian, 135
Anderson, Regina, 59
Anti-Ritualist Movement, 18
Anvil, 87
Anyplace but Here, 37, 90, 109–10, 138.
  See also They Seek a City
Apple, Louise, 92
"Arlen and Mercer," 116, 120. *See also*
  Mercer, Johnny
Armstrong, Hank, 135

"Arna Bontemps," 169
"Arna Bontemps Collection," 110
Arna Bontemps Foundation, 172
"Arna Wendell Bontemps Day," 163
Arvey, Verna (Still), 175 n.62, 178 n.31,
    180 n.35
Asch, Moe, 131
Ascot Avenue School, 35
Ashe, Betty Taylor (Thompson), 44, 187
    n.76
Asilomar Conference Center, 156
Atkins, Russell, 155
Atlantic, 66
Atlantic Monthly Press, 141
"Aunt Idoo," 21–22, 107
Avoyelles Parish, 2, 7, 163; "Bayou
    Rouge Pharrie," 4; Marksville, 10, 14;
    Mansura, 10, 14; family driven from,
    14–15. *See also* Alexandria-Marksville
"Awakening" (Chicago), 85–86
"Awakening" (Harlem), 51, 87. *See also*
    Harlem Renaissance; New Negro
    Movement

"Bad nigger" stereotype, 81
Bailey, Pearl, 116
Baker, Josephine, 54
Baldwin, James, 78, 130, 135–36, 155
"Barrel Staves," 79–80
Bass, George Houston, 147, 159, 167
Baron Rouge, Louisiana, 163
Beaumont, Texas, 26
Bennett, Gwendolyn, 63
Berea College, 166
Black Church, 50; in Alabama, 82; in
    Furlough Track, 36
Black Code, 6
Black Muslim cults, 90
Black Thunder, 75, 80–82, 88–89, 92–
    94, 102, 155
"Black Writing Today," 164–65
Blake, Eubie, 57, 169
Bland, James, 95
"Bon-Bon Buddy," 83
Bontemps, Alberta Johnson, 60–63, 70,
    72, 74, 76, 81, 86, 104, 114, 127,
    142–44, 147, 150, 156, 159–61, 167,
    170; culinary skills, 166; first date with

Arna, 62; memory of Arna, 61–62;
    wedding, 127; widowhood, 121, 160
Bontemps, "Alex," cousin of writer, 108
Bontemps, Arna Alexander ("Alex"),
    son of writer, 159, 161, 167; birth of,
    114–15, 137; infancy of, 115–16;
    youth of, 149
Bontemps, Arna Wendell:
    accomplishments of, 151; acting head
    librarian, 155; Alexandrian return, 40,
    162–66; artistic and scholarly
    contribution, 1; autobiography of, 163,
    168; birth at Alexandria, 19–20; birth
    house, 23; childhood in Alexandria,
    22–25, 32, 171; childhood in
    California, 36–39, 44–45, 156, 165,
    170–71; contacts with Adventist
    church, 46–52, 54, 63, 86–87, 101,
    103; correspondence, 159–60; Creole
    background, 1, 5, 14, 117, 156; death
    at Nashville, 23, 63, 96, 156, 166,
    170; "Depression Period," 69–83; as
    "Director of University Relations,"
    151, 154; disenchantment with poetry,
    66–67; education, 44–52, 97–98, 101–
    2, 106–7; European ancestors, 1–2, 11,
    14; first publishing efforts, 52; at Fisk,
    63, 101, 103, 153; freelance writing,
    101–2; funeral of, 63, 101, 103, 153,
    167–68; golden years, 119; in Harlem
    Renaissance, 53–67, 69; health of,
    118, 158–61, 191 n.25; interest in
    athletics, 106; lectures of, 165; literary
    feuds, 114–15; literary reputation of,
    171; mature years, 153–72; memory of
    childhood, 23, 25, 31–32, 39–41; use
    of Negro dialect, 74; nickname, 24;
    reading habits of, 44–46, 49; relocation
    in New York City, 51–53;
    reminiscences of Louisiana, 40, 170;
    residence on Geneva Circle, 150;
    retirement of, 127, 151, 162; return to
    Chicago, 158; roots of, 171; view of
    Harlem artists, 64; "Writer in
    Residence," 156, 161; writer's craft,
    162; writing habits, 70, 74; Yale
    experience of, 120, 160–61; youthful

desire to write, 47–48, 51–52. *See also*
Culture heritage; Hughes Langston

Bontemps, Camille, daughter of writer,
159, 167; birth of, 86

Bontemps, Cecelia (Swann), 16

Bontemps, Charles, 14, 16

Bontemps, Constance, daughter of writer,
99, 127, 159, 167; birth of, 86

Bontemps, Eugenia, 4

Bontemps, Hyppolite, grandfather of
writer, 3–4, 14–15; Hyppolite, the
younger, 7. *See also* Bontemps family

Bontemps, Joan Williams, daughter of
writer, 62, 72, 74, 79–81, 99, 127,
143, 159, 167

Bontemps, Jolite and Juliet, 4

Bontemps, Maria Carolina, mother of
writer, 8–9, 11; birth in Alexandria,
13; illness of, 36–37; her marriage, 13,
16–17; literary interests of, 13, 33, 35

Bontemps, Noel, great-grandfather of
writer, 4, 14

Bontemps, Paul Bismark, father of
writer, 4, 80; birth in Marksville-
Mansura, 25; brick masonry of, 13,
20, 32–34, 43; conversion to
Adventism, 33, 36; death of, 143;
devotion to family, 43–44, 49;
objection to "Uncle Buddy," 39–40,
46; opposition to son's literary
interests, 47–49, 64, 73; temperament
of, 26–28, 31–32, 48; wife, Letitia,
143. *See also* Williams, Claiborne

Bontemps, Paul Bismark, son of writer,
62, 72, 74, 80–81, 98–99, 144, 159,
167; birth of, 62

Bontemps, Pauline, grandmother of
writer, 14–15

Bontemps, Poppy, daughter of writer, 77,
80, 126, 159, 167; birth of, 77

Bontemps, Ruby Sarah (Troy), sister of
writer, 4, 8, 143, 167, 173, 177 n.5;
birth at Alexandria, 22; childhood in
Los Angeles, 30, 37

Bontemps, Victor, 4, 14, 16

Bontemps family, 2–4, 163; break with
Catholic church, 21–22, 33; Creole
speech, 33; French patois, 33;

hostilities toward power structure, 6–7;
Maria Carolina, mother of writer, 13,
16–17, 30, 43–44, 128; mixed ancestry
of, 5; "Mr. Good Times" (ancestor),
2; names of, 3–5; relocation in
California, 25–29, 32, 36–39;
temperament of, 6–7, 10; traits of, 10;
variant spelling of, 5; "White
creoles," 108; writer's immediate
survivors, 167. *See also* Pembrooke
family

Bontemps Foundation, 172

Bosley, Roberta, 59

Boston, Massachusetts, 155–56

Bowman, Preston, 22

Bradford, Roark, 71

Bragdon, Lillian, 121–22

Braithwaite, William Stanley, 47

Branch, William, 147

Brandeis University, 160

Brawley, Benjamin, 89

Breen, Robert, 155

Bremen, Paul, 147. *See also Personals*

Brewer, Nadine, 155

Brimberg, Judy, 135

Brittain, Vera, 144

Brooks, Gwendolyn (Blakely), 129, 131,
155–56, 159–60

Brown, John Mason, 120, 127

Brown, Sterling, 77, 122, 126, 147, 169

Brownlee, Fred, 151. *See also* American
Missionary Association

"Bubber Joins the Band," 83

Bunche, Ralph, 112, 140

Butcher, Philip, 141

Butler, Sandra E., 169

Caldecott Award, 125

Cambridge, Godfrey, 155

Camel Walk, the, 55

Campbell, Marie, 130

"Campus Notes," 51

Cane River, 24

Careless Love, 114

Carnegie Foundation, 118

Carolina Magazine, 67

Cartwright, Wesley, 95

Caucasian, 17

Cavalcade of the Negro Theatre, 90

Cayton, Horace, 122, 155–56
Cenla (Central Louisiana), 6, 17, 29
Century magazine, 59
Chamberlain, Wilt, 150
Chandler, Sue, 137
Chariot in the Sky, 55, 69–70, 73, 118, 122, 124–25, 145
Charleston, the, 55
Chesnutt, Charles W., 58, 122
Chesnutt Collection, 122, 129–30, 140
Chesnutt, Helen, 122, 127, 129–30
Chicago, 26, 57, 126; Federal writers project, 169; literary circle of, 85–88, 131, 156; public library of, 121; University of, 85, 97, 101–2, 107; writer's residence in, 70, 82, 85–99. *See also* WPA
Chicago Daily News, 88
Chicago Defender, 88
Chicago Renaissance, 85–87, 101
Chicago Sun, 96
Childress, Alice, 139, 156
Chocolate Dandies, 54
Choir, Eva Jessye, 155
Christian, Marcus, 95
Ciardi, John, 130
Civil War, 2, 9–10, 14, 16, 125, 171; Louisiana in, 2, 171; pre-Civil War, 90
Clarke, John Henrik, 139
College Language Association (CLA), 159
Colliers, 52
Collins, Leslie Morgan, 21–22, 106–7, 129–30, 137, 165
"Color and Democracy," 102
Columbia University, 61, 64, 85
Commonweal, 67
Connelly, Marc, 71
Conroy, Jack, 1; on Bontemps's roots, 2; in Chicago, 87–90; collaborator and friend of writer, 2, 87–90, 94, 102, 109–10, 155–57; on confusion surrounding writer's first name, 90; *The Disinherited*, 87
Cook, Mercer, 77, 144
Cooper, Wayne, 155
Cooper, William B., 167

Copeland, Aaron, 150. *See also* McDowell Colony
Cowan, Louise, 127, 130
Crabb, Alfred Leland, 124–25, 127, 130
"Crazy George," 23
Creole, 114
Cresswell, Pearl, 121, 131; Isaiah, husband of, 121
Crisis, 52, 56, 59–60, 65–67, 102, 161
Cullen, Countee, 55–56, 60, 64, 67, 69, 75–76, 78, 87, 94, 106, 129, 140; *Byword for Evil*, 112; collaborator with Bontemps, 75–77, 91–92, 110–12, 114–16, 128–29; death of, 115–16; literary squabble with White and Washington, 114–16; marriage to Ida, 94; marriage to Yolande Du Bois, 66, 94. *See also St. Louis Woman*
Cullen, Rev. Frederick, 60, 116; pastor, Salem Methodist congregation, 75, 116
Cultural heritage, African-American, 34, 45–46, 50, 53, 83, 95, 112, 117, 145–46, 153, 158, 162, 171–72. *See also* American Society of African Culture

"Dang Little Squirt," 83
Dark Renaissance, 55. *See also* Harlem Renaissance
Davis, Arthur P., 139
Davis, Frank Marshall, 95
Davis, John Paul, 158
Davis, Ossie, 154–56
Davis, Robert, 95
"Day Breakers," 59
Dee, Ruby, 155, 167
Dell, Floyd, 87
Demby, William, 135
Depression, Great, 22, 49, 61, 63, 146
"Devil Is a Conjurer," 83
De Witt Clinton literary magazine, 56
Diogenes Lantern, 138
Dodson, Owen, 116
"Dogwoods at the Spring," 67
Dorsey, Thomas A., 155
Douglas, Aaron, 63, 96, 103, 127. *See also* "Aaron Douglas"
Douglass, Frederick, 123–24, 133, 162

Dover, Cedric, 155; Maureen, his
widow, 155
Dow Award, 161
Dreiser, Theodore, 87
Drums at Dusk, 81, 89, 92–93, 102
Du Bois, W.E.B., 50, 58, 73, 118, 124;
Du Bois Memorial Committee, 155;
Yolande, daughter of, 60
Du Claire, Laurent, 4
Dunbar, Paul Laurence, 95
Dunham, Katherine, 87
Durham, Richard V., 95
Dykes, Eva B., 123

Edwards, Eli, 47
Ekomip, Joe, 8, 17
Ellington, Duke, 47, 124
Ellison, Ralph, 127, 156
Emancipation, 15; Proclamation of 1863,
45
English, Helen, 102
Engstrand, Stuart, 87
Evergreen Cemetery (Los Angeles), 43,
128

Fabre, Michel, 155
Fair, Carrole, 155
Fairless, Michael, 71
Famous Negro Athletes, 150, 155
"Famous WPA Authors," 122
Farnsworth, Robert, 155
Farrell, James T., 87
Fast Sooner Hound, 97, 102, 136, 146
Father of the Blues, 96, 102. *See also*
Handy, W. C.
Fauset, Jessie, 51, 131; *There is
Confusion*, 57
Ferguson, Blanche, 59
Field, Marshall, 96
Fillipa Polia Foundation, 90
Fire, 67
Fisher, Rudolph "Bud," 65
Fisk University, 63, 76, 81, 89, 97–99,
117, 125, 140; administration, 15, 31;
archives, 165; "Black Oral History
Program," 162; Bontemps's career at,
97–99, 101–51, 158, 161; *Forum*, 139;
Herald, 105; library, 140, 167;

memorial chapel, 125, 167, 169;
museum, 121; Negro Collection
(library), 120, 129; "Orchestrated
Crowd," 169; special collections
(library), 155; "Stagecrafters," 112–
13; theater department, 169; woodwind
quintet, 169
Fitzgerald, F. Scott, 132
Flowers, J. C. (Mrs.), 22
Folk forms, 139
Ford, Clebert, 155
Forde, Gladys Inez, 169
Fortunata, 5
Franklin, John Hope, 155
Frazier, E. Franklin, 147
*Frederick Douglass: Salve, Fighter,
Freeman*, 140, 145
"Free and Easy," 141. *See also St.
Louis Woman*
Free at Last, 162
Free Lance, 154
Free persons of color in Louisiana, 2–3;
freedmen in Louisiana, 16; free
persons owning slaves, 14–15
"Frizzly Chicken," 83
Furlough Track, 30, 36–38, 45–47, 50,
109–10. *See also* Alameda Highway;
Mud Town

Gaines, Ernest J., 73
Gallup, Donald, 120–21
Gans, "Baby Joe," 47
Gardner, Ava, 128
Garnet, Henry Highland, 46
George, Zelma Watson, 147
Gershwin, George, 65; Gershwin
Collection, 107–8, 121, 141; *Porgy
and Bess*, 65, 116, 141
"Giants," 38
Gilpin Players, 78, 92
Gilpin Theater, 88
God Sends Sunday, 69, 72–74, 76, 89,
92, 96, 102, 137
Golden Slippers, 95–96, 102, 146
"Golgotha Is a Mountain," 62, 170
"Great Disappointment," 123
Great Slave Narratives, 161
Green, Della, 141

Greenwood Cemetery, Nashville, 167
Grimke, Angelina, Papers, 141
Gross, Edward, 111, 125
Guggenheim Foundation, grants, 88, 118,
    131, 158

Hackley Memorial Collection, 161
Hamilton, Virginia, 172
Hammon, Jupiter, 46
Handy, W. C., 65, 95–96, 102, 112–13,
    128. *See also Father of the Blues*; "St.
    Louis Blues"
Hansberry, Lorraine V., 139
Harlem, 103. *See also* New York City
Harlem Academy, 54, 60–61, 70, 72, 74,
    101
Harlem literati, 64, 120, 132
Harlem: Mecca of the New Negro, 58
Harlem Renaissance, 1, 47, 52, 67, 69,
    72, 87, 97, 122, 130, 148, 171, 180–
    81 n.12; March luncheon, 156; Pre-
    Renaissance, 81, 86
"Harlem Renaissance" (course title),
    160. *See also* Negro Renaissance
"Harlem Renaissance" (essay), 147
"Harlem the Beautiful Years," 155
"Harlem Writers Guild," 58
Harper, Frances E. W., 46
Harper, 95
Harper's, 66, 155
Hayden, Robert, 103, 126, 156
Hayes, Roland, 57
Hebert, Donald J. (father), Southwest
    Louisiana Records, 6
Hecht, Ben, 87
Hemingway, Ernest, 87, 132
Henry, Dr. Oscar, 167
Hentoff, Nat, 156
Hill, Anthony, 95
Hill, Herbert, 156, 158
Hill, Mozelle, 122
Hill, Ruby, 116
Himes, Chester, 71
Hines, Ida, godmother of writer, 21, 107,
    165. *See also* "Aunt Idoo"
Hold Fast to Dreams, 161
Holtby Collection, 141, 144
"Hope," 52, 59

Horn Book, 91, 102, 159
Horne, Frank, 155
Horne, Lena, 116
Horton, George Moses, 46
Hotel Theresa, 110
Howard University, 130, 158
Howse, Beth, 137
Hughes, Langston, 51, 58, 67, 74, 77–
    78, 83, 87, 91, 110, 114, 116, 118,
    120, 122, 124, 129, 132, 135, 140,
    144, 146–47, 150–51, 153; assessment
    of Bontemps as writer, 1; biography
    of, 165, 168; collaboration with
    Bontemps, 78–79, 83, 90, 94–95, 138,
    159–60, 172; death of, 60, 126, 159;
    description of Bontemps by, 1, 63;
    estate of, 168; father's opposition to
    son's literary pursuits, 47, 64;
    friendship with Bontemps, 48–49, 53,
    55, 60, 63–64; on Great Depression,
    74; hedonism of, 132; intellectual twin
    and soulmate to Bontemps, 1, 64;
    "Negro Speaks of Rivers," 56–57;
    Weary Blues, 64. *See also Poetry of
    the Negro*
Hunter, Bernard, 167
Huntsville, Alabama, 6, 70, 72, 74–79,
    83, 103–4. *See also* Oakwood College
Hurston, Zora Neale, 56, 87, 98, 120,
    132, 172

International Institute of Arts and Letters,
    171

Jackman, Harold, 52, 55, 66, 75, 96,
    106, 116, 145; death of, 146–47
Jackson, Audrey Nabors, 162–64
Jackson, Mahalia, 141
Jackson State College (University), 167
Jam Session, 139
Jane Addams Children's Award, 134
Jeans Foundation, 130
Jim Crow sentiment, 9–10, 19–20, 25–
    28; in Alabama, 75–76, 79; in
    Chicago, 86; in Louisiana, 10, 26–28,
    30
Johnson, Alberta. *See* Bontemps, Alberta
Johnson, Ben, 135

Johnson, Charles Spurgeon, 58, 62, 76, 89, 103–5, 117, 120–21, 127, 130; death of, 135, 137, 151; "Johnson Papers," 139, 141; wife of, 140
Johnson, Dorothy Vine, 95
Johnson, Fenton, 90
Johnson, Georgia Douglass, 95
Johnson, Hank, 124
Johnson, Helene, 95
Johnson, James Weldon, 58, 67, 76, 89, 103–4, 118; collection at Yale, 120–22, 160; Johnsonia, 115. *See also* Yale University
Johnson, Lyndon Baines, 161
Jones, Kirkland C., 163–64
Jones, Quincy, 141
Jones, Thomas Elsa, 98, 101, 104–6, 117
Jubilee (play), 95; radio version of, 96
Jubilee Hall, 161
"Juneteenth," 187 n.50. *See also* Emancipation

Karamu Players, 78
Karamu Playhouse, 78, 92
Keats, John, 165
Keely Institute, 39
Kelley, William Melvin, 156
Keyes, Ulysses S., 159
Killens, John O., 139, 155–56
Kitt, Eartha, 135
Klotts, Allen T., 167–69. *See also* "Arna Bontemps"
Ku Klux Klan, 10, 14–15, 92

Ladies' Home Journal, 52
Langston, John Mercer, 140, 156
Larsen, Nella, 76
Laurent, Euphemie, 3–4; marriage to Hyppolite Bontemps, 13
Lawson, James Raymond, 161, 169
Lee Street (Alexandria, Louisiana), 24–25; streetcar line on, 32
Le Havre (French seaport), 5
"Let the Church Roll On," 82
"Liberty and Justice Book Award," 138
Life, 155
Lincoln, C. Eric, 137, 155
Lincoln University (Pennsylvania), 64

Lindsay, Vachel, 73, 87
Liveright, Horace, 58
Locke, Alain, 58, 65, 120, 140; *New Negro*, 59
Lonesome Boy, 132–33
"Lonesome Boy, Silver Trumpet," 83
"Lonesome boy" theme, 44, 132
Los Angeles, California: family's move to, 29–32; Weigand Avenue, 79–80, 90–91, 101. *See also* Furlough Track; Watts, California
Los Angeles Post Office, 51–52, 54, 121
Los Angeles Public Library, 44–46, 102
Louis, Joe, 150
Louisiana, 117; Bontemps's favorite topic for writing, 114, 142
Louisiana Education Association (LEA), 49, 162, 165
Louisiana Endowment for the Humanities, 172
Lovett, Robert Morse, 87
The Low Down on Tuberculosis, 94
Lowell, Robert, 155
Lucas, Robert, 139
Lyles, Aubrey, 57
Lyons, Rev. Jesse, 167

Magpie, The, 56
Makerere College, 145
Man's Name, 163, 168. *See also* Bontemps's autobiography
Marinov, Fania, 116, 156–57. *See also* Van Vechten, Carl
Marriage bond, required civil procedure, 175 n.60
Marshall, Thurgood, 168
Martin, George V., 87
Martin Beck Theater, 116
Marxists, 110
Masters, Edgar Lee, 87
Matthews, John, 126
Mays, Willie, 150
McCarthy (McCarthy Committee), 128, 150
McDonald, Robert, 167
McDowell Colony, 149–50
McGraw, Mike, 28

McKay, Claude, 47, 51, 58, 65, 95, 155.
   See also Eli Edwards
McKinney, Nina, 116
McPheeters, Annie L. W., 110
Meir, August, 141
Memphis, Tennessee, 142
"Men of Grainger," 138
Mercer, Johnny, 113. *See also* "Arlen
   and Mercer"
Metoyer, Rose, 163
Metro-Goldwyn-Mayer, 128
Milhouse, Katherine, 125
Miller, Arthur, 151
Miller, Flournoy, 87
Miller, William, 123. *See also* Adventists
Millet, Garland, 143
Millican, Arthenia Bates, 126, 182 n.5,
   184 n.12
"Miracles," 167
Mitchell, Loften, 147, 156, 161
Monroe, Harriet, 87
Moorland-Spingarn Collection. *See*
   Howard University
Moran, "Professor" J. L., 66, 70, 74,
   76
Morgan State College (University), 148,
   161
Morse, Mary, 125
Morton, Jelly Roll, 139
Moseley, Hardwick, 97
Moten, Etta, 90
Motley, Willard, 87, 122, 140
"Mountain Echo," 138
"Mr. Good Times," writer's ancestor, 2
Mr. Kelso's Lion, 162
Mud Town, 37–39, 109–10. *See also*
   Furlough Track
Murphy, Carl, 118

NAACP, 47, 52, 59; in Chicago, 89–90,
   148. *See also Crisis*; Spingarn Medal
Nance, Ethel Ray, 59
Nashville, Tennessee, 76; board of
   education in, 150, 155–56; during
   1940s, 104; Frontier's Club of, 139;
   public library of, 142; public library
   branch, 142; writer's contribution to,

10, 155. *See also* Fisk University;
   Peabody College; Tennessee State
   University
Native Americans, women, 2, 5, 11. *See
   also* Bontemps family; Pembrooke
   family
Negro Caravan, 52
"Negro Contribution to American
   Letters," 158
Negro Digest, 122
Negro Folklore, 138–39, 159
Negro History Bulletin, 156
Negro History Week, 133, 140, 156
Negro in Illinois, 87–90, 97, 101, 109
Negro Life and History Group, 88
Negro novel, 135
"Negro Poets Then and Now," 161
"Negro Renaissance: Jean Toomer and
   the Harlem Writers of the 20's," 158
Negro stereotype, 136, 156
New Amsterdam News, 113
Newbery Award(s), 123, 125
New Challenge, 79, 83
New Haven, Conn., 160–61. *See also*
   Yale University
New Negro Movement, 51, 53, 64. *See
   also* Harlem Renaissance
"New Negroes," 56, 65, 79. *See also*
   New Negro Movement
New Orleans (Orleans Parish), Louisiana,
   1, 5, 15–16, 39, 45, 82; during pre-
   Civil War, 114
Newsome, Lionel, 133
Newsome, Mary Effie Lee, 95
New York, 146; City University of, 102;
   literary circle of, 155
New York City, 66,97; Civic Club of,
   58; its effect on Bontemps, other
   youngartists, 54–56; riots in, 57. *See
   also* Harlem Renaissance
New York Herald Tribune, 73, 96
New York Sun, 72
New York Times, 19, 72, 95, 128, 134;
   Book Review, 130
New York University, 102
New York World, 96
Nicholas Brothers, 116

Nigger Heaven, 58, 64–65, 120. *See also* Van Vechten, Carl

Ninth and Winn Streets, 7, 23–25, 30, 163, 172. *See also* Alexandria, La.; Bontemps, Arna Wendell

Nipson, Herb, 123

Nitro, Sam, 145

Nixon murder case, 169

"Nocturne at Bethesda," 62

North Carolina Negro Library Association, 110

Nostalgia, 23, 34

Nostalgia theme, 28, 31–32, 155

"Note of Humility," 80

Oakwood College, 6, 72, 74–75, 80, 83, 98, 101, 104, 122, 143. *See also* Huntsville, Alabama

Ober, Harold and Associates, 164

O'Connel, Rev. Neal, O.F.M., 167

"Old Myth—New Negroes," 156, 162

Old South, 78, 164, 166, 169

"Ole Sis Goose," 145–46

Omega Psi Phi Fraternity, 117, 122

One-Hundred Years of Negro Freedom, 146

O'Neill, Eugene, 54, 57

Opportunity, 57–58, 62, 78, 102, 104–5

Osofsky, Gil, 158

Owens, Jesse, 150

Pacific Union College, 50–52, 101, 138

Paige, Satchel, 150

Parham, Tiny, 124

Patterson, William, 124

Peabody College, 127, 130, 132, 142

Pearl High School, 99, 114, 156–57

Pelham Bay, writer's move to, 70

Pembrooke family, 3, 5–6, 163; Anna (Stokes), 8; background, 7–13; Charlotte (Clotilde), 8–9; Joseph, grandfather of writer, 7–10, 36, 37; Lourania (Ludie), 8, 49; Mary Ellen, 8; nicknames of family, 11–12; relocation in California, 13, 25–26, 29–32; Sara Ward, grandmother of writer, 7–10, 27, 70, 127–28;

temperament, 7; traits, 7–10; Ward, 164. *See also* Bontemps, Maria Carolina; Bontemps family

Penn, William, 142. See also Toomer, Jean

People's World, 146

Perry, Clara, 166

Perry, Ludlow, writer's physician, 167; "Bishop" Perry, his brother, 167

Perry, Margaret, 73

Personals, 54, 147, 155

Peterson, Louis, 136

"Phrenologist Coon," 27

Phylon, 118, 122, 147

Pinchback (Governor), 15, 142

Pineville, La., 163. *See also* Rapides Parish

Pittsburgh Courier, 115

Poetry of the Negro, 1, 90, 118–19, 162

Popo and Fifina, 78, 108, 147

Powell, Adam Clayton, 114

Pushkin Prize, 62, 102

Rapides Parish, 2, 7, 10, 29, 163, 172; Bontemps move to, 14; Pineville, Bunkie, 10. *See also* Alexandria; Arna Bontemps Foundation

Reconstruction, in Louisiana, 15, 17; post-Reconstruction, 10, 81; terrorists during, 17

Reddick, Lawrence D., 105, 167, 169

Redding, J. Saunders, 122, 155–56

"Red Eagle," 38

Red River, 24

Rexroth, Kenneth, 156

Reynolds, Paul, 145

Richards, Beah, 155

Rider, Ione Morrison, 59, 91

Rive, Richard, 156

Riverside Church, 167

Robinson, Jackie, 150

Robinson, "Sugar" Ray, 150

"Rock, Church, Rock," 82, 109

Roosevelt, Eleanor, 134

Rose, Ernestine, 102

Rosenwald, Julius, 89

Rosenwald Fund, 89, 91, 93

Rosenwald mansion, 88, 101
"Rutland Manuscript," 146

Sad-Faced Boy, 35, 88–89, 122
Salisbury, Leah, 76, 85, 91–92, 111,
    128, 145
Sam Patch, 122, 124, 136
Sandburg, Carl, 87
San Fernando Academy, 50–52, 138
San Francisco, California, 29; 1906
    earthquake in, 32–33
Sarah Ann, 5
Scher, Jacob, 97
Schomburg, Arthur, 43, 76
Schomburg Collection, 101–2, 105, 121
Scott, Hazel, 112
Scottsboro, Alabama, 75–77; location
    near Decatur, 77; trials of, 75
Scourge, 93
Scribner, 66
Seeger, Allen, 56
Seven Arts, 47
Seventh-Day Adventists, 123–24. *See
    also* Adventism; Adventists
Shakespeare, William, 37, 165
Sheffey, Ruthe, 56
Sherman, William Tecumseh, 9
Shiloh Academy, 82, 87–88, 101
Shine Boy, 77
Shockley, Ann Allen, 66, 70–71, 136,
    155, 157, 162, 168
Shores, Louise, 104
Sinatra, Frank, 128
"Sing a Soothing Song," 140
Sissle, Noble, 54
Slappy Hooper, 110, 122, 136
Smith, Ollington, 124
Smith, Muriel, 116
"Sonny's Blues," 78. *See also* Baldwin,
    James
"Southern Mansion," 80
Southern Pacific Railway, 18, 26, 29
Southern University, 133–34
Spanish-American War, 171
"Special Collections of Negroana," 103
Spingarn, Arthur, 148
Spingarn Collection, 156
Spingarn Medal. *See* NAACP

St. Francis Xavier Church (Cathedral),
    13, 16, 163; "Father" L. Minard,
    rector of, 13, 21
"St. Louis Blues," 113, 128. *See also*
    Handy, W. C.
St. Louis Woman, 77–78, 88, 91–92,
    106, 111–12, 114–18, 125, 128–31,
    141
Sterkx, H. E., *Free Negro in Antebellum
    Louisiana*, 6
Stettheimer Collection, 121
Still, William, 123
Stokes, Anna J. (Pembrooke):
    autobiography of, 8, 35; dressmaking
    skills of, 9, 12–13, 34–35; move from
    Chicago to California, 34–35. *See also*
    Pembrooke family
Story of George Washington Carver, 131
Story of the Negro, 118, 129, 132, 134,
    139
Stowe, Harriet Beecher, 129
Straight University (New Orleans), 15–16
Strange Fruit, 115
Strode, Woody, 47
"Strolling Twenties," 55, 71. *See also*
    Harlem Renaissance
"Summer Tragedy," 78–79
Supreme Court Decision(s), 119
Survey Graphic, 58
Swados, Harvey, 156
"Syracuse Papers," 92, 114, 144
Syracuse University, George Arendts
    Research Library, 71, 96, 157

"Talented tenth," 71, 119
Taylor, Geoffrey Handley, 144
Tennessee State University, 134
Texas Southern University (Houston
    College for Negroes), 121, 124
They Seek a City, 37, 90, 109–10, 155–
    56. *See also Anyplace but Here*; Mud
    Town
"Three Visitors to Tennessee," 134
Thompson, Era Bell, 129
Thompson, Louise, 127
Thurber, James, 138
Thurman, Wallace, 52, 63, 130, 132
Times Picayune (New Orleans), 19

Tolson, Melvin B., 95–96, 124, 126, 155–56

Tomorrow, 113

Toomer, Jean, 40, 51, 130, 132, 141–42, 148–49; *Cane*, 57–58, 142; death of, 159; *Flavor of Men*, 142

Toomer, Marjorie Content, 148–49, 155

Top of the News, 140, 162

Townsend, Willard, 123

"Tribute to the Memory of Arna Bontemps," 169

"Tropics after Dark," 90

Troubled Island, 93

"Tump," 38

U.C.L.A., 155–57

"Uncle Buddy," 38–41, 46–47, 69, 73, 165

Uncle Tom's Cabin, 47. *See also* Harriet Beecher Stowe

University of Illinois, 137; Chicago Circle Campus of, 145–58, 160

University of Maryland, Eastern Shore, 164–65

University of Wisconsin, Madison, 160

Urban League, 57. *See also Opportunity*

Van Busen, Neal, 104, 106

Van Vechten, Carl, 58, 65, 87, 96–98, 107–8, 115, 118, 127, 156–57; his estrangement from Bontemps, 120–21. *See also* Marinov, Fania; *Nigger Heaven*

Vesey, Denmark, 46

"Vision of Eugene Aram" (Thomas Hood), 39

Voorhees, Lillian Welch, 105

Vosper, Robert, 155. *See also* U.C.L.A

Wabash Railway (Missouri), 97

Walker, A'lelia, 55, 133; her "Dark Tower," 71–72, 133. *See also* Walker, Madame C. J.

Walker, David, 46

Walker, Hazel, 92

Walker, Madame C. J., 71

Walker, Margaret (Alexander), 87, 126, 156, 167–69

Ward, Clara, 147

Ward family: Charlotte Ward, 8–9, 11; John Douglas, 8–9; Joseph, Jr., 18, 39, 165 (*see also* "Uncle Buddy"); Joseph, Sr., 8, 12; Nathan, 8

Ward-Steinman, Dr. Irving, 163, 165–66, 191 n.47, 192 n.48

Washington, Booker T., 15, 50, 124, 129–30, 133–34. *See also* Jeans Foundation

Washington, Freddie; her feud with Bontemps and Cullen, 114–16

Washington, Isabel, sister to Freddie, 114–16

Watkins, Ruth, 62

Watts, California, 29–30, 36–38, 82–83, 90–91, 156. *See also* Furlough Track; Los Angeles, California

Watts, Schuyler, 113–14

Weeks, Edward, 127

We Have Tomorrow, 112

Werleigh, Christian, 90

Wheatley, Phyllis, 46

When the Jack Hollers, 86, 88, 92, 114

Whetsol, Arthur, 47

"White Caps" (Ku Klux Klan), 10, 14–15

White House, 161

White Sulphur Springs, La., 8–9

White, Walter, 57, 114–15; his daughter, Jane, 115; literary feud with Bontemps and Cullen, 114–15

Whitney Foundation, 147

Wiborg, Mary Hart, 57

Wildwood, New Jersey, 127, 142–43, 149

Wiley College, 124

Wilkins, Roy, 140

"William Allen White Award," 145

Williams, Claiborne: jazz band, 14; in New Orleans, 14; writer's father as member of William's band, 14, 20, 24

Williams, William Carlos, 136

Wilson, August, 168

Winser, Ethel Reid, 92–94

Wireless telegraphy, 20

Women's International League for Peace and Freedom, 134

Worcester, Massachusetts, 155–56
Work, John Wesley, 103, 117, 125, 167;
    funeral of, 159
World Tomorrow, 67
World War I, 57, 156
World War II, 104; post-World War II,
    110
WPA (Works Project Administration),
    74, 86–88, 97; Federal Theater Project,
    87, 90, 92; Federal Writer's Project,
    72, 78, 101, 103
Wright, Richard, 70, 98, 122–23, 135,
    169, 172; death of, 139–40, 144–45;
    Native Son, 169; review of Bontemps's
    Thunder, 82; wife, Ellen, 144–45
Wright, Stephen Junius, 137, 143, 156,
    158, 161

Yaddo, writers' colony, 98, 149, 155
Yale University, 96–97, 160, 162;
    archives of, 165; *Gazette*, 102; James
    Weldon Johnson (JWJ) Collection of,
    101–2, 115, 160; library of, 102, 156–
    57; "Yale Papers," 97
Yates, Elizabeth, 125
Yerby, Frank, 87, 122, 135, 140
Yocum, Frances, 98
You Can't Pet a Possum, 79, 102
Young Booker, 162, 166

Zachary, La., 162. *See also* Baton
    Rouge, Louisiana
Zora Neale Hurston Society, 56

About the Author

KIRKLAND C. JONES is Professor of English at Lamar University, Beaumont, Texas, specializing in African-American and Third World Literatures. He contributed the entry on Bontemps, among others, to the *Dictionary of Literary Biography* and has published book chapters and articles in academic journals.

Recent Titles in
Contributions in Afro-American and African Studies

Ethiopia: Failure of Land Reform and Agricultural Crisis
Kidane Mengisteab

Anancy in the Great House: Ways of Reading West Indian Fiction
Joyce Jonas

The Poet's Africa: Africanness in the Poetry of Nicolás Guillén and
Aimé Césaire
Josaphat B. Kubayanda

Tradition and Modernity in the African Short Story: An Introduction to a
Literature in Search of Critics
F. Odun Balogun

Politics in the African-American Novel: James Weldon Johnson,
W.E.B. Du Bois, Richard Wright, and Ralph Ellison
Richard Kostelanetz

Disfigured Images: The Historical Assault on Afro-American Women
Patricia Morton

Black Journalists in Paradox: Historical Perspectives and Current Dilemmas
Clint C. Wilson II

Dream and Reality: The Modern Black Struggle for Freedom and Equality
Jeannine Swift, editor

An Unillustrious Alliance: The African American and Jewish American
Communities
William M. Phillips, Jr.

From Exclusion to Inclusion: The Long Struggle for African American
Political Power
Ralph C. Gomes and Linda Faye Williams, editors

Mental and Social Disorder in Sub-Saharan Africa: The Case of Sierra Leone,
1787–1900
Leland V. Bell

The Racial Problem in the Works of Richard Wright and James Baldwin
Jean-François Gounard; Joseph J. Rodgers, Jr., translator